THE ELUSIVE QUEST FOR EQUALITY

150 YEARS OF CHICANO/CHICANA EDUCATION

JOSÉ F. MORENO, EDITOR

EDITORIAL COMMITTEE
FRANK GARCIA BERUMEN
ROMINA G. CARRILLO
RICARDO DOBLES
ETHAN MINTZ
JULIE PEARSON STEWART
TARAJEAN YAZZIE

HARVARD EDUCATIONAL REVIEW

Seventh Printing 2016

Library of Congress Catalog Card Number 98-74040

Paperback ISBN 978-0-916690-33-5

Published by the Harvard Educational Review,
an imprint of the Harvard Education Publishing Group

Harvard Educational Review
8 Story Street
Cambridge, MA 02138

Cover Design: Manuel Hernandez-Trujillo

Contents

FOREWORD

MANUEL N. GÓMEZ

The history of educational inequality in the United States is older than the nation itself. A persistent and central tension in U.S. democracy between culture and nation has helped to both perpetuate and shape these inequities, reminding us of how narrowly we have drawn the distinction between cultural and national identity. As Oboler (1997) puts it, there has always been some difficulty in defining "American" identity because "being American had never really been solely conceived in terms of birthplace" (pp. 38–39). At the same time, though, we have relied on superficial markers of identity—race in particular—to make distinctions within "a nation of immigrants." Lighter skin color became associated with a greater degree of "civilization," while darker hues connoted "moral inferiority and social backwardness."

The historical evolution of these presumptions is complex, and has been influenced by attitudes inherited from Puritan representations of the indigenous populations, by the rise of scientific racism in the mid-nineteenth century and patterns of immigration, along with the development of slavery and the U.S. conquest of Mexico. However, the impact of these artificial distinctions is devastatingly clear: national identity has been profoundly racialized. Nowhere is this process clearer than in the historic "separate but equal" U.S. Supreme Court ruling of *Plessy v. Ferguson* (1896), in which Justice Brown argues that

> legislation is powerless to eradicate racial instincts or to abolish distinctions based upon physical differences, and the attempt to do so can only result in accentuating the difficulties of the present situation. If the civil and political rights of both races be equal one cannot be inferior to the other civilly or politically. If one race be inferior to the other socially, the Constitution of the United States cannot put them upon the same plane.

Education is one realm in which the constitutional guarantee of equal opportunity has not been adequate to promote and protect the social equity embedded in the promise of U.S. democracy. While such equality remains an ideal essential to the health of the republic, its manifestation as tangible reality remains—as the title of this book suggests—elusive. Originally presented as part of a Forum on Chicano/Chicana education after the Mexican-

American War, the chapters that follow represent both the enormous challenges facing Mexican Americans in the United States, and our progress toward social equity and opinions about how to proceed into the next century. And although opinions vary among the scholars in this volume, a unity of purpose remains fortified by the collective understanding that social equality is not possible without educational equality.

In the cover painting of this book, Manuel Hernandez-Trujillo captures, for me, the dualistic nature of the U.S. conquest of northern Mexico, reflecting both the losses and the opportunities in his *camino de espinas* (road of thorns). This tension between cynicism and optimism pervades the essays in this volume as well, something I see over and over again in discussions that focus on the significance of race in a democratic society. To what extent does the past determine our future, and to what degree do our own expectations of the future influence our interpretations of the past? It seems to me that these two interdependent questions continue to shape both our experience as Chicanos/as and our understanding of what it means to be Chicano/a in the United States at the end of the twentieth century. Is Gary Orfield correct when he characterizes a "huge young [Chicano] population" as "without the power to protect itself politically" against "demagogic attacks by those holding and maintaining a power that depends on polarizing the declining White majority against Chicanos/as"? What are the consequences of prescribing powerlessness for an entire cultural community? At the same time, how do we break through the national amnesia that continues to obscure the impact of the Mexican American War and reengage discussion within a populace that is increasingly impatient with legislative attempts to level the playing field? Where is the balance?

I believe that the lives and work of Gonzalo and Felicitas Méndez provide us with an example of this balance between awareness and expectation. The conclusion of the Forum, "150 Years of Chicano/a Education: 1848–1998," cosponsored by *Harvard Educational Review* and the University of California, Irvine, was a tribute to Felicitas Méndez, who died just before the event. Her spirit nevertheless permeated the work of the day and provided an important reminder that change is always possible, if not inevitable. I had the privilege of meeting Felicitas Méndez, who was a woman full of wonderful stories. One of my favorites is her memory of repeatedly waiting in the market, her hands full of groceries, until all the White patrons were accommodated. One day, she had had enough and, tired of waiting, she dropped her groceries and walked out of the store just as the clerk was ready to wait on her. She never had to wait in that market again. The point is clear: you are given as much or as little as you will take.

Such was also the case when Soledad Vidaurri took her children and those of her brother, Gonzalo Méndez, to register them in the 17th Street School in Westminster, California. School officials would not allow the Méndez children to attend this "White" school because they did not have the light skin and continental name of their cousins. Instead, they were instructed to attend the separate "Mexican" school. Outraged and tired of waiting for justice, Felicitas and Gonzalo Méndez challenged the school, which agreed to let the children in as "exceptions" (Arriola, 1995). Mexican American parents in other Orange County districts were experiencing similar discrimination because of their Hispanic appearance and names, and out of the protest of a small group of families, *Méndez v. Westminster* (1946, 1947) was initiated. Now regarded as a landmark desegregation case, *Méndez* has only recently enjoyed the recognition and appreciation it should have garnered upon its legislative victory for the equal educational rights of Mexican and Mexican American schoolchildren in 1947.

As his daughter, Sylvia, recounts in her comments during the Forum's Intergenerational Plática, Gonzalo Méndez "believed in the system, he was not an activist. He believed that you could do everything the right way." His wife, Felicitas, a woman of Puerto Rican descent, never doubted her children's right to the best educational opportunities offered to all U.S. citizens. Although not initially activists themselves, Felicitas and Gonzalo Méndez acted on behalf of the Chicano community, initiating legislative, political, and social movements fighting on behalf of desegregation and educational equity.

Within what often seems to be an interminable and overwhelming history of obstacles and discrimination, the work of the Méndez family remains a testament to the importance of hope and the expectation of success. For without such expectations, Chicanos/as will remain "powerless to protect themselves politically," not because of the power of other groups, but because they have no belief, and thus no desire, for positive change. On the one hand, we need the powerful memories of inequity to keep us vigilant, but at the same time, we must insist on hope if we are to move forward. The essays in *The Elusive Quest for Equality* provide us with both of these components, and in that they are most valuable when read as a whole, if not complete, dialogue. I hope that the steadfast spirit of strength of Felicitas Méndez will inspire us all, as we again envision the world we want for ourselves and our children.

REFERENCES

64 Federal Supplement. (1946). Méndez et al. v. Westminster School District of Orange County et al., District Court, S. D. California, Central Division.

161 Federal Reporter, d. S. (1947). Westminster School District of Orange County et al. vs. Méndez et al., No. 11310. Circuit Court of Appeals, 9th Circuit.

Arriola, C. (1995). Knocking on the schoolhouse door: *Méndez v. Westminster*, equal protection, public education, and Mexican Americans in the 1940s. *La Raza Law Journal, 8,* 166–207.

Oboler, S. (1997). "So far from God, so close to the United States": The roots of Hispanic homogenization. In M. Romero, P. Hondagneu-Sotelo, & V. Ortiz (Eds.), *Challenging fronteras: Structuring Latina and Latino lives in the U.S.* (pp. 31–54). New York: Routledge.

Plessy v. Ferguson. 163 U.S. 537 (1896).

Introduction

We need to be heard. I make an effort to do this work because I know
that it is something important that is going to be for the better of the
children. Every time the word goes out a little further and further, the
more the people will learn.
— *Felicitas Méndez, principal plaintiff in* Méndez v. Westminister,
in an interview about her recollections of the case

The year 1998 marks the 150th anniversary of the Treaty of Guadalupe
Hidalgo, which ended the Mexican-American War and formalized the
conquest and appropriation of half of Mexico's territory into what is
now the U.S. Southwest. The treaty guaranteed Mexican-origin people in the
appropriated territory "the enjoyment of all the rights of citizens of the
United States according to the principles of the Constitution" (Article IX).
However, the United States reneged on this promise almost immediately. In
recognition and commemoration of that unfulfilled promise, the *Harvard
Educational Review* and the University of California, Irvine, cosponsored a Forum on April 25, 1998, entitled "150 Years of Chicano/Chicana Education:
1848–1998." The purpose of this Forum was to explore critically and broadly
the state of education for Chicanos/as and their communities in the Southwest. The Forum brought together over 350 scholars, teachers, parents, community activists, and students to discuss the historical role that education has
played in Chicano communities. *The Elusive Quest for Equality: 150 Years of Chi-
cano/Chicana Education* is an outgrowth of this Forum.

Despite the precedents of the Treaty of Guadalupe Hidalgo, legal victo-
ries, and opposition expressed by voting against public referendums, the
Chicano community's quest for a just and equitable education remains elusive. *The Elusive Quest for Equality* is another step toward understanding why
this is so. We hope that understanding the evolution of current educational
issues within their historical context will better inform educators, policymakers, and our communities as they further develop and consider strategies through which true educational equity for Chicanos/as can be realized.

As we write this introduction, universities and school systems around the
country are in the midst of their 150th academic year since the signing of the
Treaty of Guadalupe Hidalgo. And for the 150th year, most high school and
university students in the United States will not be taught the history and experiences of Chicanos and Chicanas since the U.S. border cut through our
communities in 1848. Both the Forum and this volume are direct outgrowths

of our communal sense of responsibility and commitment, and that of the *HER* Editorial Board, to mark the 150th anniversary of the Treaty of Guadalupe Hidalgo. The use of the terms "Chicano" and "Chicana" in this volume reflects the ideological position from which it was conceptualized and organized. While we are mindful and respectful of every individual's freedom to refer to themselves as Mexican, Mexican American, Latino/a, etc., "Chicano/a" connotes for us an ideological stance of self-determination and political consciousness in terms of Chicano/a communities vis-à-vis dominant U.S. society. This is not to say that those who do not identify as Chicano/a do not share parts of this ideology: we simply state that the use of a particular term serves as a compass to locate where one has chosen to position oneself politically and ideologically.

The Elusive Quest for Equality emanates from our desire to document a Chicano/a educational history that, as San Miguel (1987) and Donato (1997) have noted, has received scant attention from education historians. In particular, this book focuses on our communities' educational history in the context of U.S. conquest. In documenting Chicano/a educational history, it is critical to include both the plight and the struggle of Chicano/a communities. It is not enough to simply document the injustices against Chicano/a communities, as doing so only serves to portray Chicanos/as as mere victims. For every injustice perpetrated, there has consistently been some form of reaction by Chicano/a communities. These responses varied and were largely influenced by racial and social-class hierarchies that permeated Chicano/a communities. As a consequence, at different times these responses consisted of either acquiescence, accommodation, and/or opposition, in many instances occurring side by side and simultaneously. Given these circumstances, San Miguel (1986) suggests a Chicano/a educational historiography that incorporates and analyzes what schools have provided or not provided for Chicano/a communities. San Miguel and Valencia (1998) term these two approaches the "plight" and the "struggle" of Chicano/a communities and discuss how such communities responded to the type of schooling they were receiving.

Within San Miguel's (1986) framework, the guiding themes of both the Forum and this book include the historical development of education and the effects of language, segregation, Americanization, and resistance on how and why education for Chicano/a communities developed as it did. By examining our educational history through these themes, one can discern that the locus of these policies and practices had as an objective the eradication of the identity of Mexican-origin peoples. To complete the military, economic, and political conquest of Mexican-origin people in the annexed territories, the United States depended pivotally on a cultural and intellectual conquest via the public schools. Thus, public education became an arena of struggle and resistance where self-determined Chicano/Mexicano peoples held steadfast to the spirit of the promises made via the Treaty of Guadalupe Hidalgo, and their belief that survival was inextricably tied to a just and equitable education.

As Chicanos, both of us live and struggle under the Treaty's broken promises. Our working-class parents and families persevered and sacrificed for our education, holding onto the "good faith" covenant made to our ancestors in the aftermath of the Mexican-American War. However, despite having had some well-intentioned, dedicated, and supportive teachers, we both experienced an educational system that limited our intellectual development through its hostility to our cultural identity and removal of positive vestiges of our history. While we endured these practices and graduated from high school, we know that far too many of our brothers and sisters did not, and that none of us remained unscathed by the depreciation of our identity.

In our own university experiences, both of us have encountered, much to our dismay and disillusionment, a similar pattern of educational negligence and adversity, albeit more subtle and indirect. As undergraduates we witnessed the low admission and high attrition rates of our fellow Chicanos/as at colleges and universities; courses whose syllabi and textbooks were devoid of our Chicano/a experience; an intellectual discourse confined to "Black and White" issues and perspectives, where Black is viewed as pathological and White as normal; ethnocentric professors afflicted with intellectual rigidity and historical amnesia; and a minuscule number of Chicano/a faculty to serve as mentors and researchers. But again, we endured, thanks to the intellectual nourishment of Chicano Studies courses, the development of tools of resistance through our MEChA chapters,[1] the *conciencia*-building (consciousness-building) activities that led us to serve our barrios, and the inspiration of our overworked and aging parents.

Then we came to Harvard, where history repeated itself: we found that the under-valuing and exclusion of the Chicano/a experience was alive and well at Harvard. As Chicano doctoral students, we are reminded on a daily basis, through our personal observations and ongoing experiences, of the lack of social and educational equity for our communities. Every day we are reminded by faculty, students, and our own communities of how "lucky" we are and how we must do well since "so few of us" make it this far. We are also told by conservatives that we no doubt feel "stigmatized" because we are products of affirmative action, that we "question ourselves daily" about whether we truly belong at Harvard, whether we were "given" our spots here rather than "earning" them and thus are "taking" a place in the doctoral program away from "more deserving" students.

Like many students, both White and of color, we do often privately question whether we deserve to be at this type of institution. But for us as Chicanos and for other students of color, there is another level to this questioning—a public level. Our presence in institutions of higher education is a matter of public scrutiny. What does it mean to have one's very presence go from a matter of private and personal reflection to one of public discourse and public policy? This is particularly disheartening when others from our communities are being labeled in those same public debates as being lazy,

[1] For a description of MEChA, see Intergenerational Plática (note 1, p. 213).

not studious, fatalistic, too family-oriented, and better suited for manual labor. Chicano/a students are forced to make sense of this duality and contradiction: On the one hand we are told that we do not value education, and thus are not expected to thrive and succeed in our educational endeavors. On the other hand, when we do succeed we are told that we must feel like we didn't earn it and that, in fact, we probably didn't earn it.

As we reflect on our own personal educational histories, the 1990s are drawing to a close. This has been a decade in which history has also repeated itself for Chicano/a communities specifically, and Latino communities in general. Our communities have come under vicious attack from various segments of U.S. society on issues such as immigration, affirmative action, and bilingual education. The epicenter of these attacks has been in the state of California, where in the past six years three propositions have been passed (Proposition 187 in 1994; Proposition 209 in 1996; and Proposition 227 in 1998). What is peculiar and insidious in these propositions is that at the core of each is a direct assault on the educational opportunities of Chicano/a schoolchildren.

Proposition 187, a measure calling for the denial of education and social services to undocumented immigrants, would have resulted in the expulsion of over 400,000 schoolchildren (predominantly Chicano/a), had it not been found unconstitutional by federal courts. It has, however, been appealed to the U.S. Supreme Court. Proposition 209, which formalized the demise of affirmative action, has contributed to dramatic decreases in Chicano/a admissions and enrollments in the University of California, and the segregation of University of California campuses. Proposition 227, which mandates the eradication of bilingual education, has consigned thousands of Chicano/a schoolchildren to classrooms that are ill prepared to meet their cultural and linguistic needs. Meanwhile, in Texas, the 5th Circuit Court of Appeals ruling in *Hopwood v. Texas* (1996), which banned the use of affirmative action in admissions, has had an equally negative effect on Chicano/a college participation rates.

Educators and policymakers have long agreed that the nation's ambivalent commitment to education for Chicano/a schoolchildren has resulted in an education that has been separate and unequal (Carter, 1970; San Miguel & Valencia, 1998; U.S. Commission on Civil Rights, 1971). Unfortunately, current mainstream discourse on educational matters seems conspicuously devoid of any historical understanding of the legacy of 150 years of deliberate, state-sanctioned denial of equal educational opportunities for Chicano/a communities, and also of how these communities have struggled for equity in education. In *The Elusive Quest for Equality*, scholars discuss the state of education for Chicanos/Chicanas in the Southwest in both historical and contemporary terms. In various chapters, they reveal that the current educational crises affecting Chicano/a communities are not new developments, but rather part and parcel of policies and social beliefs regarding Chicano/a communities that can be traced back through history.

In their ideological quest to eradicate Chicano/Mexicano cultural identities and values, schools, supported by mass media and corporate ethos, continue to implement socio-educational curricula that value and praise individuals rather than communities. The media images we receive highlight the Escalantes, the Selenas, and the De La Hoyas, and the disadvantages they have overcome. And, because they have overcome their disadvantages, they are now christened as heroes of our community. Rarely does the media examine why they came from disadvantaged backgrounds to begin with or seek to understand the historical circumstances that contributed to their disadvantages. Does the media highlight individual success stories because as a society we all collectively know deep down that only a few will be let out? Or is it because when individuals make it, it eases our collective conscience about the unequal and oppressive circumstances in which our society has placed entire communities of people?

Somehow, communities of color are led to believe that the individual success of a few in our community legitimizes the cult of meritocracy and "rugged individualism" that negate the extent to which poverty and prejudice predetermine outcomes. The history of Chicano/a education over the past 150 years reveals that these two ideological tenets have been used as convenient myths to anesthetize the hopes of the many for the benefit of the few. Whatever the answers, we must come to terms with the historical purpose of education for Chicano/a children and its legacy. As a Chicana colleague expressed to us in a Chicano/a group dialogue about this introduction, "It is not enough to demand more 'White' success stories in 'brown' bodies." Rather, we must collectively push to transform the way opportunities are structured so that educational systems cease to serve and perpetuate the racial and economic hierarchies both inside and outside our communities.

As is made clear in the ensuing chapters, many of today's proposals and rhetoric about education and its purpose are not new or constructive in resolving the long-term and historical marginalization and exclusion of Chicano/Mexicano peoples. Rather, they are time-tested solutions that have been consciously and systematically designed and used as tools for political, economic, social, and cultural stratification.

In light of 1998 marking the sesquicentennial of the signing of the Treaty of Guadalupe Hidalgo, we felt it an opportune time to look back and reflect on the history of Chicano/a education. We hope doing so will help us better understand the present challenges and adversities confronting our communities, as well as how we struggled against and challenged these adversities in the past and how we can continue to do so today. To help us build a bridge between the past and the present we drew from oral histories of our elders and the current experiences of Chicano/a students. To reflect our ongoing history, both the Forum and this book were organized into two parts—Historical and Contemporary—followed by an Intergenerational Plática, which is a dialogue among Chicanos/as who have experienced the U.S. education system at different periods in time.

Part One, "A History of Chicano/Chicana Education," begins with "The Treaty of Guadalupe Hidalgo and the Racialization of the Mexican People" by Martha Menchaca, in which she provides a historical context of the conditions that have shaped the educational experience of Mexican-origin people. She contends that the first stage of the racialization of Mexican-origin people began during the Spanish conquest with the institutionalization of a racial order that assigned inferior rights to Indians, mestizos, and afromestizos. This racial order was dismantled in 1821, when Mexico won its independence from Spain. However, this brief respite was blunted by the outbreak of the Mexican-American War, which ended with the signing of the Treaty of Guadalupe Hidalgo in 1848. Mexican-origin people living in the ceded territories at that time experienced a second stage of racialization when the United States violated the treaty's citizenship articles (VII and IX) and refused to extend full political rights to Mexicans because most were not Anglo. Indians and Blacks could be enslaved and indentured in most states, while mestizos could be barred from voting or becoming naturalized citizens and were held to miscegenation laws. Finally, their marginalized status guaranteed their exclusion from the education system and a lifetime of social inferiority. In summary, a legacy of racial discrimination followed the Treaty of Guadalupe Hidalgo that consigned Mexicans to a fate similar to that of other peoples of color. Denied basic civil rights, they were segregated, excluded from voting, and denied the educational opportunities granted to White citizens.

In "The Schooling of Mexicanos in the Southwest, 1848–1891," Guadalupe San Miguel provides a historical overview of the education experiences of Mexican-origin people during their first decades under U.S. rule. In the post-1848 period, the number of schools increased. Formal schooling became the dominant type of instruction, propelled largely by the dynamics of an emergent capitalist society and the Mexican community's desire to facilitate its integration into the new social order. San Miguel notes two distinct currents in the schooling of Mexican-origin people, which distinguished this era from the past. First, state-based public education became the dominant form of schooling, although schools sponsored by the Catholic Church continued to play an important role in Mexican communities. In addition, during the immediate pre–Civil War years, Protestant schools increased their presence in Mexican-origin communities, promoting conversion and "industrial" education. Second, schools had as a primary goal a mission to Americanize its new citizens, thus becoming, over time, increasingly adverse to minority ethnicity and identity. Public schools in particular sought to de-ethnicize the Mexican population and remove all vestiges of that identity.

San Miguel discerns that the decline of the Mexican population during this period contributed to a diminished presence on school boards and in elected offices. Although the population decline varied from state to state in the Southwest, it ultimately resulted in the Mexican community's inability to counter-balance negative measures such as English-only laws and Anglo-centric curricula.

Gilbert González's chapter, "Segregation and the Education of Mexican Children, 1900–1940," focuses on the first part of the twentieth century, a time in which great political and economic forces affected the social status and educational experience of Mexican Americans. The expanding Anglo capitalist system required a mass of cheap labor, which was provided by the migration of over two million Mexicans to the United States between 1900 and 1930. Alarmed by this influx of laborers, social theorists cautioned against cultural disintegration and political revolution, reinforcing public education's role to indoctrinate the citizenry with a common political culture that valued political stability and capitalist profitability.

González identifies three strategies employed by public schools to deal with the "Mexican Problem." The first was the segregation of Mexicans into "Mexican Schools." Officials justified this segregation with the belief that Mexican children had diminished mental capacity that slowed the academic progress of Anglo children, as did Mexican children's impediment of speaking only the Spanish language. The second strategy was the use of scientifically flawed intelligence testing to further justify the practice of segregation and add a veneer of legitimacy. The third strategy involved the development of a differentiated curriculum for Mexican schoolchildren, legitimized by their mismeasured intelligence. This dictated that unequals could not be given the same curriculum nor expected to learn at the same rate, thus requiring that Mexican children be schooled for manual labor and/or housework. In cases where Mexican children attended mainstream schools, they were consigned to vocational tracks or "mentally handicapped" classes.

The Mexican American community's response to these strategies was to organize and struggle to dismantle legal segregation. Instrumental in these efforts was the founding of several national organizations, including the League of United Latin American Citizens (LULAC); groundbreaking research by educator George I. Sánchez and labor leader Ernesto Galarza; and critical lawsuits. In 1930, for example, Mexican parents in Lemon Grove, California, won the first successful desegregation court case in this nation's history. This was followed by *Méndez v. Westminister* in 1947, the first successful challenge to school segregation in the federal courts. Although both court cases had only a local and regional impact, they nevertheless demonstrated the Mexican American community's resolve to persevere in the long and difficult struggle to improve their children's education.

The final chapter of the historical section is "Chicana/o Education: From the Civil Rights Era to the Present" by Dolores Delgado Bernal, who addresses the belief systems, education policies, and judicial decisions that have influenced Chicana/o education from the 1950s through the 1990s. She attributes the persistence of segregation to political, scientific, and religious theories that continued to view Mexicans as "culturally deficient."

By the 1960s, as Delgado Bernal explains, almost half of Chicana/o elementary and secondary students attended de facto segregated schools. During that decade, the emerging Chicana/o generation embraced nationalism and militancy in order to press for educational, political, and social reform.

Pivotal events such as the 1968 East Los Angeles high school walkouts galvanized the Chicana/o community, which in the process developed an activist youth movement, one that included Chicana activism and feminism. During this period the Chicana/o community pressed for such educational reforms as bilingual education, desegregation, equity in school funding, and affirmative action.

However, a sociopolitical conservative retrenchment emerged in the late 1970s and became more pronounced during the 1980s. This movement was propelled by a backlash against social equity programs, increased military spending, a decline in education spending, and a growing recession. Nevertheless, Chicana/os have made modest progress, as seen through larger numbers attending post-secondary institutions, the existence of Chicano Studies in colleges and universities, and the increase in Chicano/a scholarship and research. But this progress is small when compared to the dramatic growth of the Chicana/o population over the last fifty years. At present, Chicana/o students remain the ethnic group least likely to finish high school, or to attend or graduate from college. In recent years, they have endured the brunt of exclusionary laws like California's Propositions 187, 209, and 227, which have direct impact on their economic, political, and social well-being. This notwithstanding, Chicanas/os have a valuable historical legacy, which includes an active struggle to gain equal access to quality education. Delgado Bernal asserts that it is vital for educators, policymakers, and Chicano/a communities to persevere in active engagement and continue to struggle for the educational well-being of Chicano/a communities.

Continued engagement is precisely what the authors in Part Two, "Chicano/Chicana Education in the Contemporary Era," say is needed if Chicano/a communities are to expect substantive change, and if the United States is to live up to its promises to Chicano/a communities. In "Politics Matters: Educational Policy and Chicano Students," Gary Orfield argues that in analyzing Chicano/a education, we must remember that electoral politics matter. Through a political analysis of social policy and public referendums over the past twenty years in California, Orfield shows that a shift in racial/ethnic policy—which he calls "a counterrevolutionary reaction" to civil rights movements—has had a dramatic negative impact on Chicano/a students. He clearly lays out propositions that have had direct negative consequences on Chicano/a educational opportunities, and argues that Chicano/a communities must actively participate in the electoral process, both as a means to participate in a democracy, and also to protect ourselves and our children. Despite recent gains in electoral representation, Orfield's chapter raises fundamental questions about democracy in a system wrought with social prejudices and stereotypes of people of color.

In "Educational Testing and Mexican American Students: Problems and Prospects," Richard Valencia argues that it is these very social prejudices and stereotypes, based in the eugenics movement of the early twentieth century, that laid the foundation for intelligence and aptitude testing of schoolchildren. Valencia presents a compelling case for our need to understand fully the legacy of tests used to support racial hierarchies and constructs. Valencia erases any doubts about the legacy of racially biased testing by citing studies and current data that clearly show the gross overrepresentation of Chicano/a students in "special education" classes and the underrepresentation of Chicano/a school students in gifted and talented programs. Valencia argues for a deconstruction of current standardized measures, with a special emphasis on understanding the effects of language and culture on children's testing.

Culturally relevant curricula and pedagogues are at the center of Eugene García's chapter, "Chicanos/as in the United States: Language, Bilingual Education, and Achievement." Stressing the importance of building a true "community of learners," García critiques multicultural education as it has been practiced in the mainstream, that is, as mere cultural exchanges rather than a fulfillment of their intent to provide curricula and pedagogy that place justice and equity center stage. Focusing specifically on language and bilingualism, García outlines the theoretical, practical, and policy issues related to language that have directly affected Chicano/a educational success. García concludes his analysis by proposing a theoretical and practical framework for transforming the educational experience of Chicano/a schoolchildren.

The consequences of cultural stratification mixed with traditional views of a meritocracy and their influence on Chicano/a students' access to higher education is the focus of Patricia Gándara's chapter, "Staying in the Race: The Challenge for Chicanos/as in Higher Education." Using the metaphor of a race, where the number of hurdles placed in a runner's lane is determined by his or her racial/ethnic background and social class, Gándara deconstructs the fallacy of "colorblind" admissions and the devastating effects such practices have had on access to and attainment in higher education for Chicanos/as. She focuses on Texas and California to illustrate that in order for Chicanos/as to increase their presence in higher education, either admissions criteria must be transformed or pre-admissions factors that depress current criteria must be addressed. Gándara shows why class-based solutions are misdirected, due to their presumption that the factor of income level alone eradicates cultural differences and views by citing SAT data that shows that middle- and upper-income African American and Latino students, on average, score about the same as low-income White students. Based on her research and the evaluation of the highly successful Puente Program in California, Gándara argues that what is critical for Chicano/a educational mobility is the nourishment and sharing of social and cultural capital. Without this nourishment, argues Gándara, Chicano/a schoolchildren are more likely to fall prey to the overwhelming negative stereotypes about themselves and their community.

Much of the cultural and intellectual nourishment we receive as school-children does not come from schools, but rather from conversations with our parents, *abuelitos* (grandparents), *tias y tios* (aunts and uncles) and community elders. This book ends with a transcript of the Intergenerational Plática held at the Forum, which includes oral histories of some of the most significant acts of resistance in the Chicano/a community. As the exchanges in the plática reveal, the ways the past informs both the present and future of Chicanos/as was at the center of the day's discussions, displaying the diverse viewpoints and experiences in our communities. What is made clear through the plática is the void in school curricula about our collective history and the demand that exists among our youth for knowledge about themselves and their history.

While our focus is on Chicano/a education, we know that many of the issues outlined here, as well as the socially regressive policies currently being considered or passed, also affect other Latino communities, communities of color, and communities besieged by poverty. However, it is critically important to understand the particular ways in which education has been provided and misrepresented to each community. For Chicanos/as in the Southwest, this means considering social policies in the context of the Treaty of Guadalupe Hidalgo and the commitments, both in writing and in principle, that were made 150 years ago to those who chose to stay in the appropriated territories, and to their children. However, while it is necessary to focus on the treaty as a point of reference in achieving true justice and equity for Chicano/a communities, we must also view critically the tools we look to for our own liberation. We echo Rudy Acuña's cautionary analysis presented at the Forum that the treaty itself must be understood in its proper social context, and that we must recognize that Mexican elites agreed with Anglo elites about who gets what while at the margins remained the masses.

In order to better understand the social position of Chicano/a communities in contemporary society, we must critically examine the history of one of the very tools through which we hope to achieve social equity—education. As current education reforms and initiatives are being proposed, considered, and passed, educators and policymakers must learn from the lessons of history. As presented clearly in this volume, education has been viewed by Chicano/a communities as the cornerstone to self-determination and mobility. As a result, Chicanos/as have a long history of engagement with and struggle for equitable schooling.

As we witness an expanding Chicano middle-class and growing numbers of elected officials (albeit minimal in comparison to the demographics of the region), Acuña's admonition is particularly timely as our contemporary "elites" begin "brokering" for the welfare of our communities. As we re-enter the halls of power, will history repeat itself, with elites making agreements with elites? Or will this generation's "elites" keep at the center the needs of the masses? As we continue the legacy of engagement and struggle against the dominant class, we must also hold accountable our own political and community leaders, and each other, not to short-term political expediency and self-interest, but rather to the long-term educational well-being of our Chicano/a communities.

We wish to dedicate *The Elusive Quest for Equality* to Felicitas and Gonzalo Méndez and their family, the principal plaintiffs in *Méndez v. Westminister.* In documenting our educational histories, we hope this volume fulfills one of

Felicitas Méndez's final wishes of "being heard . . . for the better of the children." As is clear in the Intergenerational Plática, we feel that the student participants, as well as those in the audience, learned from the Forum. We are confident that readers will find a similarly enriching experience in the pages of this volume.

JOSÉ F. MORENO
FRANK GARCIA BERUMEN

REFERENCES

Acuña, R. (1988). *Occupied America: A history of Chicanos.* New York: HarperCollins.

Carter, T. (1970). *Mexican Americans in schools: A history of educational neglect.* New York: College Entrance Examination Board.

Donato, R. (1997). *The other struggle for equal schools: Mexican Americans during the civil rights era.* Albany: State University of New York Press.

Muñoz, C., Jr. (1989). *Youth, identity, power: The Chicano movement.* New York: Verso.

San Miguel, G., Jr. (1987). *"Let all of them take heed": Mexican Americans and the campaign for educational equality in Texas, 1910–1981.* Austin: University of Texas Press.

San Miguel, G., Jr. (1986). Status of the historiography of Mexican American education: A preliminary analysis. *History of Education Quarterly, 2,* 523–536.

San Miguel, G., Jr., & Valencia, R. R. (1998). From the Treaty of Guadalupe Hidalgo to *Hopwood:* The educational plight and struggle of Mexican Americans in the Southwest. *Harvard Educational Review, 68,* 353–412.

Vigil, J. D. (1998). *From Indians to Chicanos: The dynamics of Mexican culture.* Prospect Heights, IL: Wavelength Press.

ACKNOWLEDGMENTS

As with all projects, be they books or social movements, it takes a committed and coordinated effort by many people to achieve success. Such is the case both with the publication of this volume and with the Forum held at the University of California, Irvine, from which the book emerged. For over nine months, the Editorial Committee spent countless hours planning, discussing, and editing the Forum and this volume. We are especially grateful for their thoughtful and selfless efforts. On behalf of the Editorial Committee and the 1997–1998 *Harvard Educational Review* Editorial Board, we thank Manuel Gómez, Vice-Chancellor for Student Services at UC Irvine, for his moral and financial support in hosting our cosponsored Forum on April 25, 1998. Central to the success of the Forum was Santana Ruíz, Special Assistant to Dr. Gómez, as well as a UCI and Harvard alumnus, who laboriously and skillfully co-coordinated the Forum. We are also grateful to the student volunteers who provided invaluable assistance the day of the Forum. At *HER* we thank the Editorial Board for their support in making the Forum and book a possibility. We also thank Karen Maloney, Dody Riggs, and Joan Gorman for the support and patience they offered, both professionally and intellectually, in the production of the Forum and *The Elusive Quest for Equality,* and Harvard Graduate School of Education professor Julie Reuben for the use of her course title for this volume. We'd like to thank Manuel Hernandez-Trujillo for his powerfully inspiring artwork for the cover, which captures and reflects the content of the book as well as our collective histories, and also for his undying commitment to the Chicano community.

Lastly, we are deeply grateful to all the Forum participants and contributors to this book for your time and energies in helping us make these historic events possible. Your continued commitment and sacrifices for the educational advancement of Chicano/a communities through your scholarship and community work is profoundly appreciated.

¡Hasta La Victoria Siempre!

PART ONE

A History of Chicano/ Chicana Education

The Treaty of Guadalupe Hidalgo and the Racialization of the Mexican Population

MARTHA MENCHACA

n 1848, the United States and Mexico signed the Treaty of Guadalupe Hidalgo, ending the Mexican-American War. In the treaty, the U.S. government stipulated that Mexicans who lived within the newly annexed territory of the Southwest would be "incorporated into the Union of the United States" with the "enjoyment of all the rights of citizens" (Article IX). The treaty thus promised to protect the political rights of the conquered population. Tragically, within a year of the treaty's ratification, the U.S. government broke the citizenship equality statements it had enacted with Mexico and began a process of racialization that categorized Mexicans as inferiors in all domains of life, including education. This process of racialization can be defined as the use of legal process to confer legal privilege upon Whites and to discriminate against people of color.

The violation of the Treaty of Guadalupe Hidalgo was yet another stage in the legacy of discrimination that was part of Mexico's colonial history—part of the drama of empire, rooted in power and the role of the "Other," that had been played out under Spanish rule. When the U.S. government violated the treaty, the Mexican population of the U.S. Southwest found itself cast in a racialized role that reenacted the processes of categorization, repression, and domination that characterized the racialization of Mexicans under Spanish rule. When it conquered Mexico in 1521, Spain instituted a racial order assigning inferior legal rights to Indians, mestizos (people of mixed Spanish and Indian ancestry), and afromestizos (people of mixed Spanish, Indian, and African ancestry). In 1821, Mexico legally dismantled that racial order when it obtained independence from Spain. For Mexicans who lived in what would become the U.S. Southwest, however, that victory was short-lived, for the U.S. government's breach of the treaty marked the establishment of a new imperial power and racial order that again provided Mexicans with few civil rights. The repetition of the process of racialization—first by Spain and then by the United States—suggests the strong role that power and the idea of the "Other" play in this imperial drama. It further suggests that the United States' transgression of the Treaty of Guadalupe Hidalgo evolved tragically from these themes.

This historical analysis begins with the legacy of discrimination that was established in the aftermath of the Spanish conquest of Mexico and focuses on Spain's use of education to maintain and entrench their respective racial orders. It then examines the continuation of this legacy by the United States following the ratification of the Treaty of Guadalupe Hidalgo, when the next cycle of racialization commenced.

PRE-HISPANIC AND EARLY COLONIAL EDUCATION

[handwritten annotation: BEFORE SPANISH EUROPEANS]

In 1519, the Spanish began a legacy of discrimination with its colonization of Mexico (Díaz, 1963). At that time, hundreds of indigenous groups, with an estimated population of 30 million, lived in Mexico (Meyer & Sherman, 1995; Miller, 1985). Their political structure ranged from simple forms of organization, such as hunting and gathering, to highly developed state systems, such as those of the Aztec and the Maya (Gibson, 1964). The Aztec empire was the most powerful state system in Mexico; its administrative center was located in Tenochtitlán, present-day Mexico City. Its territories included the modern states of Mexico, Morelos, Puebla, Hidalgo, most of Veracruz, much of Oaxaca and Guerrero, as well as the coasts of Chiapas (Meyer & Sherman, 1995).

Spanish conqueror Hernán Cortés reported that, when he first visited Tenochtitlán, it was one of the cleanest and most beautiful cities he had seen (Díaz, 1963). Relations between the Spaniards and the Aztec emperor, Moctezuma II, were amicable at first, but soon changed. In 1521, fewer than nine hundred Spanish soldiers and eight thousand Tlaxcalans defeated the Aztecs and began the process of colonization (Díaz, 1963). In the first fifty years after the conquest, the Spanish gradually restructured central Mexico's social institutions, leaving many of the nobility in power (Liss, 1975; Powell, 1952): Aztec elites who had transferred their allegiance to the Spanish were allowed to remain in power, while those who challenged the Spaniards were replaced or murdered. During this restructuring, many indigenous institutions, including the Aztec educational system, continued to function. Because this was not immediately dismantled, we have information on its curriculum and function.

Throughout the Valley of Mexico, the Aztecs instituted two types of schools, differentiated by the economic status of students' families: the *calmecac* for the children of nobility, and the *telpochcalli* for commoners (León-Portilla, 1975; Meyer & Sherman, 1995). These schools simultaneously educated students and reproduced the Aztec social order. At the calmecac, the children of the nobility learned hieroglyphic writing, mathematics, astronomy, meteorology, zoology, botany, and history (Larroyo, 1946). Thus, the schools prepared them to be the leaders and administrators of the Aztec Empire. At the telpochcalli, commoners learned agricultural sciences, home economics, tax col-

Martha Menchaca

lection, and warfare (Larroyo, 1946). In every town in the Aztec Empire, the telpochcalli prepared students for practical professions, such as farmer, tax collector, low-level officer, and soldier. Although the dual school system effectively tracked students, it was not rigid, and students who were identified by their teachers as intellectually gifted were transferred to the calmecac schools, where they acquired the necessary skills for high-status professions (León-Portilla, 1975). Commoners were also taught Aztec history, as well as dancing, speech, and other social skills, to make them refined and honorable citizens of the community. Conceivably, these skills could help them enter the ranks of nobility, since performance in ritual was highly regarded and rewarded by the elite (Meyer & Sherman, 1995). By encouraging upward mobility through such recognition, Aztec society remained flexible and inclusive of commoners.

Before the Aztec schools were dismantled, the Catholic Church founded two educational systems for the Indians, the doctrina and the formal schools. Both systems were designed to acculturate and evangelize the Indians and to teach them the superiority of Spanish culture during a period when their own society was being destroyed and reconstructed.

DOCTRINA SCHOOLS

The evangelization of the Indians began in 1523 in Tlaxcala, Mexico (Engelhardt, 1929). The Tlaxcalans, allies of Cortés and the first Indians to choose to be Christianized, were taught a catechism that included the basic tenets of Christianity and concurrently attacked the validity of their indigenous religious beliefs. The various missionaries' styles of teaching depended on the amount of religious pluralism they were willing to tolerate (Lafaye, 1974). Many missionaries patiently allowed Indians to practice religious syncretism: that is, they were allowed to continue worshiping their deities while undergoing conversion to a Christianity that associated these deities with images of Catholic saints, Jesus Christ, and the Virgin Mary. This was an early form of bicultural education and an effective way to make the transition from one belief system to another without causing total ontological chaos among the Indians. Many priests, however, were less tolerant and refused to allow any form of religious syncretism. They punished the Indians for practicing pre-Hispanic religious rituals or for refusing to destroy their sites of worship.

By 1536, the evangelization of the Indians had spread outside the Valley of Mexico. Missionaries moved northward, as far as the present state of Jalisco, in search of Indians to convert (Engelhardt, 1929; Powell, 1952). Their movement into unknown territory was facilitated by the Spanish crown, which in 1512 had decreed under the Laws of Burgos that Indians had the legal right to learn Christian doctrine. The Laws of Burgos constituted protectionist legislation that decreed that Indians, like orphans, widows, and the wretched, would be protected and Christianized (Hanke, 1949). These laws gave the Catholic Church the responsibility to teach catechism to the Indians.[1] For this purpose, the Spanish eventually erected thousands of churches throughout Mexico.

FORMAL SCHOOLS

While catechism was used to teach the Indian masses the ways of the Spanish, other missionaries established formal schools for a select number of Indians. In 1523, the Spanish founded the first elementary school in Texcoco, now a district of Mexico City (Larroyo, 1946). Students learned writing, reading, singing, and music. Because the school became popular among Indian elites, the missionaries founded a second school, the Escuela de San Francisco, with an expanded curriculum that also included classes in advanced arts and vocational training.

By 1540, there were many Spanish elementary schools in Mexico City, Morelia, and Pátzcuaro; secondary schools offering more advanced studies did not yet exist. Instead, centers of higher learning that became interethnic meeting places under the control of Spanish friars were made available to adults (McDowell, 1980). In these schools, Indian scholars exchanged knowledge and taught missionaries about pre-Hispanic culture, in particular how to decipher hieroglyphic text (Klor de Alva, 1988). This was an important intellectual task, since the Aztec, Mixtec, Mayan, and Oaxacan peoples were among the indigenous cultures that used hieroglyphs to record their history and tax revenues, and to make mathematical and meteorological notations (Gutiérrez Solana, 1992). In turn, the missionaries taught the Indians to speak Spanish and prepared them to be interpreters and cultural brokers.

THE NOBLE SAVAGE DEBATE

Although the educational system established for the Indians illustrates a liberal phase in the colonization of Mexico, I am not suggesting that all Spaniards favored acculturating, Christianizing, and educating Indians. On the contrary, many Spanish officers and soldiers preferred to enslave them. The colonial debate over whether Indians should be enslaved encapsulates the conflicting views held by Spaniards and illustrates the important role education played in protecting the Indians' legal rights. The "Noble Savage debate" illustrates how education was used by the Catholic Church to argue that Indians were human and therefore could not be enslaved.

In Spain, Ginés de Sepúlveda, a renowned juridical scholar, was the most influential person arguing for enslaving Indians. In his works, among them

Democrates Alter, de Sepúlveda maintained that Indians were savages without souls—a view that countered the Catholic Church's interpretation of Indians as descendants of the lost tribe of Israel (Lafaye, 1974). The Church's and de Sepúlveda's divergent positions came to be known as the Noble Savage debate (Stocking, 1968). Although de Sepúlveda and his followers concurred that Indians probably were from the "promised land," he argued that on their exodus from Israel they came into contact with the devil and entered a stage of demonic savagery. De Sepúlveda claimed that Spaniards in the New World therefore had the right to enslave these savages. He cited the iconography found in hieroglyphic texts and on buildings as proof of his assertions.

On the other side of the debate was Father Francisco de Vitoria, who challenged de Sepúlveda's demonization of the Indians. De Vitoria argued for the Catholic Church and the crown to classify Indians as humans and thus to bestow on them the legal rights of human beings (Borah, 1983; Hanke, 1949). These rights included not being enslaved, being allowed to marry whomever they chose, being Christianized, being allowed to own property, and being allowed to live in towns and villages. Essentially, de Vitoria argued that Indians had the right to pursue happiness. His philosophy was reflected in the political activism of other clergy, such as Father Bartolomé de Las Casas, who moved from theory to activism by obtaining field evidence to support the position that Indians were rational beings with souls.

In 1502, de Las Casas first arrived in the New World in Hispaniola (present day Haiti and Dominican Republic) and later observed the mistreatment of the Indians throughout Latin America (Haring, 1963). In his travels, he observed the colonists overworking the Indians and treating them as animals. In essence, the colonists were breaking the religious and labor laws by denying Indians time to rest and to learn Christian doctrine (Pérez de Soto, 1774a). Most of the atrocities were committed by *encomenderos*, Spaniards who were awarded land and free Indian labor to work their *encomienda*, or estates.[2]

Although in theory the encomiendas were to be acculturation sites where Indians would be civilized and Christianized, they in fact became unofficial slave institutions (Vigil, 1984). Many missionaries, concerned about the Indians' suffering, intervened. They sent countless complaints to the Spanish king and lobbied to end the encomienda system (Borah, 1983). The king sent investigators to the New World to determine whether Indians were indeed being mistreated.

De Las Casas became the most outspoken critic of the encomiendas and launched an attack on them. Knowing that he needed evidence to prove the Indians' humanity if de Sepúlveda's claims were to be discredited, he refined the hypothesis that the Indians had migrated from Israel to the New World. De Las Casas's main argument centered on the Indians' capacity to learn Christian doctrine. He asserted that, since Indians were able to learn Christian doctrine and to read in Spanish, they had the capacity to think abstractly; this proved they were human (Wagner & Parish, 1967).[3] As a consequence of de Las Casas's research, de Vitoria successfully obtained the Indians' legal classification as human beings.

The enslavement of Indians became illegal in 1537, when Pope Paul III, in the papal bull *Sublimis Deus*, proclaimed Indians to be humans with the right to be Christianized and to own property (Hanke, 1949). The Spanish crown endorsed the proclamation and over time imposed additional protectionist laws. The position taken by the Catholic Church and the crown was a liberal stance that was not shared by the entire Spanish population or by most of the countries of Europe (Menchaca, 1996). Not until 1859 did most European countries accept that Indians and other people of color were not animals (Lyons, 1975; Menchaca, 1996).

Although the church succeeded in obtaining the legal status of human being for the Indians, it also endorsed the crown's position that they must be governed and protected. The crown therefore named the church the Indians' legal protector and gave it the responsibility to Christianize and convert them into loyal, tax-paying subjects (Polzer, 1976; Pérez de Soto, 1774a). These legal rights, which came to be known as de Vitoria's Natural Laws, in theory became standard practice in Mexico by 1550 (Hanke, 1949; Liss, 1975). As long as de Vitoria's Natural Laws did not conflict with the crown's colonization plans, officials were instructed to extend Indians their legal rights; however, if Indians resisted colonization, they were not to be given any legal rights and they could be enslaved (Pérez de Soto, 1774a).

By 1575, the Spaniards, with the assistance of the indigenous nobility, had secured military and political control of central and southern Mexico (Gibson, 1964). Once they were in control and no longer feared revolts, the Spaniards placed less significance on the welfare of the masses. Educating the Indians was no longer a priority, and schooling focused instead on the needs of Spanish children. Private schools were established for Spaniards, and Indians were admitted only on a limited basis. Ironically, in some schools Indian commoners were admitted and offered scholarships (Larroyo, 1946). It is not known when the Indian schools were dismantled, but we do know that over time their quality declined, as more emphasis was placed on teaching Indian students trades (Bayle, 1931). Schooling Indians became the exception, and catechism became the main mode of instructing them. Thus, education and/or the denial of education became entrenched as a mechanism of social control and a means by which the system of discrimination replicated itself.

MISCEGENATION LAWS AND RACIALIZATION

Coinciding with this decline in education was the passage of the first antimiscegenation decree, which also commenced the Spanish era, of officially racializing non-Whites (Pérez de Soto, 1774a). In 1575, viceroys, presidents, mayors, and all fiscal officers and their families were prohibited from marrying Indians. If any section of the decree were disobeyed, the crown required immediate dismissal of the official. Within a few years, the government expanded the decree to include all its employees; only military personnel were exempt. In 1592, it added a harsh amendment that required government employees to marry spouses born in Europe (Pérez de Soto, 1774b). Once again, breaking the decree meant immediate dismissal. The passage of these decrees signified the formation of a racial order in which race became the basis for ascribing and denying legal privileges.

By the end of the sixteenth century, Spanish officials had instituted the *casta* system, a racial order that legally distinguished Mexico's population on the basis of race (Lafaye, 1974; Mörner, 1967; Vigil, 1984). Those classified as Spaniards included *peninsulares*—individuals who had been born in Spain and were of full European descent—and *criollos*—those of full European descent who had been born in the New World.[4] The castas were mestizos—people of mixed Spanish and Indian descent—and other people of mixed blood. The Indian category included only people of full indigenous descent.[5]

Of the various racial groups, the Spaniards enjoyed the greatest social prestige and were accorded the most extensive legal and economic privileges. The legal system did not distinguish between peninsulares and criollos; nevertheless, the crown instituted policies requiring that high-level positions in the government and Catholic Church be assigned to peninsulares because it was believed that only they were fervently loyal to the Spanish crown (Haring, 1963; Meyer & Sherman, 1995). If the crown were unable to find peninsulares willing to accept appointments in colonies established along the frontier, the crown made exceptions to the decree for those areas and appointed criollos. It was required, however, that a criollo taking such an appointment be the son of a peninsulare. As a rule, peninsulares were appointed to positions such as viceroy, governor, captain-general, archbishop, and bishop, whereas criollos were appointed to less prestigious positions, such as royal exchequer (treasurer, comptroller) and judge, and, after 1618, to mid-level administrative positions in the church, such as priests or directors of schools.

The social and economic mobility of the rest of the population was seriously limited by the legal status ascribed to their ancestral groups. In theory, Indians were economically more privileged than mestizos because they held title to large parcels of communal land protected by the crown and the Catholic Church (Haring, 1963; Mörner, 1967). Despite their claim to property, however, the Indians were accorded little social prestige in Mexico and were legally confined to subservient social and economic roles regulated by the Spanish elite. Most Indians were forced to live in a perpetual state of tutelage controlled by the church, the state, or Spanish landowners.

Mestizos enjoyed greater social prestige than the Indians, but were considered inferior to the Spaniards. They were often ostracized by both Indians and Spaniards and did not enjoy certain legal privileges accorded either group. For example, most mestizos were barred by royal decree from obtaining high- and mid-level positions in the royal and ecclesiastical hierarchies (Haring, 1963; Mörner, 1967). Moreover, the Spanish crown did not reserve land for the mestizos under the *corregimiento* system—land reserved for the Indians and subject to church and royal policies—as it did for the Indians. For the most part, the only economic recourse most mestizos had was to enter the labor market or migrate toward Mexico's northern and southern frontiers. Each migrant who was the head of a household was awarded land and exempted from taxation for a period of approximately ten years (León-Portilla, 1972; Rubel, 1966; Weber, 1982).[6]

Free afromestizos—usually the children of Black male slaves and Indians —were accorded legal privileges similar to those of mestizos. Because they were of partial African descent, however, they were stigmatized and considered the social inferiors of Indians and mestizos (Love, 1971; Pi-Sunyer, 1957; Seed, 1988). Twenty-thousand Black slaves had been imported to Mexico by 1553 (Meyer & Sherman 1995); by the mid-1600s, however, 74 percent of racially mixed Blacks in Mexico were free (Aguirre Beltran, 1946; Love, 1971). The majority of afromestizos obtained their liberty with the Catholic Church's legal assistance. Although Blacks did not come under Pope Paul III's *Sublimis Deus,* the majority of them obtained their freedom under the Siete Partidas. The church had successfully obtained the freedom of children whose mothers were Indian and whose fathers were Black slaves; under the Siete Partidas, such children obtained the legal status of their Indian mothers and not the status of their slave fathers. The afromestizo children of Black women and Spaniard males did not receive similar legal protection.

By 1570, the sexual union of Spanish males and Indian females had produced 13,504 mestizos; by 1646, that population had increased to 277,610 and, in fact, outnumbered the Spaniards, afromestizos, and Blacks (Aguirre Beltrán, 1946; Meyer & Sherman, 1995). Although the mestizo population was rapidly growing, its numerical size was considerably smaller than that of the Indians who, in spite of several epidemics, numbered approximately one million in 1650 (Meyer & Sherman, 1995).

When the northern frontier was opened for settlement in 1598, Indians, mestizos, and afromestizos marched north with their colonial superiors.[7] They joined the northerly migration in an effort to improve their social position and to obtain economic opportunities not available to them in the interior of Mexico. Although the casta system allowed only Spaniards to be members of the local government assemblies and to occupy the highest positions within the government in the frontier zones, the racial order was flexible, and non-Whites were given the opportunity to enter any occupation and to establish farms and ranches. For them, this became an incentive to participate in the conquest of what would become the U.S. Southwest.

THE ESTABLISHMENT OF SCHOOLS IN THE SOUTHWEST DURING THE COLONIAL PERIOD

Spanish settlement of what is today the U.S. Southwest began in 1598; within a century, thousands of Spanish missionaries, soldiers, government officials, merchants, and farmers had erected missions, towns, garrisons, and *presidios* (regional military administrative centers) throughout the region (León-

Portilla, 1972; Weber, 1982). Permanent settlements were formed after the military gained control of an area. In most cases, the Spanish conquered the local Indians by using military force (Spicer, 1981). At times, however, Indians voluntarily complied in exchange for military protection against their indigenous enemies (Kessell, 1989; Persons, 1958).

Prior to the colonization of the area, the Spanish monarchy had decreed in the royal Ordinance of Pacification of 1573 that the region was to be colonized peacefully and that the missionaries were to be responsible for initiating the Indians' acculturation (Cutter, 1986). Throughout the Spanish period, missions became the main locus of Indian-Spanish contact (Weber, 1992). Mission records indicate, for example, that twenty-one thousand neophytes were baptized in 1821 and became registered members of the California missions (Hornbeck, 1978, 1989).[8] Between 1770 and 1834, nearly a half million Indians had lived in these missions at one time or another (Bowman, 1958).

Spanish-Indian contact was also common in Indian villages that had been incorporated as ally settlements, or Christian *rancherías* (Morfí, 1778/1977).[9] These alliances often commenced after a mission was founded and the missionaries befriended nearby Indian communities. Contact usually began with the use of Christianized Indians as interpreters (Bolton, 1960; Pérez de Soto, 1774a). When the church established new missions, it commonly transferred three Indian neophytes to assist the friars in the conversion of the Indians. If friendly relations followed, the conversion of the Indian settlements into Christian rancherías began. This conversion process, in some cases, took months or years; however, the transformation of Indian villages into Christian rancherías occurred only after the Indians voluntarily agreed to be baptized, to adopt Spanish customs—that is, to believe in Catholic doctrines, to speak Spanish, and to wear Spanish clothing—and to register the rancherías in the presidios as ally settlements (Polzer, 1976). The church also required that the Indians prove their goodwill by sending a high-ranking male youth to live in a mission or by allowing him to enter a religious college in the interior of Mexico. In this way, Christian rancherías officially became part of Spanish municipalities and the Indians became legal wards of the crown and church (see *Byrne v. Alas et al.*, 1888; Weber, 1982). Throughout the Southwest, eighty-one missions were established and became the centers of Spanish society (Chipman, 1992; Kessell, 1976; Merriam, 1955; Polzer, 1976; Weber, 1982). Most were able to establish a stable economic base to sustain the neophyte Indian population, as well as to assist the settlers.

TEXAS

The Spanish colonists were dispersed in the towns, presidios, missions, and ranches. The missions became the most important educational centers, where Indians were taught catechism and a select number were taught to read and write (Engelhardt, 1930). Schooling was a liberal practice employed by missionaries who sought to acculturate Indian children and prepare them to live among the colonists. Throughout the colonized region, the missionaries also offered schooling to the children of the colonists on a fee basis. This type of instruction, however, was temporary and generally lasted as long as the missionary was stationed on the frontier. Children usually learned to read and write from their parents (Sánchez, 1967). It was also common for high-level Spanish officers to educate their children by sending them to schools in the interior of Mexico, a form of private education unavailable to the commoner. Indians were sent to schools in the interior of Mexico only when the church chose to educate a child of a ranchería chief (see Polzer, 1976).

Texas was the first Southwest territory to establish a formal school that employed a professional teacher to develop curriculum and to instruct students on a regular basis. Founded in San Antonio in 1746, the first formal school was a private Catholic school limited to children whose parents were able to pay tuition (Berger, 1947). Forty years later, a second school was founded in San Antonio; this one lasted only three years because the parents had the teacher removed and could find no replacement. After 1782, the church ordered the missionaries to increase the secular education of the Indians in the areas of agriculture, horticulture, mechanical arts, and stock raising (Engelhardt, 1930). In essence, they were to prepare the Indians to become self-sustaining ranchers. Every mission began offering classes in agriculture and in other industrial occupations (Berger, 1947). Unfortunately, most of the missions in Texas were secularized within a decade, which led to the closing of the mission schools and to a decrease in agricultural science classes.

Although in San Antonio only one school remained open continuously, the educational system improved in Texas following the royal decree of 1793, which ordered local governments in the Southwest to establish public schools (Engelhardt, 1930). The decree was part of the crown's liberal philosophy to improve the cultural lifestyle of the colonies by schooling the children of the settlers and the Christianized Indians. Under this decree, school attendance was to be compulsory, and the schools were to be funded by taxes levied by local governments and from private donations. Indian children were allowed to attend public schools, but were not allowed to speak their native languages. If Indian students could not speak Spanish, they were to be taught Spanish, as all instruction was to be in that language. The royal decree was ambitious for its time and difficult to implement. Nonetheless, in Texas, government officers established schools in the garrisons, although the type of education they offered is unknown. Government officials in Texas also attempted to enforce the spirit of the decree by pressuring parents to send their children to school. In 1803, Texas passed an additional territorial compulsory educational law to put further pressure on parents (Berger, 1947). Although Texas required school attendance, resources were scarce and there were more students than there were schools in which to teach them.

CALIFORNIA

In California, the application of the royal decree of 1793 was successful, and Governor Diego de Borica enthusiastically prepared plans to establish schools in all major settlements. Although professional teachers were not hired, officers who were literate and willing to act as teachers were relieved from military duties. Within two years of the decree, the government in California had established five public schools—four in the presidial towns of Santa Barbara, San Diego, Monterey, and San Francisco, and one in the civilian township of San Jose (Engelhardt, 1930).[10]

The first public schools in California were founded in 1795 in San Jose and Monterey. Both schools were in areas with large civilian populations and stable local economies that depended on goods produced on ranches and missions (Garrison, 1930; Mason, 1986). The first teachers were Manuel Vargas, stationed at the garrison at San Jose, and José Rodríguez in Monterey. In 1796, a third school was established in Santa Barbara, a thriving community with one of California's most successful mission economies and a large afromestizo population (Forbes, 1966; Weber, 1992). The teacher was José Manuel Toca, a sailor who taught a class of thirty-two students. The fourth school was established in 1796 in San Diego, and Manuel Vargas from San Jose was recruited to open it. Vargas departed for San Diego after stabilizing the school in San Jose, leaving his twenty-seven pupils with their new teacher, retired ensign Ramón Lasso de la Vega. The fifth school was established in San Francisco in 1797 by Manuel Boronda, who also acted as the town's carpenter. Like the other teachers, he taught students to read and write; but as a devout Catholic, he also emphasized religion as a central part of his curriculum. In 1817, a sixth school opened in Los Angeles (Wess, 1978). Its first instructor was Máximo Pino, a disabled soldier who transferred to Los Angeles and was commissioned to start a school. After Pino, Los Angeles continued to offer schooling with only brief interruptions.

The teachers' wages differed, depending on the parents' financial status and the local government assemblies' ability to raise funds. In San Jose, parents paid the teacher an equivalent of 37 cents a month. In San Diego, twenty-seven parents paid the school teacher the equivalent of $100 annually, but parents who could not contribute were allowed to keep their children in school. In Santa Barbara, the cost of schooling was passed on to the soldiers, who voluntarily paid the teacher an annual sum of $125, the highest salary paid in the Southwest at that time. Why the soldiers chose to pay for local children's education is uncertain; one can surmise that they felt some sense of obligation. In Monterey and San Francisco, the teachers taught the children without pay.

Throughout the Spanish and Mexican periods, schools in California closed down temporarily when the teachers moved, but reopened as soon as a new teacher was available. As in Texas, school supplies such as books, charts, paper, pencils, and slates were scarce. This limited the curriculum teachers could offer. Since few textbooks were available, teachers used outdated government reports and books to teach children the alphabet (Tyler, 1974).

NEW MEXICO

Public education got under way in New Mexico after 1813. Unlike in California, where students were allowed to attend public schools irrespective of their parents' or the local government assemblies' ability to pay teachers' salaries, only the children whose parents contributed to the individual teacher's salary, or *dotación,* were allowed to attend school. Apparently, the royal decree of 1793 was ignored by the local government. Government administrators, who were part of New Mexico's elite class, did not consider public education important. The effort to institute public education in Mexico was again promoted by the royal government. In 1812, the Cortes, the Spanish parliament, ruled that all towns in Mexico were to establish public schools. Once again, New Mexico's government ignored the order. To motivate the local assembly residents to establish an educational system, the Cortes issued a direct order on January 26, 1813, that public education must be made available in New Mexico. New Mexico's governor was also ordered to establish plans for offering some form of higher education in Santa Fe, the capital (Barreiro, 1832, in Carroll & Haggard, 1942).

Following this decree, New Mexico established six schools. The date of their founding is uncertain; however, an 1832 report by government inspector Antonio Barreiro entitled *Ojeada: Sobre Nuevo México,* or *A Glimpse of New Mexico,* tells us that the schools were established during the Spanish period and that they remained in operation during the Mexican period (Barreiro, 1832, in Carroll & Haggard, 1942). According to Barreiro, the schools were founded after 1813 in the towns of Santa Fe, Albuquerque, Cañada, and in the Indian—*genízaro*—towns of Belén, San Miguel del Vado, and Taos.[11] Apparently these schools were badly funded and had limited supplies.

During the Spanish period, the schools in New Mexico generally emphasized reading and writing and did not offer expanded curricula. Only Santa Fe had textbooks and a professional teacher, Guadalupe Miranda, who offered advanced schooling to a select number of literate students in the home of Rafael Rascón, New Mexico's vicar general. Though supplies were limited, Barreiro found that New Mexico's teachers were paid well. Their stipends ranged from 250 to 500 pesos, but parents supplemented these modest salaries with gifts of cattle, food, and luxury items (Barreiro, 1832, Table 2, in Carroll & Haggard, 1942). While Santa Fe's teachers received the highest salaries, teachers in the Indian-genízaro towns received the lowest. Children whose parents could not pay school fees learned to read and write only if their parents were literate or if they were taught by missionaries.

ARIZONA

In Arizona, public schools were not available during the Spanish period, and few children were schooled by missionaries. The missionaries, who traditionally played important roles in schooling children in other regions, were preoccupied with their multiple duties as soldiers, farmers, and medical aides (Kessel, 1976). Their missionary work required that they travel hundreds of miles to reach their Christian rancherías, which left little time to teach children. Arizona settlers, however, contemplated opening two public schools in Tucson following the Cortes decree of 1812 and the visit of friar Juan Baptista de Cevallos. In 1814, the crown assigned Cevallos, the commissary prefect, to inspect Arizona settlements (Dobyns, 1974). He found no schools in Arizona and immediately ordered the settlers to hire two teachers to establish schools in Tucson and in Mission San Francisco Xavier del Bac.

Neither Cevallos nor the settlers acquired the necessary funds to establish the schools, but Cevallos's enthusiastic educational plans illustrate the dedication that many people had for the educational orders passed by the Cortes. These plans were part of a spirit of equality professed by the Cortes, largely to avert revolutionary independence movements in Mexico, including what would become the U.S. Southwest. The Cortes realized that, to avoid revolution, the hierarchical racial order had to be dismantled. The casta system was producing serious conflicts, and reforms were badly needed to improve the social and economic mobility of the non-peninsulare population.

PUBLIC EDUCATION DURING THE MEXICAN PERIOD, 1821 TO 1848

Toward the latter part of the Spanish period, the crown legislated racial reforms to improve the civil rights of the non-White population in Mexico. Indians and mestizos were the targeted groups of these reforms, for they constituted the majority population. The Cortes's aim at this time was to make these sectors loyal subjects by accelerating the Indians' assimilation and opening up economic opportunities for both mestizos and Indians. To reach these objectives, the Cortes abolished the casta system and gave Indians, mestizos, and free afromestizos the legal rights of Whites.

The first reforms were aimed at the Indians. On September 25, 1810, they were released from paying tribute to the crown and to local government (Borah, 1983), and were to be taxed in the same manner as other subjects.[12] On February 9, 1811, the crown decreed that Indians were permitted to raise any crop they chose, to enter any profession, and to transact business with anyone (Borah, 1983; Hutchinson, 1969). In sum, all economic and occupational restrictions were lifted.

The 1811 decree also abolished racial restrictions in the craft guilds and was directed to all non-Whites, excluding Black slaves. Prior to the decree, only peninsulares and criollos were allowed to work as master craftsmen, while mestizos and afromestizos were restricted to working as journeymen or unskilled laborers (Chance & Taylor, 1977; McAlister, 1963). Indians, of course, had been barred from the craft guilds. Lifting the racial restrictions in the guilds was of utmost importance to non-Whites, for whom the guilds were the main method of advancing economically (Poyo, 1991; Seed, 1982). Finally, the Cortes abolished most racial restrictions on citizenship with the 1812 Law of Cadiz, which proclaimed that Indians, mestizos, free afromestizos, criollos, and peninsulares were legally equal (Goodrich, 1926; Hutchinson, 1969; Menchaca, 1993). Previously, non-Whites had been able to obtain the legal rights of White citizens only by performing heroic acts during time of war (Pérez de Soto, 1774b). After 1795, they could also gain these rights by buying *cédulas* that gave them the legal status of Whites (Haring, 1963; McAlister, 1963).[13] In the area of education, the Cortes ruled in 1812 that public education was to be made available to all free children, irrespective of their parents' ability to pay (Larroyo, 1946).[14] Essentially, the Cortes removed all racial restrictions not related to Black slaves.

In what would become the U.S. Southwest, the Cortes's changes had only minimal economic impact, since many of the racial reforms were already in place before being legally mandated (Poyo, 1991). On the southwestern frontier, unlike the interior of Mexico, racial restrictions had traditionally been less rigid. For example, the Spanish crown had never enforced the craft guild racial restrictions (de la Teja, 1991; Persons, 1958; Tjarks, 1974). Non-Whites, including Indians, were able to enter any profession—tanner, blacksmith, carpenter, mason, printer, or artist.

Although the reforms had little economic impact in the Southwest, they allowed non-Whites to improve their standing within the political and social spheres. During the colonial period, non-Whites had been prohibited from participating in local government and were barred from positions as generals of garrisons or presidios (Haring, 1963; Pérez de Soto, 1774b). After the reforms, non-Whites could run for local offices and be eligible for high-level appointments within the government and the Catholic Church.

Throughout Mexico, the reform movement experienced a temporary setback when Ferdinand VII, the Spanish monarch, halted Mexico's political liberalism (Hall & Weber, 1984). Perceiving the Cortes as encroaching on his power, Ferdinand disbanded it in 1814 and nullified the racial reforms. In 1820, however, protests by the criollo elite and the masses forced Ferdinand to reinstitute the reforms (Haring, 1963).

In 1821, the Spanish monarch was no longer able to avert revolution, and Mexico obtained its independence from Spain. That year, the Plan de Iguala became Mexico's provisional constitution. It guaranteed citizenship and equality under the law to Whites, Indians, mestizos, and free afromestizos. Although the provisional constitution did not address the issue of slavery, Mexico's newly elected congressional delegates began the process of eradicating it in 1823, when they met to convert Mexico into a federal republic (Meyer & Sherman, 1995).[15]

After independence, the main problem in passing a national emancipation proclamation involved immigration reforms in Texas, which needed immigrants from the United States to assist the Mexican colonists in protecting their settlements against Indian raids. To attract immigrants, the Mexican government delayed reforming its slave code and temporarily allowed Anglo-American immigrants to bring slaves into Texas (Bugbee, 1898). Although only immigrants were permitted to bring slaves into Mexican territory, abolitionists pressured congressional delegates to suspend this practice.

In 1823, the government began to comply with the abolitionists and prohibited the purchase and sale of slaves in Mexico. Slave owners were ordered to free all slave children born in Mexico when they became fourteen years old; all adults slaves were to be set free after ten years in bondage. Finally, in 1829, President Vicente Guerrero issued Mexico's emancipation proclamation and released the last 10,000 slaves in bondage in Mexico, including those in Texas.[16] All former slaves became citizens of Mexico (Meyer & Sherman, 1995).

With respect to education, the Mexican government formed grand plans for educating the masses immediately after the War of Independence, but it lacked sufficient funds to implement them because Spanish officials had emptied the royal treasury, leaving the country bankrupt when Spain's hold over Mexico ended (Lafaye, 1974; Miller, 1985). In spite of its economic problems, however, the new republic pushed forward in the area of education and began to set up an elementary public school system. It considered public education a practical way to level the economic disparities caused by Spain's racially biased system (de la Peña, 1993). At the national level, under the Constitution of 1824, Mexico's Congress ruled that the federal government would promote public education by assisting the states and territories in developing educational policies. Selecting a curriculum, hiring teachers, and school funding would be the responsibility of the state and territorial governments (Berger, 1947; Tyler, 1974).

It was not until 1833 that a senior government official took an active stand toward educating the masses. Vice-President Valentín Gómez Farías lobbied for federal control of education to ensure that the masses, and not solely the elites, would benefit from educational reforms (Larroyo, 1946). He realized that responsibility for establishing a public school system would have to be taken from the states and territories and given to the federal government. He was unsuccessful in gaining federal control, but was able to enact educational reforms. Under his influence, a federal education agency was established to oversee the administration of public education. The Dirección General de Instrucción Pública (Administrative Center for Public Education) was charged with planning ways to make public education available to as many people as possible (Larroyo, 1946; Tyler, 1974). The Dirección began by secularizing public schools, requiring teachers to be certified, and reviewing textbooks every two years. Three years later, the federal government passed the Act of 1836, which required that primary schooling be compulsory and that schools be established in every town (Tyler, 1974). Local governments were responsible for raising the necessary funds by collecting an education tax. To assist local officials, the federal government ruled in 1842 that one-third of every centavo collected through its tax system was to be used for public education (Tyler, 1974). Though the taxes earmarked for public education were outrageously inadequate, the idea of federal funding for public education had finally begun.

In the meantime, public education had improved in Texas and California. These territorial governments enthusiastically endorsed educational reforms by passing compulsory public education acts several years before such action was taken by Mexico's new federal government. In 1827, the Constitution of the Territory of Coahuila y Tejas required all municipalities to establish compulsory primary public schools (Berger, 1947), and in 1833, California passed a public education act ordering a similar plan (Tyler, 1974).

CALIFORNIA AND NEW MEXICO

In California, during the Mexican period, the public schools established during the Spanish period continued to function. The missions also continued to school children. In 1834, to assist the badly funded yet energetic educational system in California, the Mexican government commissioned twenty teachers to open schools (Hutchinson, 1969). They arrived at San Diego as part of the Padres-Hijara Colony, which brought 239 colonists, many of whom were professionals, including teachers, lawyers, doctors, carpenters, distillers, tailors, and shoemakers (Weber, 1982). Only 20 percent of the group were farmers. Upon their arrival, these colonists dispersed to areas throughout California such as Monterey, San Jose, and Sonoma. Many of the teachers became important community members, as they replaced teachers in Monterey, Los Angeles, and Santa Barbara. They also taught in several of the missions (Hutchinson, 1969).

In New Mexico, the educational system did not expand during the Mexican period; the only improvement was in the availability of textbooks. Father Antonio José Martínez, the teacher at Taos, became a popular advocate for New Mexico's public educational system. Father Martínez confronted what he perceived as the main obstacle to improving the quality of public education in the schools—the absence of textbooks—by obtaining a printing press, writing and printing his own textbooks, and distributing them throughout the schools (Tyler, 1974). This dramatically improved the students' ability to learn, as they now had the opportunity for self-paced education, which helped them overcome the unavailability of teachers.

TEXAS

After Mexico's War of Independence, the public schools in Texas temporarily closed. In San Antonio, one private school remained open, and four private schools were established in Austin by Anglo-American teachers. Unlike the private school in San Antonio, which was well funded, the schools in Austin were transitory and lasted only until the teachers found better paying jobs (Berger, 1947).

Public schools were reinstated in 1828, following the Coahuila y Tejas constitutional ruling requiring them: San Antonio, La Bahía, and Nacogdoches each opened a public school (Berger, 1947). San Antonio's school used the Lancasterian system of education, and it became the model for the rest of the settlements.[17] In San Antonio, a professional teacher was hired, 150 pupils attended school on a regular basis, slate and pencils were available to students, one hundred school charts were used to assist in instruction, and thirty-six catechisms functioned as texts (Tyler, 1974). In La Bahía and Nacogdoches, supplies were scarce because, unlike in San Antonio where the school was funded completely by local taxes, teachers had to depend on the charity of the local population. The latter two settlements also did not hire professional teachers because of a lack of funds. Schooling improved in Nacogdoches when it became dominated by Anglo-Americans, who built a schoolhouse in 1831. Unfortunately, the number of Mexican students declined at that time; only one out of ten students was Mexican (Berger, 1947). Sadly, the situation in Nacogdoches would soon be replicated throughout the Southwest, when the United States annexed most of Mexico's northern frontier after the Mexican-American War.

THE TREATY OF GUADALUPE HIDALGO AND THE RACIALIZATION OF THE MEXICAN POPULATION

Mexico began to lose its hold over the Southwest in 1836, when Anglo-American immigrants won the Texas War of Independence and separated from Mexico (Weber, 1982). In 1845, matters worsened when the United States annexed Texas and continued its conquest of other parts of the Southwest. The following year, the United States declared war on Mexico. The final blow was struck in 1848 when the United States won the Mexican-American War and took possession of Mexico's northern territories—the present-day states of California, Arizona, New Mexico, and Texas. Mexico also lost parts of its northern frontier that today include Nevada, Utah, parts of Colorado, and small sections of Oklahoma, Kansas, and Wyoming. The Treaty of Guadalupe Hidalgo, which ended the war, was executed on February 2, 1848, in Guadalupe Hidalgo, Mexico, and ratified and exchanged at Querétaro, Mexico, on May 30, 1848 (Tate, 1969; Nine Statutes at Large, 1862). It stipulated the political rights of the inhabitants of the ceded territories, set the U.S.-Mexico border, and put several binational agreements on economic relations into effect.

Within a year, however, the United States violated the treaty's citizenship articles and refused to extend Mexicans full political rights because most of them were not White (Menchaca, 1993). Instead, the United States initiated a new cycle of racialization. When the United States took over the new territories, it nullified Mexico's liberal racial legislation and began the process of racializing the Mexican population.[18] Much as Spain had done, the United States gave full citizenship to Mexicans who were considered White and ascribed inferior legal status to people of color on the basis of race. At the time of the ratification of the treaty, the United States conferred full political rights only upon free Whites, while Blacks and Indians could be enslaved and indentured in most states. People of mixed European and Indian ancestry could not be enslaved, but they could be barred from voting, practicing law, becoming naturalized citizens, and, in many states, marrying Anglo-Americans (Konvitz, 1946; Menchaca, 1993).

The United States chose to violate Articles VIII and IX of the treaty, which gave all Mexicans U.S. citizenship. Article VIII stated that the United States agreed to extend citizenship to all Mexican citizens who remained in the ceded territories. If those individuals did not want citizenship, they had to so indicate within one year; otherwise, they would automatically become U.S. citizens (cited in Tate, 1969). Under Article IX, the United States further agreed that Mexicans who chose to become citizens would have all attendant rights of citizenship: "Mexicans who, in the territories aforesaid, shall not preserve the character of citizens of the Mexican Republic . . . shall be incorporated into the Union of the United States, and be admitted at the proper time . . . to the enjoyment of all the rights of citizens of the United States" (cited in Tate, 1969).

Almost immediately, the U.S. government abandoned its federal responsibilities to its new citizens. In 1849, Congress gave the legislators of the ceded territories and states the right to determine the Mexicans' citizenship status.[19] This move had a severe impact on Mexicans, as the state legislators chose not to give most of them the legal rights enjoyed by White citizens. Making matters worse for thousands of Mexicans, the Christian Indian population came under cruel governmental legislation. The Indian Intercourse Act of 1834, which stipulated that Indians were to be placed on reservations, governed the political status of these Indians. If they refused to be relocated, they could be punished, even sentenced to death (Dale, 1951; Four United States Statutes at Large, 1850). In effect, the Indian Intercourse Act of 1834 was designed to contain Indians on the reservations at all cost (Forbes, 1982; Takaki, 1990).

In 1849, Congress continued to place the Indians who had come from Mexico under the jurisdiction of the Intercourse Act; however, it gave the states and territories of the Southwest the right to "protect" its Christian Indian population. If the legislators chose, the Christian Indian population did not have to be placed on reservations. (Dale, 1951; Nine Statutes at Large, 1862). The exemption given to the Christian Indians was enacted by the federal government in recognition of the fact that they were peaceful people who had been civilized by the former governments of Spain and Mexico (Dale, 1951; *United States v. Lucero*, 1869). This right was to be held by the states and territories as long as the Indians were sedentary and did not behave as nomadic Indians. If the Christian Indians became vagrants, they immediately came under the jurisdiction of the Indian Intercourse Act (Heizer & Almquist, 1977; Jackson, 1903). Through this legal process, the Indian population was differentiated and racialized from the rest of the Mexican population.

CALIFORNIA

In California, the state constitution of 1849 granted only Whites full citizenship and gave only U.S. males and White Mexican males the right of suffrage; Indians, mestizos, and afromestizos were ineligible to vote and therefore were stripped of most political rights (California Constitution, 1849). Afromestizos were allowed to remain in California and were not placed in bondage or deported (Heizer & Almquist, 1977). Although the Christianized Indians were not placed in bondage, their property rights were rescinded; many became homeless and thus fell under the policies of the Indian Intercourse Act of 1834.

Making matters worse for Indians in general, Congress commissioned the U.S. War Department to clear the native population from hundreds of thousands of acres in preparation for the arrival of Anglo-American settlers (Takaki, 1990). This resulted in the massive reduction of the Indian population in California, from 310,000 in 1850 to 50,000 in 1855 (Cook, 1976; Hurtado, 1988). Those Christianized Indians who survived the extermination campaigns faced serious problems unless they could pass in public for a Mexican mestizo, as the U.S. government did not distinguish between nomadic or Christian Indians if the latter were homeless. Under California's Act of 1850, commonly known as the Indentured Act, if Indians became vagrants or orphaned minors, they could be placed in indentured servitude (Goodrich, 1926; Heizer & Almquist, 1977); if Indian paupers committed any punishable offense, they could be placed in bondage. In 1860, the Indentured Act was amended to order that, if an Anglo-American lodged a complaint against the moral or public behavior of an Indian—that is, loitering, strolling, or begging—within twenty-four hours that person could be placed in bondage and sold at auction.

TEXAS

In Texas, the racialization of the Mexican population began in 1836, immediately after the Texas War of Independence. After the Treaty of Guadalupe Hidalgo in 1848, the racialization process continued, although more humane Mexican Indian policies were instituted. The Texas Constitution of 1845 and the amendments of 1850 extended the rights of citizenship and voting to free Whites, to non-Black Mexicans, and to detribalized, taxpaying Indians (Judd & Hall, 1932).[20] To acquire the right of citizenship, however, Mexicans had to have resided in Texas prior to 1845 (Padilla, 1979); any Mexican immigrant arriving after that date was not eligible for naturalization and was thus prevented from becoming a qualified elector (Menchaca, 1993). At that time, only Whites were allowed to apply for naturalization (Naturalization Act of 1790; Naturalization Act of 1802). By 1850, most nomadic Indians had been exterminated or pushed into Mexico and were no longer a "problem" (Newcomb, 1986).

In 1849, Christianized Indians, although distinguished from Mexicans, were given property rights if they could prove they were culturally Mexican. Under Texas's state supreme court ruling in *McMullen v. Hodge and Others* (1849), Indians were granted property rights if they held perfect land titles and if they could prove that they or their ancestors were released by missionaries; spoke Spanish; passed a two-year secularization probationary period where they were observed to have practiced Mexican traditions; had been Spanish subjects or practicing Mexican citizens—that is, voted, ran for office, or practiced the holy Catholic sacraments; obtained property alienation rights releasing their land from the tutelage of the church and government; and had land that was surveyed according to U.S. laws (*McMullen v. Hodge and Others*, 1849).

In the case of afromestizos, Texas was not so kind. Most decisions pertaining to afromestizos were made after Texas won independence and were later ratified by the U.S. government upon the annexation of Texas. In 1836, afromestizos were given the dubious choice of remaining in Texas and becoming slaves or being deported to Mexico (Schwartz, 1975). This policy was consistent with the pro-slavery position instituted in the Republic of Texas after it gained independence from Mexico and again after being annexed by the United States.

NEW MEXICO

In New Mexico, the Mexican constitutional delegates, who were in the majority at the first territorial assembly, resisted the racialization of the population. From 1850 to the mid-1870s, a period during which Mexican mestizos retained considerable negotiating power, relatively liberal legislation was passed (Lamar, 1966).

At the constitutional convention on May 15, 1850, a delegation of eleven Mexicans and nine Anglo-Americans drafted New Mexico's first territorial constitution, the Organic Act (Larson, 1968). Father Antonio José Martínez, Taos's teacher and the author of New Mexico's first textbook, served as the president of the delegates. The Organic Act conferred full rights of citizenship on free Whites and those citizens of Mexico who had become citizens of the United States as a result of the Treaty of Guadalupe Hidalgo (New Mexico First Legislative Assembly, 1851). Within days, confusion arose over two issues: were the Pueblo Indians part of the conquered Mexican population that had obtained U.S. citizenship under the Treaty of Guadalupe Hidalgo? If so, did they thereby acquire the right of suffrage? A month after the constitution was drafted, the Cochiti Indians (part of the Pueblo Indians) sent a delegation to Santa Fe, where it met with government officials to discuss the Cochiti citizenship status (Larson, 1968). The Cochitis were assured that they counted as part of the conquered Mexican population and were therefore eligible to vote, which they did in New Mexico's first territorial election. Father Martínez was instrumental in this decision, as he advised several Indian groups to assert their rights.

On September 5, 1853, however, the U.S. Congress rescinded the Pueblo Indians' voting rights (Larson, 1968). In defense of the Indians' political rights, New Mexico's legislators attempted to bypass Congress's hostile response by giving Pueblo Indians full citizenship rights at the county and township levels (Deavenport, 1856). New Mexico's courts also prohibited federal Indian agents from relocating any Pueblo Indian to a reservation. The courts reasoned that, because the Pueblo Indians had adopted Spanish culture and the Mexican township system, they had the right to obtain special privileges not extended to other Indian groups. In *United States v. Lucero* (1869), for example, New Mexico's supreme court prohibited homesteaders from settling in Pueblo territory. The main purpose of the ruling was to ensure that the Pueblo Indians would not be converted into landless paupers, and thus come under the jurisdiction of the Indian Intercourse Act of 1834. The court reasoned that they deserved special privileges because generations of Spanish cultural indoctrination had uplifted their race. The court concluded that the Pueblo Indians had become a Mexicanized Indian race that had adopted the culture, names, and traditions of their Mexican neighbors:

> At the date of the treaty [*sic*] of Guadalupe Hidalgo the Indian race, in the Spanish sense of the term, were as much and fully citizens of the republic of Mexico as Europeans. . . . This court . . . does not consider it proper to assent to the withdrawal of eight thousand citizens of New Mexico . . . and consign their liberty and property to a system of laws and trade made for wandering savages and administered by the agents of the Indian department. . . . The Pueblo Indians of New Mexico are not within the provisions of the intercourse act [*sic*] of 1834. . . . In the absence of law or decision on the subject, are we not at liberty to conclude from these facts that the laws, the decision of the courts, and the acquiescence of the people, all recognized the Pueblo Indians as citizens, as "Mexicans?" We do so conclude. (*United States v. Lucero,* 1869, pp. 422, 432, 441, 456)

In short, the court decided that the Cochiti and other Pueblo were part of the conquered Mexican people who had obtained U.S. citizenship under the Treaty of Guadalupe Hidalgo.

The liberal New Mexico supreme court ruling and territorial laws were, however, short-lived. In 1876, the U.S. Supreme Court rescinded the Pueblos' claim to U.S. citizenship under the Treaty of Guadalupe Hidalgo (Davis & Mechem, 1915; *United States v. Joseph,* 1876). The revocation of these citizenship rights coincided with the growth of the Anglo-American community in the territory. In the late 1870s, the Anglo-American population gradually increased; by 1880 it had become the majority, numbering ninety thousand (Lamar, 1966). With this population growth had come political power.

The political status of the afromestizo population following the Mexican American War was tragic. Under the Organic Act of 1850, citizenship was extended to all former citizens of Mexico. That year, however, the U.S. Congress refused to recognize that Mexico had "ever" extended citizenship to Blacks (Larson, 1968). Congress also ruled that Blacks could not become citizens anyway, since Hispanos had to pledge allegiance to the new government to become citizens, and under the new system of law Blacks did not have this privilege. Thus, since Blacks were not allowed to take the oath of citizenship, the Organic Act could not apply to them.

Although Congress refused to confer U.S. citizenship on afromestizos, it did uphold the antislavery position passed by New Mexico's delegates in the first constitutional assembly (Larson, 1968). The delegates appended a statement to the Organic Act entitled "To the People of N. Mexico," in which they openly expressed hostility toward slavery. This document contained the declaration of rights of the inhabitants of New Mexico:

> Slavery in New Mexico is naturally impracticable, and can never, in reality, exist here; wherever it has existed it has proved a curse and a blight to the State upon which it has been inflicted—a moral, social and political evil . . . we have unanimously agreed to reject it—if forever. (cited in Larson, 1968, pp. 33–34)

As the slavery debate continued throughout the United States, congressmen from Texas and other pro-slavery states pressured New Mexico's legislators to change their position on slavery. New Mexico's representatives to Congress were issued a warning—unless New Mexico supported slavery, pro-slavery legislators would vote against New Mexico's becoming a state. New Mexico's citizens were also warned that Washington would withhold all favors until their legislators passed a slave code. In 1856, Miguel A. Otero, the territorial congressional delegate, finally succumbed to the pressure and offered a compromise: New Mexico would not become a slave state, yet it would prohibit Blacks from living in the territory for more than thirty days (Larson, 1968). Unfortunately, the Mexican delegates acceded to the racialization pressures that the U.S. Congress pressed upon New Mexico.

ARIZONA

Arizona was governed by the laws of New Mexico until 1863, when the United States gave it separate territorial status. Once it obtained its separate status, Arizona's legislators decided to base parts of their new constitution on the California model. It adopted California's constitutional citizenship and electoral eligibility requirements, and only White males and White Mexican males were incorporated as citizens with full attendant rights (Organic Act of Arizona 1863, cited in Hoyt, 1877). By 1873, most of the Indians in Arizona were relocated onto reservations; only a few thousand were allowed to remain in their homes (Hall, 1989; Wagoner, 1970). An exception was made in the case of some Mexicanized Papago Indians (Dale, 1951; see also Spicer, 1981). Bureau of Indian Affairs officers recommended that these Papagos be left undisturbed as they were deemed to be civilized. By 1890, the U.S. Census reported that the surviving 28,469 or so Indians in Arizona had been relocated to reservations (U.S. Census, 1904).

CONCLUSION: THE LEGACY OF DISCRIMINATION

Through such legislative action in Arizona and throughout the U.S. Southwest, the U.S. government institutionalized the legacy of discrimination. It was a legacy that the United States maintained through an electoral process that radically reduced the size of the qualified Mexican electorate and later enabled federal, state, and local governments to replicate the racialized status of Mexican Americans through education. Without the protection of civil rights promised in the Treaty of Guadalupe Hidalgo, Mexican Americans had no legal protections against the processes of racialization that were already in place for other people of color in the United States. Accordingly, they were consigned to an educational system of de jure and de facto segregation that entrenched the systems of power and furthered the perception of Mexicans as "other" in the context of U.S. society. It is a legacy of discrimination bequeathed by earlier empires—a legacy that continues today.

REFERENCES

Aguirre Beltrán, G. (1946). *La población negra de México, 1519–1810.* Mexico City: Ediciones Fuente Cultural.

Bannon, J. F. (1970). *The Spanish borderlands frontier, 1513–1821.* New York: Holt, Rinehart and Winston.

Bayle, C. (1931). España y el clero indígena de América. *Revista Quincenal Hispano Americana, 94,* 213–225.

Berger, M. (1947). Education in Texas during the Spanish and Mexican periods. *Southwestern Historical Quarterly, 51,* 41–53.

Bolton, H. E. (1960). *The mission as a frontier institution in the Spanish-American colonies.* El Paso: Texas College Press for Academic Reprints.

Bonifaz de Novello, M. E. (1975). *La mujer mexicana: Análisis histórico.* Mexico City: Empresa Mexicana.

Borah, W. (1983). *Justice by insurance: The general Indian court of colonial Mexico and the legal aides of the half-Real.* Berkeley: University of California Press.

Bowman, J. N. (1958). The resident neophytes of the California missions: 1769–1834. *Historical Society of Southern California Quarterly, 40,* 138–148.

Bugbee, L. G. (1898). Slavery in early Texas. *Political Science Quarterly, 13,* 389–413.

Byrne v. Alas et al., 16 Pacific Reporter 523-529 (1888).

California Constitution, Article ll, Section 1 (1849).

Carroll, H. B., & Haggard, J. V. (1942). *Three New Mexico chronicles.* Albuquerque, NM: Quivira Society.

Chance, J. K., & Taylor, W. B. (1977). Estate and class in a colonial city: Oaxaca in 1792. *Comparative Studies in Society and History, 19,* 454–487.

Chipman, D. E. (1992). *Spanish Texas 1519–1821.* Austin: University of Texas Press.

Cook, S. F. (1976). *The population of the California Indians 1769–1970.* Berkeley: University of California Press.

Cutter, C. R. (1986). *The protector of Indios in colonial New Mexico, 1659–1821.* Albuquerque: University of New Mexico Press.

Dale, E. E. (1951). *The Indians of the Southwest: A century of development and the United States.* Norman: University of Oklahoma Press.

Davis, S., & Mechem, M. (1915). *New Mexico statutes annotated.* Denver: W. H. Courtright.

Deavenport, J. J. (Comp.). (1856). *Revised statutes of the Territory of New Mexico.* Santa Fe, NM: Santa Fe Weekly Gazette.

de la Peña, G. (1993). Individuo, etnia, nación: Paradojas y antinomias de la identidad colectiva. In E. Garzón Valdín & F. Salmerón (Eds.), *Epistemología y cultura: En torno a la obra de Luis Villoro* (pp. 243–261). Mexico City: Universidad Nacional Autónoma de México, Instituto de Investigaciones Filosóficas.

de la Teja, J. (1991). Forgotten founders: The military settlers of eighteenth-century San Antonio de Béxar. In G. E. Poyo & G. M. Hinojosa (Eds.), *Tejano origins in eighteenth-century San Antonio* (pp. 27–39). Austin: University of Texas Press.

Díaz, B. (1963). *The conquest of New Spain* (6th ed., J. M. Cohen, Trans.) New York: Penguin Classics. (Original work written 1570)

Dobyns, H. F. (1974). *Spanish colonial Tucson: A demographic history.* Tucson: University of Arizona Press.

Engelhardt, Z. (1929). *Missions and missionaries of California: Vol. 1. Lower California* (2nd ed.). Santa Barbara, CA: Mission Santa Barbara.

Engelhardt, Z. (1930). *Missions and missionaries of California: Vol. 2. Upper California.* Santa Barbara, CA: Mission Santa Barbara.

Forbes, J. D. (1966). Black pioneers: The Spanish-speaking Afroamericans of the Southwest. *Phylon, 27,* 233–246.

Forbes, J. D. (1982). *Native Americans of California.* Happy Camp, CA: Naturegraph.

Four United States Statutes at Large, 1798–1845 (1850).

Garrison, M. (1930). *Romance and history of California ranchos.* San Francisco: Harr Wagner.

Gibson, C. (1964). *Aztecs under Spanish rule: A history of the Indians of the valley of Mexico.* Stanford, CA: Stanford University Press.

Goodrich, C. S. (1926). The legal status of the California Indian. *California Law Review, 24*(2), 83–100.

Gutiérrez, R. A. (1991). *When Jesus came, the corn mothers went away: Marriage, sexuality, and power in New Mexico, 1500–1846.* Palo Alto, CA: Stanford University Press.

Gutiérrez Solana, N. (1992). *Códices de México.* Mexico City: Panorama Editorial.

Hall, T. D. (1989). *Social change in the Southwest, 1350–1880.* Lawrence: University Press of Kansas.

Hall, T. D., & Weber, D. J. (1984). Mexican liberals and the Pueblo Indians, 1821–1829. *New Mexico Historical Review, 59,* 5–32.

Hanke, L. (1949). *The Spanish struggle for justice in the conquest of America.* Philadelphia: University of Pennsylvania Press.

Haring, C. H. (1963). *The Spanish empire in America.* New York: Harbinger.

Heizer, R., & Almquist, A. F. (1977). *The other Californians: Prejudice and discrimination under Spain, Mexico, and the United States.* Berkeley: University of California Press.

Hornbeck, D. (1978). Mission population of Alta California, 1810–1830. *Historical Geography, 8* (Supplement), 1–9.

Hornbeck, D. (1989). Economic growth and change at the missions of Alta California, 1769–1846. In D. H. Thomas (Ed.), *Columbian consequences: Vol. 1. Archaeological and historical perspectives on the Spanish borderlands west* (pp. 423–433). Washington, DC: Smithsonian Institution Press.

Hoyt, J. P., (1877). *The compiled laws of the Territory of Arizona.* Detroit, MI: Richmond, Backus.

Hurtado, A. (1988). *Indian survival on the California frontier.* New Haven, CT: Yale University Press.

Hutchinson, C. A. (1969). *Frontier settlement in Mexican California: The Hijar-Padres colony, and its origins, 1769–1835.* New Haven, CT: Yale University Press.

Hyman, H. M., & Wiecek, W. M. (1982). *Equal justice under law: Constitutional development, 1835–1875.* New York: Harper & Row.

Jackson, H. H. (1903). *California and the missions.* Boston: Little, Brown.

Judd, C. D., & Hall, C. Y. (1932). *The Texas constitution: Explained and analyzed.* Dallas, TX: Banks, Upshaw.

Kessell, J. L. (1976). *Friars, soldiers, and reformers: Arizona and the Sonora mission frontier, 1767–1856.* Tucson: University of Arizona Press.

Kessel, J. L. (1989). Spaniards and Pueblos: From crusading intolerance to pragmatic accommodation. In D. H. Thomas (Ed.), *Columbian consequences: Vol. 1. Archaeological and historical perspectives on the Spanish borderlands west* (pp. 127–138). Washington, DC: Smithsonian Institution Press.

Klor de Alva, J. J. (1988). *The work of Bernardino de Sahagun: Pioneer ethnographer of sixteenth century Aztec Mexico.* Albany: State University of New York Press.

Konvitz, M. R. (1946). *The alien and the Asiatic in American law.* Ithaca, NY: Cornell University Press.

Lafaye, J. (1974). *Quetzalcoatl and Guadalupe.* Chicago: University of Chicago Press.

Lamar, H. R. (1966). *The far Southwest, 1846–1912: A territorial history.* New Haven, CT: Yale University Press.

Larroyo, F. (1946). La educación. In A. Barocio et al. (Eds.), *México y la cultura* (pp. 584–625). Mexico City: Secretaría de Educación Pública.

Larson, R. W. (1968). *New Mexico's quest for statehood, 1846–1912.* Albuquerque: University of New Mexico Press.

León-Portilla, M. (1972). The Norteño variety of Mexican culture: An ethnohistorical approach. In E. Spicer & R. H. Thompson (Eds.), *Plural society in the Southwest* (pp. 77–101). New York: Weatherhead Foundation.

León-Portilla, M. (1975). *Pre-Columbian literatures of Mexico.* Norman: University of Oklahoma Press.

Liss, P. K. (1975). *Mexico under Spain, 1521–1556: Society and the origins of nationality.* Chicago: University of Chicago Press.

Love, E. F. (1971). Marriage patterns of African descent in a colonial Mexico parish. *Hispanic American Historical Review, 51,* 79–91.

Lyons, C. H. (1975). *To wash an Aethiop White: British ideas about Black African educability.* New York: Teachers College Press.

Mason, W. M. (1986). Alta California during the mission period, 1769–1835. *Masterkey, 60*(2/3) 4–14.

McAlister, L. (1963). Social structure and social change in New Spain. *Hispanic American Historical Review, 43,* 366–369.

McDowell, B. (1980). The Aztecs. *National Geographic, 158,* 714–751.

McMullen v. Hodge and Others, 9 Texas Reports (Texas State Supreme Court) 34-87 (1849).

Menchaca, M. (1993). Chicano Indianism: A historical account of racial repression in the United States. *American Ethnologist, 20,* 583–603.

Menchaca, M. (1996). Early racist discourses: The roots of deficit thinking. In R. R. Valencia (Ed.), *The evolution of deficit thinking: Educational thought and practice* (pp. 13–40). London: Falmer Press.

Merriam, C. H. (1955). *Studies of California Indians.* Berkeley: University of California Press.

Meyer, M., & Sherman, W. L. (1995). *The course of Mexican history.* New York: Oxford University Press.

Miller, R. R. (1985). *Mexico: A history.* Norman: University of Oklahoma Press.

Morfí, Fr. J. A. (1977). *Account of disorders in New Mexico* (M. Simmons, Trans. and Ed.) Isleta Pueblo, NM: St. Augustine Church. (Original work published 1778)

Mörner, M. (1967). *Race mixture in the history of Latin America.* Boston: Little, Brown.

Naturalization Act of 1790, ch. 3, sec. 1.

Naturalization Act of 1802, ch. 28, stat. 1.

New Mexico First Legislative Assembly. (1851). New Mexico Organic Law [Act] of 1850. In *Laws of the Territory of New Mexico* (pp. 17-24). Santa Fe, NM: James L. Collins.

Newcomb, W. W., Jr. (1986). *The Indians of Texas: From prehistoric to modern times.* Austin: University of Texas Press.

Nine Statutes at Large and Treaties of the United States of America, 1845–1851 (1862).

Padilla, F. (1979). Early Chicano legal recognition, 1846–1897. *Journal of Popular Culture, 13,* 564–574.

Pérez de Soto, A. (Comp.). (1774a). *Recopilación de leyes de los reynos de las Indias: Vol. 1* (3rd ed., books 1, 2). Madrid, Spain: Published under the royal orders of Don Carlos II, King of Spain. (Original work published 1681)

Pérez de Soto, A. (Comp.). (1774b). *Recopilación de leyes de los reynos de las Indias: Vol. 2* (3rd ed., books 3, 4, 6, 7). Madrid, Spain: Published under the royal orders of Don Carlos II, King of Spain. (Original work published 1681)

Persons, B. (1958). Secular life in the San Antonio missions. *Southwestern Historical Quarterly, 62,* 45–62.

Pi-Sunyer, O. (1957). Historical background of the Negro in Mexico. *Journal of Negro History, 42,* 237–246.

Polzer, C. W. (1976). *Rules and precepts of the Jesuit missions of northwestern New Spain.* Tucson: University of Arizona Press.

Powell, P. W. (1952). *Soldiers, Indians and silver: The northward advance of New Spain, 1550–1600.* Berkely: University of California Press.

Poyo, G. E. (1991). The Canary Islands immigrants of San Antonio: From ethnic exclusivity to community in eighteenth-century Béxar. In G. E. Poyo & G. M. Hinojosa (Eds.), *Tejano origins in eighteenth-century San Antonio* (pp. 41–60). Austin: University of Texas Press.

Robinson, W. W. (1948). *Land in California.* Berkeley: University of California Press.

Rubel, A. (1966). *Across the tracks.* Austin: University of Texas Press.

Sánchez, G. I. (1967). *Forgotten people: A study of New Mexicans.* Albuquerque, NM: Calvin Horn.

Schwartz, R. (1975). *Across the rio to freedom: United States Negroes in Mexico.* El Paso: University of Texas at El Paso.

Seed, P. (1982). Social dimensions of race: Mexico City, 1753. *Hispanic American Historical Review, 62,* 569–606.

Seed, P. (1988). *To love, honor, and obey in colonial Mexico: Conflicts over marriage choice, 1574–1821.* Stanford, CA: Stanford University Press.

Spicer, E. (1981). *Cycles of conquest: The impact of Spain, Mexico, and the United States on the Indians of the Southwest 1533–1960.* Tucson: University of Arizona Press.

Stocking, G. W., Jr. (1968). *Race, culture and evolution.* New York: Free Press.

Takaki, R. (1990). *Iron cages: Race and culture in nineteenth century America* (2nd ed.). New York: Alfred A. Knopf.

Tate, B. (1969). *Guadalupe Hidalgo Treaty of Peace 1848 and the Gadsen Treaty with Mexico 1853.* Truchas, NM: Tate Gallery and Rio Grand Sun Press.

Tjarks, A. (1974). Comparative demographic analysis of Texas, 1777–1793. *Southwestern Historical Quarterly, 77,* 291–338.

Tyler, D. (1974). The Mexican teacher. *Red River Valley Historical Review, 1,* 207–221.

U.S. Census Bureau. (1904). *Abstracts of the twelfth census of the United States 1900* (3d ed.). Washington, DC: Government Printing Office.

United States v. Joseph, 94 U.S. 614-619 (1876).

United States v. Lucero, 1 S. Ct. Territory New Mexico 423-458 (1869).

Vigil, D. (1984). *From Indians to Chicanos.* Prospect Heights, IL: Waveland Press.

Wagner, H., & Parish, H. R. (1967). *The life and writings of Bartolomé de Las Casas.* Albuquerque: University of New Mexico Press.

Wagoner, J. J. (1970). *Arizona territory 1863–1912: A political history.* Tucson: University of Arizona Press.

Weber, D. J. (1982). *The Mexican frontier, 1821 to 1846: The American Southwest under Mexico.* Albuquerque: University of New Mexico Press.

Weber, D. J. (1992). *The Spanish frontier in North America.* New Haven, CT: Yale University Press.

Wess, M. (1978). Education, literacy and the community of Los Angeles in 1850. *Southern California Quarterly, 60,* 117–142.

NOTES

1. The Laws of Burgos were an extension of the Siete Partidas code of law enacted in Spain in 1265.

2. As part of the agreement between the crown and the *encomenderos*, an encomendero had the right to receive Indian tribute in the form of free labor, as well as to take possession of part of the Indians' property (Meyer & Sherman, 1995). Indians were allowed to work their own land but were also required to plow, seed, and harvest the encomenderos' land without recompense.

3. Father Bartolomé de Las Casas conceded to his opponents that Indians were culturally inferior and barbarous, a condition easily resolved by Christianizing them. He favored replacing the encomienda system with a mission system in which Indians could live under the tutelage of the friars rather than the encomenderos.

4. As miscegenation increased among the Spanish elite, the criollo category was redefined. This occurred around 1774 (Bonifaz de Novello, 1975; Mörner, 1967).

5. The analysis of Mexico's racial order is partly based on my research published in Menchaca (1993).

6. After 1680, mestizos were allowed to become parish priests in Mexico's frontier settlements or in sparsely populated areas (see Haring, 1963, pp. 194–218).

7. The Chichimeca Indians prevented Spaniards from establishing colonies in Northern Mexico. After decades of battles, they were defeated in 1591 (see Powell, 1952).

8. Bolton (1960), Bowman (1958), and Mason (1986) found mission records that indicate it was common for some California missions to have over two thousand Indians in residence.

9. Scholars use the term *ranchería* to refer to permanent Indian villages.

10. Scholars disagree on which Spanish settlements in California can be considered towns. Officially, only San Jose, Santa Cruz, and Los Angeles were founded as towns; however, since the presidios acquired a township structure when the colonists arrived and these settlements functioned as towns during the Mexican period, some scholars refer to presidio settlements as presidial towns. For differing interpretations, see Bannon(1970), Mason (1986), Robinson (1948), and Weber (1992).

11. A *genízaro* is a mestizo of Spanish and Pueblo Indian descent, or a detribalized Indian. Genízaro towns were settlements occupied predominantly by detribalized Indians who adopted the lifestyle of colonists and mestizos of Pueblo Indian and Spanish descent. See Gutiérrez (1991) for a discussion of the genízaros.

12. Hutchinson (1969) claims that the Cortes released the Indians from paying tribute on May 26, 1810.

13. A *cédula* was a legal document giving special privileges to individuals. In the case of race, it gave a non-White person the legal status of a Spaniard.

14. In 1814, the Spanish monarch returned to the throne, disbanded the Cortes, and brought the reform movement to a halt. In 1820, he reinstituted the reforms to avert independence movements (see Hall & Weber, 1984).

15. Mexico became a federal republic under the Constitution of 1824, which was drafted on November 27, 1823 (Meyer & Sherman, 1995).

16. In Texas, Anglo-American slave owners refused to comply with the emancipation proclamation. This issue became one of the major issues leading to the Texas War of Independence (Bugbee, 1898; Schwartz, 1975; Weber, 1982).

17. California, Texas, and New Mexico began implementing the Lancasterian system of public education commonly employed in the interior of Mexico. Mexico had adopted the Lancasterian mode of teaching from England, as it was considered to be the best method of educating a large number of students at minimal expense. Under this system, one professional teacher supervised twenty student teachers who, in turn, instructed students (Larroyo, 1946). The professional teacher selected the best students and taught them an advanced curriculum. These student teachers were placed in classrooms and the professional teacher supervised their work. The Lancasterian system was adopted in the Southwest, but succeeded only in Texas. In California and New Mexico, it was soon abandoned (Tyler, 1974).

18. I define racialization as the legal process used to confer legal privileges upon Whites and to discriminate against people of color. After the signing of the Treaty of Guadalupe Hidalgo, this process culminated in the denial of basic civil rights to people of color, as Mexicans were differentiated and assigned legal status on the basis of race.

19. At this time, the United States had the power to determine citizenship eligibility requirements, a power given to them by the Constitution of the United States (U.S. Constitution, cited in Hyman & Wiecek, 1982).

20. In 1868, when the federal government passed the Fourteenth Amendment with the intention of legislating a uniform citizenship law, it eliminated the states' right to extend voting to Indians (Menchaca, 1993).

THE SCHOOLING OF MEXICANOS IN THE SOUTHWEST, 1848–1891

GUADALUPE SAN MIGUEL, JR.

After the signing of the Treaty of Guadalupe Hidalgo in 1848, which ended the Mexican-American War, people of Mexican origin in what is now the U.S. Southwest found their world dramatically changed.[1] The ways Mexicans were educated also changed dramatically during the first decades of U.S. rule. As in earlier decades, education comprised both informal and formal forms,[2] but unlike in the Spanish colonial and the Mexican periods when informal education dominated, formal schooling under U.S. rule assumed an increasingly important role, particularly in the Mexican community. The needs of an emerging Protestant capitalist economy and polity, along with the community's desire for the knowledge to facilitate its integration into this new social order, was the impetus for the growing importance of schooling.[3]

Schooling was not a novelty in the Southwest. Before the Anglo-Americans arrived, the political leaders of far northern Mexico had established schools. Although those schools were not centralized, widespread, or permanent, they were part of Mexican community life and contributed to the promotion of literacy and culture in these frontier regions.[4]

The schools established after the Mexican-American War differed from earlier ones in at least two ways. First, they were sponsored not only by the Catholic Church, but also by a variety of other religious, secular, and public authorities. Despite these different sponsors, however, state-based public education became the dominant form of schooling in the Southwest by the late 1870s. Second, post-1848 education assumed a new social goal of Americanization and became increasingly inhospitable to minority ethnicities and identities. Schools, especially public schools, became subtractive institutions, meaning that they sought to "de-ethnicize" the Mexican-origin population and to remove all vestiges of ethnicity from their operations and curriculum.

EMERGENCE OF SCHOOLING AND DOMINANCE OF PUBLIC EDUCATION

Before the Mexican-American War, schooling for the general population was sponsored primarily by the Catholic Church.[5] In the post-1848 period, the Church continued to promote and expand education for Mexican children, but unlike in earlier decades, other groups also established schools, as noted above. Among the most important of these were Protestant groups, public officials, and, to some extent, Mexican community members.

CATHOLIC SCHOOLS IN THE SOUTHWEST

Catholic schooling was very much a part of Mexican culture in the Southwest before the Mexican-American War. After 1848, it expanded significantly as the Church strengthened its role in the emerging American social order. As part of this effort, the Church rebuilt its churches, reaffirmed its authority over religious practices, and reestablished control over its flock. It also established educational institutions in the Southwest, including academies and convents for girls, colleges and seminaries for boys, and parish schools for working-class children.[6] The need to maintain patriarchal ideals in the frontier and to teach the appropriate gender roles for participation in the emerging social order led to the establishment of separate male and female institutions.[7]

The Church's primary reason for building schools throughout the region was initially to strengthen the religious tenets promoted during the years prior to American annexation and to eliminate ignorance in general. The Roman Catholic Bishop in New Mexico, J. B. Lamy, for instance, was struck by the deplorable state of education in New Mexico when he arrived in 1851. He noted: "Every vestige of school had vanished [and] churches and school houses were in a crumbling state." He believed that this deterioration had resulted in widespread ignorance, illiteracy, and immorality. Schooling, especially in Catholic institutions, was necessary to eliminate ignorance and to uplift the moral and "mental" culture of the native Mexican population residing in the territory.[8] The proselytizing efforts of various Protestant denominations, the increasing secularization of American institutions—especially the emerging public school—and the attacks against the church in various parts of the country later encouraged Catholic officials to promote the construction of additional parishes and schools through which to propagate an American Catholicism.[9]

The establishment of Catholic schools for Mexican children began almost simultaneously throughout the Southwest during the 1850s and continued for the next several decades. In New Mexico, between fifteen and twenty schools in as many cities were established between 1853 and 1874. The first Catholic schools for Mexican children were established in Santa Fe. Nuestra Señora de la Luz (for girls) opened in 1853, and the Colegio de San Miguel (for boys) began operations in 1857.[10]

In California, schools were established for Mexican boys and girls in several cities, including Santa Barbara, Ventura, and Los Angeles.[11] Among the

Guadalupe San Miguel, Jr.

first Catholic schools for Mexican children in Los Angeles were the Picpus School for boys (1851) and the Institución Caritativa for girls (1856). Both provided religious instruction and basic reading and writing for the poor children of Los Angeles.[12]

In Texas, a handful of schools for Mexican children were established in cities such as El Paso, Brownsville, Corpus Christi, and San Antonio.[13] The first school for Mexican girls was Ursuline Academy in San Antonio, established in 1851 by the Order of Saint Ursula. In 1852, the San Fernando Boys' School, established by the same order, opened in San Antonio.[14]

The successful establishment of Catholic schooling for Mexican children was due to three major factors: the recruitment of foreign teaching orders willing to work for subsistence wages; the support of large numbers of Spanish-speaking Catholics who wanted to preserve their identity; and the church's willingness to meet the cultural demands of its Spanish-speaking flock.

Foreign Teaching Orders

Foreign teaching orders became crucial in the establishment of Catholic schools for Mexican children in the early decades of U.S. rule. In New Mexico, for instance, four religious orders dominated Catholic schooling during the period from 1853 to 1874—Sisters of Loretto, the Christian Brothers, Sisters of Charity, and the Jesuits.[15] In California, at least nine religious orders established and staffed these new schools.[16] Religious orders also were asked to assist in the establishment of Catholic schools in Texas. In his massive study of the Catholic heritage in Texas, Carlos E. Castañeda identifies over twenty religious orders that came from Europe to establish missions, convents, and schools during the second half of the nineteenth century.[17]

The Support of Spanish-Speaking Catholics

The presence and support of large numbers of Spanish-speaking Catholics who wanted to maintain their cultural values was also a crucial factor in the establishment and expansion of Catholic schools in the Southwest. Mexican Americans generally accepted U.S. rule and the necessity of learning new rules and patterns of communication, but most of them also wanted to maintain their identity. They promoted the acquisition of a distinct bicultural and bilingual identity in the emerging Anglo social order and demanded that religious, educational, and governmental institutions value that identity.[18] Many of these individuals heartily supported the establishment of Catholic schools with the expectation that religious leaders shared their values, including those of cultural maintenance in an emerging Anglo order. Support was not limited to schools taught by religious orders, but was also given to parish and parochial schools.

The Support of the Catholic Church

A final factor in the origins and expansion of Catholic schools in the Southwest was the Catholic Church's willingness to meet the cultural and spiritual demands of Mexican Americans. By the mid-1850s, the Catholic Church hierarchy on the East Coast already had an informal policy in place to provide ethnically homogeneous schools segregated by nationality to meet the needs of non-English-speaking Catholic immigrants who demanded church support of their efforts at cultural preservation.[19] Newly appointed church leaders in the Southwest responded to the Mexican population and its demands for cultural maintenance in a similar manner. If Mexicans demanded it, the church established ethnically segregated parishes and schools for them; if they did not, it established territorial parishes and schools open to all children in their jurisdiction, including Mexican Americans.

PROTESTANT SCHOOLS IN THE SOUTHWEST

Protestants began building schools in the Southwest in the 1850s with the coming of lay missionaries interested in converting Mexicans to their beliefs. Various denominations, including Baptists and Congregationalists, were involved, but the most active were the Presbyterians. Although preaching and congregation-building were the primary means for evangelizing the Mexican-origin population before the Civil War, education was not ignored. In Texas, for instance, at least four Presbyterian missionaries sought to convert the Mexican population between 1836 and 1860—Sumner Bacon, W. C. Blair, John McCollough, and Melinda Rankin. In addition to preaching Protestant ideals to adults, they proposed teaching them to children in the schools. For these missionaries, education was an indirect means of converting Mexican youth to Protestant beliefs.[20]

Baptist missionaries in New Mexico also promoted and used education in their evangelization efforts during the 1850s. Lack of funds and opposition from Catholic bishops and priests, however, stifled their efforts in the early decades of U.S. rule.[21]

During the post–Civil War years, Protestant denominations increased their proselytizing activities in the Southwest and began to emphasize the importance of schooling and to establish mission schools in various parts of the country.[22] Protestant school-building succeeded in this period because of several factors: missionaries' efforts, Presbyterian evangelization policy, the lack of public schools, and the support of the Women's Executive Committee. Determined missionaries such as Sheldon Jackson, David F. McFarland, John A. Annin, and James A. Roberts believed that schools would enable them to reach Mexican children more effectively.[23] The Presbyterian Church's new evangelization policy favored the establishment of schools for members of the "exceptional" populations in areas without any public education facilities.[24] The vigorous financial and moral support of the newly established Women's Executive Committee of the Presbyterian Church also facilitated the establishment of these schools.[25]

Presbyterians established a variety of elementary and secondary schools for Mexican children to convert the Mexican population and to promote Americanization. In the words of Presbyterian missionary Melinda Rankin, the primary purpose of elementary schools was "to give them the Gospel, which is the antidote for all moral evils."[26] Forty-nine mission schools, also known as plaza schools, were established for Mexican children between 1879 and 1890.[27] Their number decreased significantly in the 1890s as communities established their own public educational facilities, but new mission schools continued to be founded during the next two decades.[28]

Protestant groups also established secondary schools. Between 1868 and 1896, Protestant ministers and laypersons established at least nine secondary boarding schools in New Mexico, Texas, and California.[29]

The purpose of these secondary schools was to train a Christian leadership that would promote Protestantism and Americanization. Although occasionally labeled "industrial," these schools aimed at providing Mexican-origin individuals with instruction suitable for economic mobility and for leadership positions in the larger society. They were similar to post-bellum schools and colleges established in the South by northern philanthropists and religious organizations such as the American Missionary Association.

These southern mission schools had assumed the task of training a Black professional elite and an educated leadership after most states failed to provide quality public education in the late 1860s.[30] Despite the fact that they were called "colleges," most focused on pre-college instruction. Protestant schools in the Southwest were similar to these schools, for they provided Mexican-origin children with some trade training, a traditional academic curriculum, and experience in civic affairs.

PRIVATE SECULAR SCHOOLS IN THE SOUTHWEST

Members of the Mexican community also established schools in selected urban and rural areas. Although there is insufficient data to describe the nature and extent of these community-sponsored secular schools of the nineteenth century, evidence abounds of their existence throughout the Southwest. Private schools, for instance, were found in northern and southern California. In Los Angeles, a variety of schools were established in the 1850s. One author noted that there were as many as six "little educational groups" that met privately in 1851.[31] In the mid-1850s, Antonio Jimeno del Recio established a school in his own home for instructing Spanish-speaking children, but it lasted only as long as donations supported it.[32] On September 27, 1856, *El Clamor Público*, a Spanish-language newspaper published in Los Angeles, noted that José R. Nielson, an Anglo linguist, had opened a school for Spanish-speaking children in Cristobal Aguilar's home near the plaza.

Nielson, who taught in Spanish and English, called the school "La Mexicanita." In Monterey County, California, T. S. Robert, the area superintendent, noted that in 1860 the Mexicano population in the area had two private schools that taught in Spanish.[33]

Private schools for Mexican children existed in various parts of New Mexico and Texas as well.[34] In New Mexico, for example, one resident reported that "perhaps there was one [private school] in La Plaza de los Manzanares, as my father heard people speak of *el maestro Barela,* who is not mentioned in public school records, but evidently had a school there." Private school attendance by Mexican children was also reported in Rosa, New Mexico, where the teacher lived in each student's home for a period of time.[35]

The first report of Mexican children's enrollment in a private school in Texas was in 1871. The school, established at Martha's Ranch near Isleta, was taught in Spanish by E. N. Ronquillo until the 1890s.[36] In 1857, Mexican children began to attend Aoy School in El Paso. Its founder, O. V. Aoy, used his own money to rent the building, furnish it, and buy supplies for the students.[37] Although complete data on these schools are missing, their presence suggests a strong desire for schooling among Mexican Americans.

PUBLIC SCHOOLS IN THE SOUTHWEST

Local officials also established public schools for Mexican children in this period, but, unlike Catholics and Protestants, they were in no hurry to do so. During the first two decades of U.S. rule, few public schools were provided for Mexican children in Texas or California.[38] New Mexican officials wanted to open schools, but were unable to do so because of lack of money, dependence on federal authorities, and political differences among themselves.[39]

The only exceptions to this pattern of delayed schooling were in San Antonio, Texas, and in a few California cities where local officials established schools for Mexican children or allowed them to enroll in regular public schools. Commitment to the principle of public education for all children and to the belief that the schools were instruments of assimilation motivated public officials in these cities to establish these schools and to include Mexican children in public school systems.[40]

After 1880, the number of schools for Mexican children in general increased dramatically because of popular demand, legal mandates, increasing financial ability of local government, and a greater acceptance of the ideal of common schooling. Provision of public schooling, however, occurred in the context of increasing social discrimination and a general subordination of the Mexican-origin population. The interaction of society and education produced a pattern of institutional discrimination reflected in the establishment of segregated public schools.

In Texas, officials established segregated schools for Mexican working-class children in the rural areas during the 1880s and in the urban areas in the 1890s. The need to maintain a cheap labor source on the ranches probably accounted for the earlier presence of Mexican schools in the rural areas, since schools, in combination with adequate housing, discouraged Mexican farm workers from migrating to other job sites.[41] In New Mexico, officials established segregated schools in 1872. Within the next two decades, enrollment skyrocketed. The schools were so successful that, by 1891, approximately 54 percent of New Mexico's children were enrolled in public schools.[42]

California officials did not build additional schools for Mexican children until the influx of Mexican immigrant students at the turn of the century. Schools that existed continued to be segregated and, in some cases, were inferior to the Anglo schools.[43]

The availability of public schools throughout the Southwest led to increased enrollment, but the numbers varied significantly within regions, across time, and by immigrant status.[44] Variations in the political and economic circumstances of Mexico and the border areas may have been responsible for these fluctuating enrollment rates.[45]

Enrollment rates of Anglos and Mexican Americans also varied significantly in the Southwest, with Mexican Americans in general having lower enrollment rates than Anglos. Although the enrollment gap decreased over time, there were still significant differences between Anglo and Mexican-origin enrollment rates. English-only policies, community distrust of English-only public schools, and poverty influenced educational development and led to the enrollment gap between Mexicans and Anglos.[46]

Despite the various forms of schooling in the Southwest, by the 1880s public education was emerging as the dominant form. Catholic and Protestant schooling was still extremely important, but educated a decreasing portion of the Mexican population. Most church schools were small and scattered in a few cities and towns throughout the Southwest. Public schooling, on the other hand, rapidly increased and became more important over time. Unlike religious or private secular schools, public schools were located in most cities and counties of each territory and state in the Southwest.

New Mexico is illustrative of this trend. In 1870, there were five public schools and thirty-six private institutions. Total enrollment stood at 1,798, and the majority of these students were enrolled in private schools. By 1876, there were 133 public schools and less than forty private institutions. Public school enrollment stood at 5,625—almost five times greater than private school enrollment. Eleven years later, private school enrollment had increased slightly, but public school enrollment had exploded to approximately 13,136. By the turn of the century, public education in New Mexico was clearly the dominant form of schooling for Mexican children. Similar developments occurred in other parts of the Southwest.[47]

AMERICANIZATION AND THE SCHOOLS

The schools that emerged in the Southwest after 1848 were more diverse in the goals they pursued. In the decades prior to U.S. rule, schools were primarily responsible for teaching reading and writing and some religion. Beginning at mid-century, however, they underwent significant changes and took on the new task of transforming the cultural identities of groups perceived to be foreigners. In other words, the schools assumed the function of Americanization.[48]

In historical literature, Americanization usually refers to an organized national political movement that compelled immigrants during the second decade of the twentieth century to adopt "Anglo-American ways while remaining at the bottom socioeconomic strata of society."[49] But this policy was more than a coercive twentieth-century political movement to promote the adoption of U.S. economic, political, religious, and cultural forms. It was a complex social and institutional development that originated in the colonial period to inculcate American ways and to discourage other immigrant and minority group cultures.[50] Occasionally, it promoted the maintenance of these cultures, but this was rare. I refer to the former process as subtractive Americanization and to the latter as additive Americanization.[51]

Both processes of Americanization were integral aspects of school development in this period. Subtractive Americanization occurred when schools devalued particular minority groups and their specific cultural heritages, when they sought to replace the identities of these groups with an idealized American one, or when they sought to remove minority communities, languages, and cultures from the curriculum and educational structures. Additive Americanization occurred when the schools promoted cultural maintenance or when they specifically valued minority participation in education, encouraged the development of a bicultural identity, and promoted minority communities, languages, and cultures in their curriculum and operations.[52]

CATHOLIC SCHOOLS AND AMERICANIZATION

Most of the Mexican schools in the Southwest promoted either subtractive or additive Americanization, but there were significant differences between their approaches. Catholic schools, for instance, took a stand in favor of Mexican Americans and their cultural heritage. For the most part, they validated rather than disparaged this group and its cultural heritage in the process of teaching them American social, economic, and political ideals.[53] This accommodative approach to Americanization, as noted earlier, was due primarily to official Catholic Church policy on national parishes and influenced by demography, geography, immigrant desires, and the threat of Protestant evangelization efforts.[54]

School operations and practices reflected the Catholic Church's approach to Americanization. Catholic authorities, for instance, used Spanish as a tool of instruction, named these institutions after well-known Mexican religious figures, and encouraged the Mexican-origin population to participate in the schools' support and maintenance.[55] Because of this accommodative stance, Mexican Americans, despite their distrust of formal church policies and practices, strongly supported the establishment of Catholic schools in the Southwest. They donated materials, volunteered their labor, and generously gave money to establish and maintain them.[56]

PROTESTANT SCHOOLS AND AMERICANIZATION

The Protestant schools also took a position on Mexican Americans and their identity—in contrast to Catholic schools, they were hostile to them. Protestant school leaders viewed Mexicans as illiterate, perversely immoral, superstitious, "densely ignorant," and lacking in "civilized" customs.[57] They often viewed their secular and Catholic-based culture in negative terms.[58] One of the central purposes of Protestant schools, therefore, was to transform this group into Americans by stamping out their distinct religious and ethnic identity and replacing it with an idealized Protestant-based American identity.

Over time, however, Protestant schools became somewhat accommodating because of Mexican American resistance to Protestant teachings. Resistance eventually led to a more favorable but still paternalistic view of Mexicans and their cultural heritage and to the selective use of their language and culture in schools. Many Protestant schools, for instance, occasionally used Spanish-language materials and instruction in the classroom. They also used secular aspects of the Mexican cultural tradition in the curriculum and promoted certain secular patriotic celebrations such as the dieciseis de septiembre (Mexican Independence Day) or cinco de mayo (the date on which Mexicans defeated the invasion of their country by the French).[59]

Protestant schools used Spanish and Mexican culture to accomplish a more rapid and less painful method of Americanization. Language and cultural maintenance, if it occurred, was probably an unintentional outcome of Protestant methods.

PUBLIC SCHOOLS AND AMERICANIZATION

Public schools, like Catholic ones, originally promoted additive Americanization. In the early years of U.S. rule, they promoted the use of Spanish in the schools, included Mexican cultural heritage in the curriculum, and encouraged members of the Catholic and Mexican communities to participate in them. The major reason for this accommodation to minority group members and their heritage in the early decades of U.S. rule was structural. Public schools, unlike those established by religious groups, were local institutions, controlled by members of the local communities. In many parts of the Southwest, local communities were composed primarily of Mexican American individuals and officials who were members of the Catholic Church. Under these circumstances, Mexican Americans and Church officials assumed important governance, administrative, and instructional positions in the schools and made decisions favoring the use of Spanish as the language of instruction and the use of Catholic printed materials, including the Bible, in the curriculum.

The use of Spanish and Catholic materials in the curriculum and the presence of Mexican Americans and Catholic officials in the schools, however, made public education suspect in the eyes of many Southwestern Anglo officials. Because many public schools used non-English languages and often included non-Anglos at all levels of school decisionmaking, many Anglo officials did not view public education as "American" in character. The primary task of these individuals was not to Americanize Mexican children, but to Americanize the public school. Their goal was to transform public schooling into an essentially American institution before they could successfully embark on the transformation of the ethnic identities of those perceived to be foreigners. In practical terms, this meant that Mexican Americans and Catholics—as well as the languages they spoke or the cultures they embraced—had to be replaced by American individuals and cultural forms, including the English language and nonsectarianism. In acquiring these American characteristics, the public schools themselves became increasingly subtractive institutions.

AMERICANIZATION AND THE TRANSFORMATION OF PUBLIC EDUCATION

The process of transforming an accommodative institution into an essentially "American" public school system in the Southwest was a constant but uneven one that began in the mid-1800s and continued into the early twentieth century. This transformation was achieved through a process of subtraction—that is, the "official" removal of all minority communities, languages, and cultures from the governance, administration, and content of public education. Occasional opposition from people of Mexican origin, concerned Catholic officials, and sympathetic educators slowed but did not halt these efforts.

MEXICAN AMERICAN PARTICIPATION

In the early years of U.S. rule, Mexican Americans assumed important elective positions at various levels of government throughout the Southwest and made significant decisions about public education. The presence of Mexican Americans in decisionmaking positions in general and in school decisionmaking positions in particular varied across region and time. It was most significant in New Mexico and less so in California and Texas.

In Texas, few Mexican Americans were elected to public office because of their relatively low representation in the general population, high poverty and illiteracy rates, low naturalization rates, and Anglo intimidation.[60] In central and south Texas, however, they represented a significant proportion of the voting public and were thus able to elect a few community members to office. Most served in the legislature, but few held positions on the committees responsible for public education policy. Between 1850 and the 1880s, only eight Mexican Americans held legislative positions in Texas, all of them in the lower house. At the county and local levels, the participation of Mexican Americans was practically nil.[61]

In California, Mexican Americans served in various capacities in the state legislature, on county school boards, and in local school positions. From

1849 to 1864, for instance, six people of Mexican origin were elected to the California State Senate and twelve to the State Assembly.[62] Between 1852 and 1865, approximately six of 293 county superintendents were Mexican Americans.[63] In communities such as Santa Barbara and Los Angeles, Mexican Americans were elected to local school boards and comprised either the majority or a significant proportion of those elected to these positions during the first half of the 1850s.[64]

The importance Mexican Americans held in public education is indicated by the role Mariano Vallejo, a state legislator from the San Francisco Bay area, played in establishing California's education system. In 1849, he served on a committee responsible for supporting a provision to the first state constitution that outlined the California public school system. At the constitutional convention in Monterey, California, the provision's strongest support came from Robert Semple, the convention president, and six of his lieutenants, including Vallejo. Semple and the others blocked amendments that could have modified the proposed educational provisions. As a result of their actions, California enacted one of the nation's most comprehensive public school provisions in 1850.[65]

Mexican Americans in elective offices also supported bilingual instruction, participation by Catholic officials, and the use of Catholic materials in instruction. For example, in 1850 in Los Angeles, Mexican Americans were the dominant group in local city councils and school boards. During this period, they enacted local ordinances supporting the establishment of public schools for Mexicans and Anglos, bilingualism in the schools, and public funding of Catholic schools. Although some of these decisions were rescinded years later, their passage indicated the role Mexican American officials played in promoting decisions favorable to their political and cultural interests.[66]

In New Mexico, participation at all levels of school decisionmaking was significant. Unlike in Texas and California, Mexicans were the numerical majority in New Mexico throughout the entire nineteenth century. In 1850, they were 90 percent of the territorial population; half a century later, they were 64 percent of the total population.[67] Because of their numerical representation in the population, they were elected to the senate and assemblies in large numbers during the first three decades of U.S. rule and served on important constitutional and legislative committees responsible for enacting school law. Ten out of eighteen delegates elected to the 1850 constitutional convention were Mexican Americans. Mexicans were also elected in large numbers to the territorial legislatures from 1850 to 1890. Throughout this period, with few exceptions, they comprised more than 50 percent of all legislators and sat on all major senate and assembly committees responsible for enacting educational legislation.[68]

Mexican Americans in New Mexico also served in many county and local school positions. For example, in the 1873–1874 school year, they comprised approximately 77 percent of the total number of county superintendents in the territory. In several areas, they comprised the majority of the local school boards.[69] As members of these decisionmaking structures, Mexican Americans supported the establishment of public education facilities for all children, the participation of various groups in the schools' maintenance, and the use of Spanish in the schools.[70]

As in California's school system, Mexican Americans also played key roles in establishing New Mexico's public school system. In 1850, ten elected Mexican delegates to the 1850 constitutional convention collaborated with other delegates to establish the educational provisions of the 1850 constitution that would lay the foundation for a system of public schools throughout the territory. Mexican Americans also sat on state and assembly committees responsible for enacting educational legislation. From 1850 to the 1890s, they enacted over six major school bills. During the same period, they appealed to Washington for direct appropriations to fund establishment of adequate public schools for the entire population.[71]

Over time, however, Mexican American participation in school decisionmaking throughout the Southwest decreased, largely for demographic and racial reasons. Increasing Anglo immigration to the Southwest led to dramatic declines in the Mexican-origin population and in its ability to elect or appoint Mexican Americans to important decisionmaking positions. In those areas where they remained a significant part of the population, Anglos used a variety of schemes to ensure that they would not assume these positions.[72]

The pattern of declining participation varied tremendously across the Southwest. In California, Mexican American representation in the state legislature and in local and county positions for all intents and purposes disappeared by the mid-1860s. In Texas, all forms of participation disappeared by the 1870s. In New Mexico, the process was more gradual and less traumatic; still, by 1891, no Mexican Americans were found in city superintendent positions, only a few on county school boards, and proportionally fewer on committees responsible for public education legislation.[73]

CATHOLIC OFFICIALS' PARTICIPATION

Another important aspect in the Americanization of public education involved the removal of Catholic officials from the schools. In Texas and California, their removal was accomplished quickly because of the numerical and political dominance of Protestant Anglos, the rapid subordination of the Mexican population, and the relatively powerless position of the Catholic Church in civic matters. In the New Mexico Territory, however, Catholic participation in public education lasted several decades after U.S. rule was established. For example, in New Mexico, the Catholic bishop served on the Territorial Board of Education into the late 1870s, and Catholic officials served on county and local school boards in the 1880s.[74]

Anglo officials, most of whom were avid Protestants, vehemently opposed Catholic involvement in public education and sought to remove Catholic Church officials from school-related positions. From the 1870s until the early 1890s, public officials and school reformers conducted a campaign to remove Church officials from public schools. Most historians refer to this campaign to separate church and state as the "school question."[75] Many contemporary Mexican Americans, however, viewed it as an attack on their centuries-old heritage.[76] Protestant hostility decreased in 1891 with the passage of an English-only public school law that officially removed the Catholic Church from the governance of public education.[77]

THE "SUBTRACTION" OF SPANISH

Public officials also removed the Spanish language from the public schools. The campaign to remove Spanish from public education was part of a general nativist phenomenon that affected all non-English languages and cultures and all public institutions across the nation. It was in part a response to increasing diversity in the United States. The presence of diverse ethnic groups raised anxieties and fears among the Anglo population, including the impact that immigrants could have on American culture, on social and political unity, and on the political hegemony of White America.[78] In response, White educators and other policymakers initiated campaigns against diversity. The primary goals of this movement were the promotion of Anglo cultural purity, unification of the nation through establishment of a common culture and a common language, and maintenance of White political dominance. In many ways, the campaign to remove Spanish from the public schools in the Southwest was merely the regional expression of a national campaign.

The subtraction of Spanish from public education was accomplished through the enactment of progressively stronger English language policies. These policies not only prescribed English as the medium of instruction in the schools; they also discouraged, inhibited, or prohibited the use of Spanish.[79] In some cases, language designation was usually accompanied by discriminatory legislation and practices against the minorities who spoke the language.[80]

The subtraction of Spanish from the schools occurred in two phases. In the first phase, mostly during the 1850s, Spanish was usually only discouraged from being used as a medium of instruction in the schools. Both Texas and California, for instance, enacted legislation in this decade mandating English in the schools and restricting the use of Spanish.[81] During the 1850s, Anglo officials in New Mexico tried to enact an English-language law and to remove Spanish from the schools, but they were unsuccessful because of the size and political strength of the Mexican American population.[82]

During the second phase, from 1870 to the early 1890s, Spanish was banned from the public schools. In 1870, Texas and California passed English-only laws prohibiting the use of Spanish in the public schools.[83] A similar English-only law was passed in New Mexico in 1891.[84] Anglos' increased anxieties over the continued growth of minority groups and their increasing impact on American religion, culture, politics, and social life served as the impetus for the passage of these laws.[85]

The passage of progressively stronger English-language laws and the restrictions on use of the Spanish language did not have an immediate impact on minority group members or public officials; many of them continued to use this language despite policy restrictions. It did, however, affect the language's status in the schools and Anglo attitudes toward it. In most cases, these restrictions reaffirmed the primacy of one language—English—at the expense of others.

Most Mexican Americans opposed subtractive language policies. More specifically, they opposed English policies that failed to protect the importance of Spanish to the Mexican population or that favored its removal from the schools.[86] The strongest opposition came from New Mexico because of the size and influence of its Mexican American community, but there was also resistance in California and Texas. In the New Mexico Territory, for instance, Mexican Americans consistently opposed the establishment of a public school system that did not support the use of Spanish as a language of instruction.[87] In California and Texas, the Mexican community also consistently opposed English-only rulings and practices in the schools.[88]

THE "SUBTRACTION" OF MEXICAN CULTURE

Finally, school officials subtracted Mexican culture from the public school curriculum. Public officials were able to remove courses pertaining to Catholic topics and Mexican history from the public schools in California and Texas by the mid-1850s because of the small size of the Mexican population and the relatively weak position of the Catholic Church in those states.[89] In New Mexico, however, school officials encountered significant opposition from Catholic officials and Mexican Americans, due largely to the combined efforts of the politically influential Catholic Church and the large Mexican American leadership. Both groups fought to have Catholic topics in general and Mexican history courses in particular taught in the public schools until the 1890s.

Mexican heritage classes were eventually replaced by new courses and instructional materials that reflected the American experience. The Mexican American presence in the Southwest was now interpreted through the eyes of the dominant Anglo group—an interpretation that generally tended to omit the contributions of Mexican Americans and to provide a distorted, stereotypical view of them and their cultural heritage.[90]

The curriculum became Anglocentric by the 1870s, as indicated by history textbooks used in the schools. History books, which began to appear a decade after the Mexican American War ended in 1848, contained only disparaging comments about the Mexican presence in the Southwest. These books consistently denounced the character of the Mexican people, and stressed the nobility of the Anglos.[91]

Most of the late nineteenth- and even early twentieth-century history textbooks presented Texas history through a narrow focus and omitted or minimized the cultural contributions of Spain and Mexico to the development of

Texas. According to the authors of these textbooks, little or nothing transpired in Texas worthy of record before the coming of the first Anglo settlers from the United States.[92]

CONCLUSION

The establishment of Catholic, Protestant, secular, and public schools in the Southwest during the second half of the nineteenth century indicated that schooling, especially public education, was assuming an increasingly important role in the new American social order for a variety of social, economic, religious, and political reasons. Although Mexican children were excluded from public education during the first decades of U.S. rule, the availability of these diverse forms of schooling also means that, they had varying degrees of access to Catholic, Protestant, and community schools.

Beginning in the 1850s, the schools took on the Americanization of the Mexican-origin population. Both Catholic and Protestant schools and, to some extent, private secular ones quickly assumed this role. Public education, however, faced a dilemma: it could not Americanize because of the presence and influence of Mexican Americans and Catholic officials in its governance and administration. Thus, before the public schools could fulfill their role of transforming the identities of those viewed as "foreigners," public education itself had to be Americanized. This was achieved through a process whereby all forms of "foreignism" were "officially" removed from the governance, administration, and content of public education. In doing so, the public school itself became an increasingly subtractive institution. By century's end, public education had become an essentially American public institution ready to assume its role of Americanizer in the Southwest.

NOTES

1. In the text, "Mexican," "Mexican American," and "Mexican-origin" are used interchangeably. "Anglo" is a common term used to refer to Anglo-Americans and European immigrants in the Southwest. It is important to note, as does Montejano, that the use of "Mexican" and "Anglo" conceals considerable diversity in the way members of these groups have identified themselves. Mexicans, for instance, have called themselves Mexicano, Castilian, Spanish, Hispano, Latin American, Chicano, and Hispanic. Each identity reflects a class character as well as a political context. Likewise, Anglo-Americans and European immigrants, including such non-Anglo groups as Irish, Italian, and Jewish, were referred to by many in the Southwest as simply "Anglos" or "Whites." See David Montejano, *Anglos and Mexicans in the Making of Texas, 1836-1986* (Austin: University of Texas Press, 1987), p. 10.
2. About schooling and literacy in the colonial period, see Bernardo P. Gallegos, *Literacy, Education, and Society in New Mexico, 1693–1821* (Albuquerque: University of New Mexico Press, 1991).
3. Carl F. Kaestle, *Pillars of the Republic* (New York: Hill & Wang, 1983). Kaestle argues that economic, demographic, cultural, and political influences encouraged U.S. acceptance of increased state involvement in public education in general and support for schooling dedicated to moral education, good citizenship, and assimilation. See especially pp. 62–74.

4. Gallegos, *Literacy*.

5. As early as the 1790s, a few schools were established by the state, but with little success. For examples of these early state-sponsored schools, see Gallegos, Literacy, pp. 21–36.

6. The Catholic Church hierarchy expressed dismay over the moral and religious beliefs of the Mexican-origin population, expelled Mexican-origin priests and replaced them with European ones, and eliminated Mexican traditions from the church. They also condemned the Penitentes, a religious organization of Mexican laymen, the lack of regular church attendance, and the Mexican community's failure to support its new policies of taxation and moral regeneration. The church's view of Mexican Americans and their religious practices in many cases led to misunderstandings and conflicts between the institutional church and the Mexican-origin community. Despite these misunderstandings, the Mexican community continued to support the church and its teachings. See Jay P. Dolan and Gilberto M. Hinojosa, eds., *Mexican Americans and the Catholic Church, 1900–1965* (Notre Dame, IN: University of Notre Dame Press, 1994). See also Odie B. Faulk, ed., *John Baptist Salpointe: Soldier of the Cross* (Tucson, AZ: Diocese of Tucson, 1966), and Carlos Castañeda, *The Church in Texas Since Independence, 1836–1950, Vol. 7, Our Catholic Heritage in Texas, 1519–1936* (1958; rpt. New York: Arno Press, 1976).

7. On the establishment and modification of patriarchy in the Southwest during the second half of the nineteenth century, see Richard Griswold del Castillo, *La Familia* (Notre Dame, IN: University of Notre Dame Press, 1984). On the role that private institutions played in teaching gender roles, see David Tyack and Elisabeth Hansot, *Learning Together: A History of Coeducation in American Schools* (New Haven, CT: Yale University Press, 1990).

8. Ellen Lucille Riser, "St. Michael's High School: A Beacon of Light," *New Mexico Historical Review, 55,* No. 2 (1980), 140.

9. Lazerson notes that most Catholic historians agree that the growth of a separate Catholic school system was a response to the rapid development of a Protestant-based public school system. But public schools were rare in the Southwest during the first decades of American rule. See Marvin Lazerson, "Understanding Catholic Educational History," *History of Education Quarterly, 17* (1977), 297–317.

10. *St. Michael's College, 100 Years of Service* (Santa Fe, NM: St. Michael's College, 1959); Sister M. Lilliana Owens, S.L., "Our Lady of Light Academy, Santa Fe," *New Mexico Historical Review, 13,* No. 2 (1938), 129–145.

11. These Catholic schools initially were state supported, but in 1852, a new law prohibited religious schools from sharing in the apportionment of state funds. California Superintendent of Public Instruction, *First Biennial Report* (Sacramento: State Printer, 1866), p. 248.

12. Sister Rose I.H.M, Society of Southern Emanuel, "The Parish Schools of Our Lady Queen of the Angels," *Historical California Quarterly, 43* (1961), 446–459, quote from p. 447.

13. Castañeda, *The Church in Texas*, pp. 285–347.

14. M. S. Friedman, "An Appraisal of the Role of Public School as an Acculturating Agency of Mexican Americans in Texas, 1850–1868," Diss., New York University, 1978, pp. 142, 145.

15. The Sisters of Loretto first came to the New Mexico Territory in 1853. The Christian Brothers came from France to New Mexico in 1859. The Sisters of Charity and the Jesuits arrived in New Mexico in 1865 and 1870, respectively. Louis Avant, "History of Catholic Education in New Mexico since the American Occupation," Diss., University of New Mexico, 1940, pp. 100–104.

16. William F. North, "Catholic Education in Southern California," Diss., Catholic University of America, 1936, pp. 123–150.

17. Castañeda, *The Church in Texas*, pp. 285–347.

18. Richard Milk, "The Issue of Language in Education in Territorial New Mexico," *Bilingual Review/Revista Bilingüe, 7* (1980), 212–221; Guadalupe San Miguel, Jr., "Status of the Historiography of Mexican American Education: A Preliminary Analysis," *History of Education Quarterly, 26* (1986), 523–536; Richard Griswold del Castillo, *The Treaty of Guadalupe Hidalgo: A Legacy of Conflict* (Norman: Univeristy of Oklahoma Press), pp. 88–89.

19. Lazerson, "Understanding Catholic Educational History," pp. 299–301.

20. Douglas R. Brackenridge, Francisco O. García-Treto, and John Stover, "Presbyterian Missions to Mexican Americans in Texas in the Nineteenth Century," *Journal of Presbyterian History, 49,* No. 2 (1971), 103–132.

21. W. G. Ritch Notebooks, vol. 3, p. 18, William G. Ritch Collection, Huntington Library, Los Angeles, CA. These notebooks are a compilation of the notes and personal memories of W. G. Ritch and are dated circa 1873.

22. Norman Bender, *Winning the West for Christ* (Albuquerque: University of New Mexico Press, 1993), pp. 11–34.

23. These missionaries also believed that their version of Christian education offered the best means to regenerate these "anomalous" peoples. M. T. Banker, *Presbyterian Missions and Cultural Interaction in the Far Southwest, 1850–1950* (Chicago: University of Illinois Press, 1993), p. 49.

24. This new policy stipulated the following points: 1) every application for the establishment and maintenance of a school by the Presbyterian Church's Board of Home Missions would be judged on its own merits; 2) no school would be established or supported by the board in any territory that already had or was likely to have schools, unless there were strong and special reasons for making an exception to the rule; 3) only teachers endorsed by the church would be hired; 4) all financial assistance for education would be the responsibility of the Women's Board of Home Missions; and 5) only among "populations that cannot be reached as yet by churches" would the board undertake and establish schools. The populations affected by this policy were "Mormons, Mexicans, Aztecs, Indians, Chinese, and the natives of Alaska." See Presbyterian Church, *Minutes of the General Assembly* (New York: Presbyterian Church of the U.S.A., 1878), p. 167; Lucius Buck, "An Inquiry into the History of Presbyterian Educational Missions in New Mexico," Diss., University of Southern California, 1949, p. 23.

25. The General Assembly, the Presbyterian's governing body, approved the organization of the Woman's Executive Committee in 1878. This group was founded expressly to care for mission schools in the new West. Sheldon Jackson publicized the need for churches and schools in the Southwest and made appeals for more missionaries and especially for more teachers. Through printed appeals—speeches, letters, a newspaper, and personal magnetism—he was able to recruit volunteers, raise funds, and increase interest among laypersons and other Presbyterians. See *Presbyterian Panorama* (New York: Presbyterian Church of the U.S.A., 1952), pp. 175–200; Edith Agnew and Ruth Barber, "The Unique Presbyterian School System of New Mexico, *Journal of Presbyterian History,* 49 (1970), 205–206. For information on Sheldon Jackson, see Alvin K. Bailey, "Sheldon Jackson, Planter of Churches," *Journal of the Presbyterian Historical Society,* 26 (1948), 129–148; Norman Bender, "Sheldon Jackson's Crusade to Win the West for Christ, 1869–1880," *Midwest Review,* 4 (1982), 1–12; Robert Laird Stewart, *Sheldon Jackson* (New York: Fleming H. Revell, 1908).

26. Melinda Rankin, *Texas in 1850* (Waco, TX: Texian Press, 1966), p. 58.

27. The majority of these schools operated in the northern counties, although several of them were found south of Albuquerque. They operated from three months to eighty years; the average life was probably one to three years. These schools generally taught Protestant and American ideals and condemned "popery" and negative Mexican traits. Agnew and Barber, "The Unique Presbyterian"; Carolyn Zeleny, "Relations between Spanish-Americans and Anglo-Americans in New Mexico: A Study of Conflict and Accommodation in a Dual Ethnic Situation," Diss., Yale University, 1944, pp. 270–271.

   In 1889, there were more than thirty-three schools in New Mexico with a total enrollment of 1,131 (Agnew and Barber, "The Unique Presbyterian"). Protestant schools were also found in other parts of the Southwest. The first in Texas was known as the Rio Grande Female Institute. In addition to the regular academic subjects, it taught Bible and the English language. It opened in the spring of 1852, but temporarily closed in December of the same year. For the next year and a half, its founder, Melinda Rankin, sought funds from the Presbyterian Board of Education in Philadelphia. On May 3, 1854, she bought land in Brownsville and reopened the school for Mexican women. Between thirty and forty Mexican women enrolled in Rankin's school. See J. C. Rayburn, "Introduction," in Rankin, *Texas in 1850*, pp. vi–xiii; W. H. Chatfield, *The Twin Cities of the Border and the Country of the Lower Rio Grande* (New Orleans: E. P. Brandao, 1893), p. 18.

28. By 1908, the Board of Home Missions reported that it was responsible for the establishment of over sixty schools in the territory, enrolling over 1,500 students. C. Atkins,

"Menaul School: 1881–1930: Not Leaders Merely, But Christian Leaders," *Journal of Presbyterian History, 58* (1980), 284.

29. The first secondary school, Aranama College, was founded in Goliad in 1852 by William C. Blair, the first Presbyterian missionary to work with Mexican origin individuals in Texas. Aranama College was sponsored by the Western Texas Presbytery. See Brackenridge, García-Treto, and Stover, "Presbyterian Missions." The other boarding schools were: Presbyterian-Allison School for Mexican Girls, Santa Fe, New Mexico, 1868; Mora Boarding School in Mora, New Mexico, 1882; Menaul Training School for Boys, Albuquerque, New Mexico, 1895; Rio Grande Female Institute, Brownsville, Texas, 1852; Bible Training School for Christian Workers, Laredo, Texas, 1896; Methodist-Harwood School for Boys and Girls, Tiptonville, New Mexico, 1870; Holding Institute, Laredo, Texas, 1880. For more information on these schools, see Agnew and Barber, "The Unique Presbyterian"; Buck, "An Inquiry"; Rankin, *Texas in 1850;* Chatfield, *The Twin Cities;* Brackenridge, García-Treto, and Stover, "Presbyterian Missions."

30. For a history of industrial education for Blacks in the South, see James D. Anderson, *The Education of Blacks in the South, 1860–1935* (Chapel Hill: University of North Carolina Press, 1988).

31. H. W. Splitter, "Education in Los Angeles, 1850–1900," *Historical Society of Southern California Quarterly, 33* (1951), 101–118.

32. Leonard Pitt, *The Decline of the Californios* (Berkeley: University of California Press, 1966), p. 226.

33. *El Clamor Público,* September 27, 1856, n.p.

34. Mention is made of these schools in Francisco Hernández, "Mexican Schools in the Southwest," unpublished paper, pp. 20–22; Arnoldo De León, *The Tejano Community, 1836–1900* (Albuquerque: University of New Mexico Press, 1982); Bertha Archer Schaer, *Historical Sketch of Aoy School* (El Paso, TX: El Paso Public Schools, 1951); and Jovita González, *Social Life in Cameron, Starr, and Zapata Counties,* Diss., University of Texas, Austin, 1930, p. 75.

35. Hernández, "Mexican Schools."

36. Hernández, "Mexican Schools."

37. Schaer, *Historical Sketch of Aoy School.*

38. David Frederic Ferris, *Judge Marvin and the Founding of the California Public School System* (Berkeley: University of California Press, 1962), p. 56; Frederick Eby, *The Development of Education in Texas* (New York: Macmillan, 1925).

39. Dianna Everett, "The Public School Debate in New Mexico, 1850–1891," *Arizona and the West, 26,* No. 2 (1984), 107–134.

40. For information on the San Antonio school, see "First Public School Still Standing Haunted with Many Memories," manuscript for publication in the *San Antonio Light,* December 12, 1909, p. 2; found in "School-History" file, local history room, San Antonio Public Library, San Antonio, Texas. On the California schools, see John C. Pelton, "California's First Public School and Its Founder," *Golden Era, 40* (1891), 845–850; Ferris, *Judge Marvin,* p. 56; and Robert N. Christian, "A Study of the Historical Development of the Santa Barbara School District," Diss., University of Southern California, 1963.

41. De León, *The Tejano Community,* pp. 187–194.

42. J. C. Atkins, Who Will Educate? The Schooling Question in Territorial New Mexico, 1846–1911, Diss., University of New Mexico, Albuquerque, 1978, p. 402.

43. R. N. Christian, *A Study of the Historical Development of the Santa Barbara School District,* Master's thesis, University of Southern California, Los Angeles, 1963; Richard Griswold del Castillo, *The Los Angeles Barrio, 1850–1890* (Los Angeles: University of California Press, 1979), pp. 84–88.

44. In Los Angeles, for instance, the proportion of Mexican-origin students enrolled in the schools declined drastically from 43 percent in 1860 to 25 percent in 1870. The following decade, it increased to 38 percent. The pattern of fluctuating enrollment was also apparent in Texas. Data from El Paso County show that enrollment decreased between 1850 and 1900. The opposite was true in Bexar County, where it increased from 8.3 percent to 30.7 percent. School enrollment remained constant in the lower Rio Grande Valley. Kenneth L. Stewart and Arnoldo De León, "Literacy among *Inmigrantes* in Texas, 1850–1900," *Latin American Research Review, 20* (1985), 180–187.

45. Political conflicts such as the Civil War in the United States or the French Intervention in Mexico in the 1860s, as well as border conflict in the 1870s, might have affected these rates. Stewart and De León, "Literacy among *Inmigrantes*."

46. Griswold del Castillo, *The Los Angeles Barrio*, pp. 84–88; De León, *The Tejano Community*, p. 187.

47. For data on New Mexico school enrollment in the 1870s, see William H. Rideling, "A Trail in the Far Southwest," *Harper's New Monthly Magazine, 53* (1876), 15–24. For data on school enrollment in the 1880s and 1890s, see Atkins, *Who Will Educate?* p. 388.

48. Oscar Handlin notes that by the mid-1800s, the schools underwent a significant transformation from being instruments of academic transmission to ones of cultural socialization. He argues that this reform impulse was not due to class imposition or to urbanization and industrialization, but to "vague aspirations" of some Americans interested in conversion— that is, in persuading those in "darkness" to walk "in the way of light." Oscar Handlin, "Education and the European Immigrant, 1820–1920," in *American Education and the European Immigrant: 1840–1940,* ed. Bernard J. Weiss (Chicago: University of Illinois Press, 1982), p. 7.

49. Eileen Tamura, *Americanization, Acculturation, and Ethnic Identity* (Chicago: University of Illinois Press, 1994), p. 52.

50. Robert A. Carlson, *The Quest for Conformity: Americanization through Education* (New York: Wiley, 1975).

51. The literature on Americanization usually refers to the "subtractive" concept as "coercive." This term, however, implies an imposition to repress or compel. The subtractive notion, in my view, is less judgmental. For an overview of Americanization as applied to education, see Nicholas V. Montalto, *A History of the Intercultural Movement, 1924–1941* (New York: Garland, 1982), pp. 1–21.

52. The notion of subtractive and additive Americanization is taken from similar concepts applied to bilingual education. For further elaboration, see W. E. Lambert, "Bilingualism and Language Acquisition," in *Native Language and Foreign Language Acquisition,* ed. H. Wintz (New York: New York Academy of Sciences, 1981), pp. 9–22; Eduardo Hernández-Chávez, *The Inadequacy of English Immersion Education* (Sacramento: California State Department of Education, 1984), pp. 144–183.

53. Frances Campbell, "Missiology in New Mexico, 1850–1900: The Success and Failure of Catholic Education," in *Religion and Society in the American West,* ed. Carl Guerneri and David Alvarez (Lantham, MD: University Press of America, 1987), pp. 59–78.

54. Lazerson, "Understanding Catholic Educational History," pp. 297–317.

55. For an overview of the church's relationship to Mexican-origin communities during the period from 1836 to 1890, see Moisés Sandoval, *On the Move: A History of the Hispanic Church in the United States* (New York: Orbis Press, 1990), pp. 25–40.

56. Campbell, *Missiology in New Mexico*, pp. 68–69.

57. Katherine R. Crowell, *Our Mexican Mission Schools* (New York: Woman's Board of Home Missions of the Presbyterian Church in the USA, n.d.), p. 10.

58. For a Protestant view of Mexicans in the 1850s, see Melinda Rankin, *Twenty Years among the Mexicans: A Narrative of Missionary Labor* (Cincinnati, OH: Central Book Concerns, 1875).

59. Banker, *Presbyterian Missions.*

60. De León, *The Tejano Community.* De León further notes that census data indicate that 53 percent of the Mexican males twenty-one years of age and older in 1850 and 60 percent in 1900 were not native born and were therefore ineligible to vote in local, county, or state elections. Additionally, only 13 percent of Tejano males of voting age, in contrast to 88 percent of the Anglo population, were literate in 1900.

61. The individuals elected prior to 1880 were Basilio Benavides, Santos Benavides, J. A. Chavis (*sic*), Gregorio N. García, Angel Navarro, T. A. Rodríguez, and T. P. Rodríguez. For a listing of members of the Texas legislature from 1846 to the late 1880s, see Texas Legislature, *Members of the Texas Legislature, 1846–1962* (Austin, TX: Fifty-Seventh Legislature, 1962). For the varied roles Mexican American politicians assumed in south, central, and east Texas during the latter half of the nineteenth century, see De León, *The Tejano Community,* and Mario García, *Desert Immigrants* (New Haven, CT: Yale University Press, 1979).

62. For elaboration on Mexican American representation in the state legislature, see Fernando V. Padilla and Carlos B. Ramírez, "Patterns of Chicano Representation in California, Colorado, and Nuevo Méjico," *Aztlán*, 5 (1974), 189–234.

63. California Superintendent of Public Instruction, *First Biennial Report* (Sacramento: California Superintendent of Public Instruction, 1866), pp. 294–296.

64. *Chronological Records of Los Angeles City Officials, 1850–1938* (Los Angeles: Los Angeles Public Library, 1938), pp. 1–2.

65. The other members of the group were Captain Henry W. Holleck, Stephan Botts, Lansford W. Hastings, Francis J. Lippitt, and William M. Gwin. For a discussion of their efforts, see Ferris, *Judge Marvin.*

66. "Mayor's Message," *L.A. Star,* May 14, 1853, n.p.

67. Richard L. Nostrand, *The Hispano Homeland* (Norman: University of Oklahoma Press, 1982).

68. See C. E. Hodgin, *The Early School Laws of New Mexico*, New Mexico University, Bulletin #41, Vol. 1, Art. 1 (Albuquerque: University of New Mexico Press, 1906) for a list of these laws.

69. William Ritch, *Education in New Mexico* (Santa Fe, NM: Manderfield and Tucker, 1874).

70. Chronological Records of Los Angeles City Officials, 1850–1938; "Mayor's Message."

71. Hodgin, The Early School Laws of New Mexico, p. 14. For details on these laws, see Ritch, *Education in New Mexico,* p. 134.

72. Padilla and Ramírez, "Patterns of Chicano Representation."

73. Padilla and Ramírez, "Patterns of Chicano Representation."

74. For a history of Catholic participation in public education, see Everett, "The Public School Debate in New Mexico," pp. 107–134.

75. Everett, "The Public School Debate in New Mexico," pp. 107–134.

76. Lynn Marie Getz, *Schools of Their Own: The Education of Hispanos in New Mexico, 1850–1940* (Albuquerque: Univeristy of New Mexico Press), pp. 6, 15.

77. Everett, "The Public School Debate in New Mexico," pp. 107–134.

78. Many Whites believed that the infusion of ethnic and racial minorities, most of which were "inferior," could lead to the decline of Anglo-American culture. Others believed that allowing the use of non-English languages could lead to the replacement of English and could cause social and political fragmentation. Others, especially politicians, found diversity troubling because racial and ethnic groups tended to vote for their own kind. For a history of the campaign against diversity, see the following: Shirley Brice Heath, "Language and Politics in the United States," in Muriel Saville-Trioke, ed., *Georgetown University Roundtable on Language and Linguistics* (Washington, DC: Georgetown University Press, 1977), pp. 267–296; James A. Banks, *Multiethnic Education: Theory and Practice,* 2nd ed. (Boston: Allyn & Bacon, 1986), pp. 1–30.

79. Arnold Leibowitz, "Language and the Law: The Exercise of Power through Official Designation of Language," in *Language and Politics,* eds. W. O'Barr and J. O'Barr (The Hague, Netherlands: Mouton, 1976), pp. 449–466.

80. Leibowitz, "Language and the Law," p. 6.

81. Texas passed a law in 1858 stipulating that no school would receive state funding unless English was principally taught in it. See F. Eby, *The Development of Education in Texas* (New York: Macmillan, 1925), p. 336. California, unlike Texas, took several actions. In the 1850s, the legislature suspended the 1849 Constitutional provision allowing the state government to publish its laws in Spanish. In 1855, the State Bureau of Public Instruction issued an administrative ruling requiring all schools to teach strictly in English. See Nicolas Patrick Beck, "The Other Children: Minority Education in California Public Schools from Statehood to 1890," Diss., University of California, Los Angeles, 1975, p. 18; H. Kloss, *The American Bilingual Tradition* (Rowley, MA: Newberry House, 1977), pp. 181–182; Pitt, *The Decline of the Californios,* p. 226.

82. Governor William Lane, for instance, proposed in the early 1850s that, for efficiency's sake, the legislature should replace Spanish with English as the official state language. Fierce resistance on the part of the large Spanish-speaking community resulted in the resounding defeat of his proposal in the territorial legislature. Anglo legislators in 1856 proposed the establishment of an English-only public school system. Mexican American voters rejected the monolingual public school system by a wide margin. See David Martin Eiband, "The Dual Language Policy in New Mexico," Diss., University of Texas, Austin, 1978, p. 33.

83. On the Texas law, see "School Law of 1870," in Frederick Eby, *Education in Texas: Source Materials*, Bulletin 1824 (Austin: University of Texas Press, 1919), p. 526. For the law in California, see *California Statutes*, ch. 556, sec. 55 (1870). The California provision was strengthened and broadened to include all public institutions in 1879 with the passage of a new constitution that made English the "official language of the state." *California Constitution*, Art. 4, sec. 24 (1879).

84. *School Law of 1891*, Art. 16, cited in D. L. Meyer, "The Language Issue in New Mexico, 1880–1900: Mexican American Resistance against Cultural Erosion," *Bilingual Review, 4* (1977), 101. For a Mexican American response to this law and its aftermath, see Aurelio M. Espinosa, "Speech Mixture in New Mexico: The Influence of the English Language on New Mexican Spanish," in *The Pacific Ocean in History*, eds. H. M. Stephens and H. E. Bolton (New York: MacMillan, 1917), p. 411.

85. Irving G. Hendrick, *California Education: A Brief History* (San Francisco: Boyd & Fraser, 1980), p. 56.; Robert A. Calvert and Arnoldo De León, *The History of Texas* (Arlington Heights, IL: Harlan Davidson, 1990), p. 173; Rupert Norval Richardson, Ernest Wallace, and Adrian N. Anderson, *Texas: The Lone Star State* (Englewood Cliffs, NJ: Prentice-Hall, 1981), p. 182.

86. *El Clamor Público.*

87. See Milk, "The Issue of Language in Education in Territorial New Mexico" and Meyer, "The Language Issue in New Mexico," pp. 99–106; Griswold del Castillo, *The Treaty of Guadalupe Hidalgo*, pp. 88–89; Leibowitz, "Language and the Law," pp. 449–466.

88. See Griswold del Castillo, *The Treaty of Guadalupe Hidalgo*, pp. 88–89, and Leibowitz, "Language and the Law," p. 48.

89. Some schools in different parts of the Southwest, however, did not fully remove Catholic heritage classes until the early 1880s. In Los Angeles, the largest Mexican community in California, the public schools taught "la doctrina Católica" as part of its curriculum until 1882. See Pitt, *The Decline of the Californios*, p. 226; Griswold del Castillo, *The Treaty of Guadalupe Hidalgo*, p. 87.

90. García, *Desert Immigrants*, pp. 110–126; James William Cameron, "The History of Mexican Public Education in Los Angeles, 1910–1930," Diss., University of Southern California, 1976, pp. 60–91.

91. See Carlos E. Castañeda, "The Broadening Concept of History Teaching in Texas," in *Proceedings of the Inter-American Conference on Intellectual Inter-Change, June 16–17, 1943* (Austin: University of Texas, Austin, Institute of Latin American Studies, 1943), p. 100.

92. The trivialization of Spanish and Mexican contributions to Texas in the history books existed into the 1930s. Castañeda quotes Lone Star State, a popular history textbook written by Clarence Wharton and published in 1932, to illustrate the narrow scope of Texas history. The author's view of early Texas history is reflected in the following comment on Anglo-American colonization: "We are now at the real beginning of Texas history. All that happened in 300 years after Pineda sailed along our shores and Cabeza de Vaca tramped from Galveston Island to the Rio Grande was of little importance." See Castañeda, "The Broadening Concept," pp. 99–103.

Segregation and the Education of Mexican Children, 1900–1940

Gilbert G. González

I n the aftermath of the 1848 war between Mexico and the United States, the newly acquired U.S. territory in the Southwest underwent a radical social transformation. Using a variety of legal, extralegal, and generally violent means, Anglo-American capitalist society first dominated then decimated the pre-capitalist Mexican system. At the heart of the transformation was a continually expanding labor-intensive production system that required an inexhaustible labor supply; this system replaced the old Mexican self-subsistence economy. As the new century opened to a national imperialist expansionism that engulfed the Caribbean, Mexico, and Latin America, the entrenched monopolistic economy of the Southwest demanded an army of cheap, mobile, unorganized, and dependable labor.

In Porfirian Mexico (1880–1910) and later in post-revolutionary Mexico, governmental policies complemented that demand and ensured the availability of labor for U.S. business. Porfirio Díaz's and revolutionary Mexico's open-door foreign investment policy (demanded by Washington), coupled with large-scale corporations' voracious appetite for Mexican labor, functioned as an international infrastructure that stabilized the Mexican immigrant community as a permanent component and ethnicity within the U.S. working class. An incipient sector of the regional working class was formed in the early 1900s, and it continued to grow with the help of legal and illegal immigration in response to capital's requirements for workers. More often than not, "illegal" immigration constituted a form of state-sanctioned labor crossing of the border to satisfy corporate demand.

Indeed, the Mexican community emerged as a major participant in the capitalist development of the Southwest. It became integrated into the corporate industries then experiencing unprecedented growth. These same economically productive workers were segregated in terms of work, religion, occupation, recreation, housing, and education. An apparent irony was set in motion as they were integrated into a system of production dominated by monopolistic capital and yet segregated from nearly every other aspect of society. The social and economic conditions that have characterized the Mexican community in the United States throughout the twentieth century were especially evident during the first two decades, a period during which the modern Chicano community made its entrance.

IMMIGRATION AND SETTLEMENT

Well over a million Mexican migrants streamed into the United States between 1900 and 1930. The majority arrived in the 1920s to settle in mining zones, irrigated agricultural valleys, manufacturing centers, and railroad construction sites. Laborers, with families in tow, were coveted and actively recruited by employers. They entered into the lowest-wage employment in the packing houses of Southern California, the sugar beet fields of Colorado, the smelters of El Paso, the garment factories of San Antonio, the copper mines of Arizona, the cotton farms of Texas, and railroad construction across the United States. As the Mexican community in the Southwest grew, a new lexicon entered the vocabulary of the dominant community. Mexicans, it was said, were naturally suited to physical labor, as their short stature made it easier for them to pick, hoe, and lift. Nature adapted them to a subordinate status in which they took orders from a paternalistic boss and lived on meager wages. Though humble, they nevertheless enjoyed the simple pleasures of life to the fullest.

Charles Teague, longtime CEO of the Southern California Fruit Growers Exchange (the forerunner of Sunkist) in the interwar years, casually remarked that "Mexicans are naturally adapted to agricultural work, particularly in the handling of fruits and vegetables. . . . Many of them have a natural skill in the handling of tools and are resourceful in matters requiring manual ability."[1] Teague knew where the interests of the corporation lay: over 90 percent of the picking force of twenty-five thousand were Mexican laborers.[2] Although Mexicans were praised for their manual dexterity, they were seldom compensated for it. "Mexican wage" meant working for less than Anglo-American workers, and "Mexican work" meant undesirable, lowest-paid manual labor.

A settlement pattern quickly formed along the U.S.-Mexican border, where about 85 percent of migrants put down roots. They established permanent communities in company towns sponsored by mining companies, citrus associations, and cotton farms; covenants forced them to live "across the tracks," where they created *colonias* in the cities' outskirts and *campos* on the edges of agricultural towns. Throughout the Southwest, the increasing number of Mexican settlements kept pace with the economic development of the region. Mexican customs, traditions, celebrations, organizations, and activities were transplanted into the inhospitable environment. Before long, the residents established a new identity embodied in their communities and, except for leaving to work or to find some form of recreation, life was spent within the colonia or campo.

Gilbert G. González

Integration into the economic sphere carried a price: segregation in theaters, parks, politics, and restaurants marked relations between Mexican society and the dominant community. In spite of the strength of community organizations and structures, Mexican barrios became associated, in the popular mind, with the outcast: Mexicans were foreigners, immigrants, transients, poor, delinquent, uncultured, and unskilled. Soon enough, the "Mexican problem," which encapsulated a host of alleged dangers to society's fundamental institutions, became a topic of widespread discussion in public policy venues. Los Angeles City Schools Superintendent Susan B. Dorsey lamented having to administer the educational mission of the schools with high enrollments of Mexican children. In one talk to district administrators she addressed the widely deplored educational problem:

> It is unfortunate and unfair for Los Angeles, the third largest Mexican city in the world, to bear the burdens of taking care educationally of this enormous group. We do have to bear a spiritual burden quite disproportionate to the return from this great number of aliens in our midst. This burden comes to us merely because we are near the border.[3]

Another complaint expressed by many educators accused Mexicans of increased crime, welfare cases, schooling problems, vice, and threats to the racial and cultural homogeneity of the nation.[4]

PUBLIC SCHOOLS AND THE SEGREGATION OF MEXICAN CHILDREN

As these communities formed, the public education system underwent a major overhaul and assumed a prominent position among the institutions shaping the political culture and social structure of the nation. In the late nineteenth century, periodic labor strikes convulsed the nation, and socialism and communism made inroads among the working classes. In response to these threats, leading social theorists cautioned that modern society contained dangerous and volatile social elements that threatened cultural disintegration, even a political revolution, if not properly controlled and neutralized.[5] Indeed, the public education system emerged transformed from a small-scale volunteer endeavor to a centralized, mass, compulsory state agency organized to indoctrinate the citizenry with a common political culture aimed at strengthening political stability, while inculcating the skills necessary for optimal economic growth and profitability.[6] At no time, however, did the schooling enterprise propose to alter existing class relations. Schools actively represented the status quo, with all of its attendant public policies, inequalities, and prejudices, and shouldered the task of creating an efficient,[7] organic, clock-like society. Across the nation, expanding public schooling placed the maintenance of the status quo high on its agenda while simultaneously assimilating the unfolding social relations, including class and racial hierarchies, dominant political ideologies, and economic operations.[8] Within this context, the Mexican problem compelled Southwestern school districts, which were enrolling significant numbers of Spanish-speaking children, to design a curriculum adapted to Mexican children. Acceptance of schooling intended to resolve the Mexican problem ensured the reproduction of the Mexican community as a source of cheap labor.

How did school systems treat the Mexican problem? What objectives guided school administrators? What methods did they employ to realize those objectives? The first administrative proposal for solving the Mexican problem was simple: segregation into all-Mexican schools. Several reasons were proffered for separating Mexican children from Anglo-American children. First, educators and academicians claimed that segregation provided a fitting environment in which to meet the educational needs of the culturally distinctive Mexican child. Administrators and educators confidently insisted that Anglo- American and Mexican children were substantially distinct culturally. Moreover, the culture of the Mexican child diminished his or her capacity to learn to such a degree that it was unwise to place both in the same school setting. The crux of the learning problem pivoted around language. Slowed by speaking Spanish, Mexican children progressively fell behind through the grades. Simultaneously, segregation unburdened the Anglo-American child from the "slower" Mexican pupils, who in turn benefited by avoiding competition with "faster students." Second, the inherited intelligence of Mexican children, as measured by IQ tests, purportedly fell well below that of the average Anglo child. This also required segregation to educate at the special ability levels of Mexican children. Third, the level of measured intelligence and the employment pattern peculiar to Mexicans (which parents seemed to pass on to their children) appeared to contain the seeds of a social inevitability. Educators therefore implemented a strict emphasis on vocational education in the segregated environment.

THE CULTURE CONCEPT

In school districts throughout the region, a variety of segregation practices appeared. Initially, separating children into "foreign" classrooms seemed to solve the educational problem; eventually the first experiments grew into complete separation. In urban school districts such as Los Angeles, district lines created officially named "neighborhood schools" that only "foreign" (i.e., Mexican) students attended. The procedure most often applied, however, was the classic "Mexican School." In towns and cities where a Mexican colonia had been established, a separate school for Mexican children became a high priority for boards of education. Nearly all school districts separated Mexican children in one fashion or another, ostensibly because of the need to cleanse them of cultural defects by means of proper guidance and control. Schools bore the responsibility for teaching them the English language and American customs, values, and norms—that is, of Americanizing them. Mexicans were alleged to hold a Pandora's box of cultural dilemmas that, if allowed to escape, could move beyond the confines of the colonia and subvert the desirable and healthy cultural norms of society. If Mexicans were left to themselves, it was believed that certain destruction would threaten the superior (Anglo) culture and all that it had created. Educators and political leaders worried over Mexican habits thought to be antithetical to the national culture: uncleanliness, shiftlessness, irresponsibility, lack of ambition, unthriftiness, fatalism, promiscuity, and proneness to alcohol abuse.

E. E. Davis of the University of Texas confidently asserted in a report on illiteracy in Texas that "there is but one choice in the matter of educating these unfortunate [Mexican] children and that is to put the 'dirty' ones into separate schools till they learn how to 'clean-up' and become eligible to better society."[9] A deeply perplexed Phoenix principal argued that Mexicans' propensity to "steal cars, break windows, wreck recreational centers"[10] required that "more time should be spent teaching the [Mexican] child clean habits and positive attitudes towards others, public property, and their community in general." One Southern California teacher of Americanization wrote that "Mexican apathy . . . the infirmity of the will, forever the promise of mañana [dragged] upon the wheels of such progress as might exist."[11] An assistant supervisor in the Los Angeles city schools bluntly summarized the widely discussed Mexican problem:

> The Mexican problem . . . is principally the product of poverty in the home, which, in turn, is largely the appendage of the influx of immigrants from the Republic south of us. . . . The infusions of Spanish blood into Aztec and Maya veins has Latinized later generations since the sixteenth century. The mixture of the two is fundamentally responsible for the carefree, if not indolent, characteristic of the race.[12]

At a meeting of administrators in 1925, Susan B. Dorsey, the Los Angeles School District superintendent, recommended to her supervisors the antidote most often applied: "We have these [Mexican] immigrants to live with, and if we can Americanize them, we can live with them . . .". She, like many of her colleagues, believed that Americanization controlled the cultural defects while bringing Mexicans "to the light" so that they could embark on the process of social betterment.[13]

To fulfill the objectives of the Americanization program, however, proficiency in English and the elimination of Spanish were paramount, for language was considered the linchpin of culture. Backward cultural beliefs could be eliminated, it was claimed, once the core of the belief system, the Spanish language, was replaced by the heart of the superior culture, English. Thus, in district after district, English instruction via immersion and the forced removal of Spanish (and any traces of bilingualism) occupied the first two years of instruction in segregated schools. The first and second grades were generally known as the "Americanization" rooms, the locus of cultural change and guided entrance into American society.

Classroom rewards and punishments revolved around the child's willingness to adapt to speaking English exclusively. Schools incorporated practices that valued and rewarded proficiency in English, a practice that implicitly branded the language of the parents and the community as inferior and undesirable. Many an adult who lived through that era recalls the signs that warned "No Spanish" or "Speak English" and punishment by detention, corporal punishment, loss of privileges, or bad grades. One graduate of a segregated school bitterly recalled that "teachers warned us, 'I don't want to catch you speaking Spanish' . . . [but] we couldn't help it. That's all we knew at home. They'd tell us 'we're going to send you back to Mexico' because they wanted to scare us that way. . . . That's about all we used to hear. . . . I forced myself to learn English."[14] The curriculum of Mexican schools correlated with the identification of the language barrier as the internal enemy arrayed against America's basic institutions.

Language, however, encapsulated a complex pedagogical equation for the education of Mexican children. Gender figured prominently. Females were considered the social "gene" that, when properly socialized, could transform Mexican colonias from islands of cultural degradation into solid, American enclaves in one generation. Towards this objective, Americanization classes for adult women and home economics for girls in school took center stage. Americanization teachers taught cooking, childrearing, housekeeping, thrift, and manners, and sponsored competitive projects like "Better Homes Week," during which women were urged to learn "acceptable" standards of housekeeping. Graduation ceremonies awarded diplomas to adult women able to speak a modicum of English. Schooling, however, did not have the interests of the women or of the community in mind.[15]

Beneath the educational surface, however, larger political issues were in command. Mexicans were alleged to harbor a culture that threatened not only to undermine prevailing norms, but also to create political mischief. The Americanization program in California, for example, initiated in 1915, targeted language because it was believed that all non-English-speaking sectors of the population held the potential to develop a class consciousness capable of evolving into radical, even communistic, organization and activities. In the Americanization agenda, more than ethnic rivalry was at stake; clear political objectives grounded the exercise.[16] Americanization, fundamental to the agenda of the segregated school, served as a preventive measure that promised the elimination of cultural disintegration and political disaster that loomed within the Mexican psyche.

THE BELL CURVE, 1920S STYLE

Justification of the selection of Mexican children for special educational experiences went beyond culture to include genetic "stock." No other pedagogical device controlled classroom practice and curriculum as did the IQ test. Segregation may have accomplished the removal of Mexican children from the "normal" class, but it was the concept of intelligence and its operational contrivance, the IQ test, that "scientifically" legitimized and guaranteed unequal outcomes. Moreover, prevalent psychological theory laid the cultural "backwardness" of the Mexican immigrant community on the genetic material from which they descended.

The foremost psychologists and educators of the period, particularly in the 1920s, held that nature behaved in a most undemocratic fashion, bestowing intellectual abilities unequally. An ancillary premise of intelligence theory was that culture reflected intelligence; thus, a superior stock created a superior culture. Furthermore, a device called the IQ test could measure with great accuracy the mental variations among any population. The specter of race hovered over intelligence testing research that sought to define exactly how nature divvied up shares of intelligence. A politically saturated science that found nature's unfortunates—those endowed with degrees of intelligence below the "norm"—predominated. If the theoretical novelty had been confined there, perhaps the grosser consequences of the widespread segregation of Chicano children might have been avoided. But there were social implications in intelligence theory that affected the curriculum as well.

William James, Lewis Terman, Henry Goddard, E. L. Thorndike, and a host of social scientists who embraced the commonly accepted doctrine of the racial distribution of intelligence contended that social inequality, the division of labor, and the gross disparities in wealth and political power were passed from one generation to the next via the genes.[17] Moreover, only those with superior intelligence were capable of entering the professional occupations; the less intelligent were fitted for slots suitable to their level of mental ability in the lower quarters of the division of labor. Thus, class structure mirrored the distribution of intelligence, and neither conscious choice nor institutional practice molded the social order.

Schools across the nation rapidly adopted IQ testing and ignored all of its theoretical shortcomings and heavy-handed biases. Departments of psychological testing and research were instituted between 1910 and 1920 in the school systems of Los Angeles, El Paso, Phoenix, and San Antonio to survey the intellectual ability of students and to adjust individual school curricula to group averages. In classic doublespeak, they also embraced a new definition of democratic education: unequals could not be given the same curriculum nor expected to learn at the same pace. Differing intellectual abilities meant differing educational experiences, and therefore unequal outcomes. Educators concluded that such results were inevitable when understood in the context of prevailing theories that identified the "low-mentality" individual with low achievement (and the working class).

The principal of a Southern California school repeated the message broadcast during the 1920s by many experts when he wrote that "stupid parents are apt to have stupid children." Sensing that a critic might suggest environment as a factor, he flatly denied the environment thesis, contending that environment "never made a stupid child intelligent." So it was not unexpected that, as one Los Angeles supervisor put it, "nothing is so unequal as the equal treatment of unequals."[18] The principal at an all-Mexican school joined the broadening denunciation of the notion of equality: "The doctrine that 'all men are born free and equal' applies to man's political equality. . . . In no way can this idea of equality be applied to intellectual endowment."[19] Democratizing the schools mandated an internally differentiated schooling process accommodated to the intellectual diversity contained within any student universe. An entirely new lexicon gained footing in school administrative offices, as terms like "gifted," "bright," "superior," "average," "subnormal," "dull," "moron," "low grade moron," "borderline moron," "low mentality," and "feebleminded" were used to describe the children under their charge. Accordingly, a twentieth-century democratic education required unequals to be prepared differently for the inevitable reality that faced them in later life. Effective schools trained the diverse pool of children to assume the kinds of occupations that their inherited intelligence presaged. Under such a charge, school systems became training grounds not only for the superiors, but also for the slow learners and the feebleminded.

But much more was at stake. Adherents of IQ theory postulated an antidemocratic corollary: nature destined intellectual superiors to occupy positions of political power as well. The genetically less well endowed required government by their genetic superiors. Those whom nature allocated substantially fewer mental abilities required a tailored education administered by a paternal state that trained (recruited?) manual labor for employment possibilities in the Southwest's burgeoning enterprises. Although the widespread use of IQ tests appeared to have particular bearing upon Mexican children in the region, we should not ignore the national scope of the testing movement. Racialized policies enforcing the use of testing, segregation, and tracking affected children across the United States.

In segregating Mexican children, unequal education justified by a theory of inborn racial traits (and therefore inborn cultural traits) assumed center stage in the nation's state-run schools. Racial inequality—the foundation for and consequence of widespread pedagogical practices—rested on the near religious acceptance and universal application of the intelligence test. But racially inspired educational theory and practice, buttressed by scientific claims, reflected existing social relations and the division of labor in the production of commodities and sought to maintain them over generations. Moreover, dominant political and economic classes tethered those discourses and schooling practices to their interests.

Dozens of research projects simulated the scientific racism of Lewis Terman at Stanford. They were set up to identify the intellectual level of Mexican children. Over nine thousand Mexicans served as research subjects

Domestic employment training in the industrial education curriculum, Los Angeles City Schools, ca. 1930

for nearly forty intelligence studies between 1915 and 1950. In survey after survey, a dismal conclusion was reached: Mexican children consistently scored lower than the norm for Anglo-American children, that mythical average 1.00. And even when the language "handicap" was controlled for, the test results hardly varied. Scores clustered around the .90 range in study after study. According to investigations in Los Angeles completed during the 1920s, about 47 percent of Mexican children scored below the .90 level, and only 22 percent scored at the normal step (a figure that paralleled general studies carried out on Mexican children by a host of psychologists). In 1932, the statistician for the Los Angeles district offered her reasons for the poor performance of Mexican children: "There is some selection in the type of Mexican family who comes to Los Angeles. Most of the children represented in the group belong to the laboring class."[20]

A 1928 investigation in California concluded that Mexican children scored on average at .86, and that 60 percent scored in the nonacademically inclined range.[21] At Belvedere Junior High in Los Angeles, with a student population that was 50 percent Mexican, 55 percent of all students scored below .90. At Lafayette Junior High School, not far from Belvedere, over half of all Mexican students were channeled into the nonacademic group. Statistics gathered for 1929 by the Los Angeles School District reported that the majority of "mentally retarded children" came from districts with the largest number of immigrants; the reverse was true for the "children of superior mentality," who were found "most frequently in the Normal Type school" or neighborhood.[22]

Many educationists and policymakers thought like the vice-principal of an urban elementary school that enrolled only "low mentality" children. He wrote that the "pupil of low intelligence" was prone to "failure, tardiness, lying, cheating, truancy." He confidently asserted that "inheritance" explained the problem.[23] California State Superintendent of Public Instruction William J. Cooper offered similar advice to the teachers under his supervision. His 1927 public policy statements on the subject added little to contemporary views of the relationship of biology and social conditions, but they demonstrate the confidence in such theoretical discourse. Like his contemporaries, Cooper contended that "we build on a biological foundation. We cannot make a black child white, a deaf child hear, a blind baby see, nor can we create a genius from a child whose ancestors endowed him with a defective brain. Within the limits set by heredity we can do much." He then recommended that "teachers should study biology."[24]

These theoretical premises and racialized cultural stereotypes had important bearing on teacher training during the period under study. In some cases, administrators were trained by leading authorities in the field of intelligence psychology. Dr. Frances Gaw, psychologist with the Los Angeles City Schools' Division of Psychology and Educational Research, earned her doctorate under Cyril Burt at the University of London. The division's director, Elizabeth Sullivan, and the agency's statistician, Alice McAnulty, were tutored by Lewis Terman at Stanford University. The clinician in charge of social service, Dorothy Henry, completed her master's degree under E. L. Thorndike at Columbia.

Of course, not all had the opportunity to study under the masters; the next best thing was to read their books. Teachers' colleges commonly used texts by leading psychological and pedagogical authorities of the day. Works by eugenicist Lathrop Stoddard and psychologists Lewis Terman and E. L. Thorndike, together with a host of others, found their way into course reading lists. Included in the lists one finds titles relating to Mexico and interpretations of Mexican culture from the perspective of these same social scientists and like-minded visitors to Mexico. Common reference texts emerged from the first cohort of scholars dabbling in Mexico, later known as Latin Amercanists, which included Wallace Thompson (*The Mexican Mind*) and Edward A. Ross (*Social Revolution in Mexico*), both of whom disparaged all things Mexican, and the paternalistic and romanticized versions of Stuart Chase, Carleton Beals, Frank Tannenbaum, and Ernest Gruening, who found things of value in the Indian background and culture of Mexico. Neither the romanticized nor the racially inspired readings held any promise for enabling students to better understand Mexico and the Mexican immigrant. Both viewpoints essentially bolstered the belief in a fundamental distinction between Mexican and Anglo-American, a belief that corresponded with U.S. foreign policy in the region and provided the theoretical beginning point in the segregationist policy. One need read only a few of the dozens of master's theses on the education of Mexican children written by budding school administrators to appreciate their blind faith in the conventional pathway elaborated by the acknowledged experts.[25]

The scientific method held such sway over the education corps that the common contention that Mexican children, and the entire Mexican community, for that matter, comprised inferior genetic material appeared incontrovertible. In step with learned opinion, superintendents authoritatively cautioned principals, counselors, and teachers that the Mexican child could expect to achieve only two-thirds of the educational potential of the Anglo-American child. El Paso, Los Angeles, San Antonio, and Phoenix, like many smaller rural districts, adjusted their curriculum to the range of intelligence of the student body. All children who scored between .50 and .90 were considered "nonacademic types" who could excel with their hands but not their minds, fine material for manual labor but not the "book learning" type. In Los Angeles, the research and testing arm of the district, the Division of Psychology and Educational Research, found that at least half of all Mexican children fell into the slow-learning to feeble-minded categories and were ideal material for nonacademic course work "suited to their needs." And since the remaining half still fell below the norm, it was an easy solution to the Mexican problem to design a curriculum that revolved around below-average learners. School administrators believed that the problem of the slow learner was not that he or she learned at a slower pace, but that his or her capacity to learn limited the range of curriculum that could be adequately mastered.

INDUSTRIAL EDUCATION[26]

As segregated schools matured into the convention, a policy enforced by counselors armed with IQ tests affirmed that slow learners were quite capable of mastering the world of manual, nonacademic education; college-level preparation could never be considered for the slow learner. This conclusion became the bedrock of the education of Mexican children. In relation to Mexican children, school officials resolved that the curriculum would comprise heavy doses of industrial education, and would derive in part from counselor surveys of the group's intelligence, the kinds of occupations open to Mexicans in the local area, and the cultural qualities attached to Mexicans.

Segregated schools resembled industrial schools, and in some districts these were (rightly) referred to as the "industrial school." These schools should not be confused with trade schools, however. Trade schools stipulated that applicants score at the norm on the intelligence test; in the trade classes of the Mexican schools, it was assumed that such courses were admirably suited to the intelligence and temperament of Mexican children. On the basis of scores on any intelligence test then in use, Mexican children found themselves placed in slow-learner tracks in numbers far out of proportion to their population. For boys, course work often included body shop, agriculture, basket weaving, upholstery, and animal husbandry. Girls learned to keep a neat house, care for children, serve as a domestic servant, keep house for an employer, and sewing and needlework.

In 1923, the copper mining enclave of Miami, Arizona, opened a school for the children of Mexican miners that was equipped "with a view to emphasizing industrial and homemaking courses for these children." Zavala Mexican School in Austin, Texas, paralleled Miami's plan; the school represented the "only elementary school in Austin . . . equipped with an industrial arts shop and home economics laboratory." Sidney Lanier Junior High School in San Antonio, Texas, attended exclusively by Mexican students, offered "special courses, flexible programs, home making, and industrial activities" based on courses in "sewing, cooking and art work for the girls; machine shop practice, auto repair, auto painting, top making, sheet metal work, plain bench and cabinet work in wood and a department in which type setting and job printing are taught to boys."[27] These examples from the 1920s and 1930s demonstrate the assumption that two goals were met simultaneously by industrial education: the cultural and intellectual needs of the Mexican community and the wider labor requirements of employers were satisfied in a single curriculum.

The assumption that Mexican children inevitably gravitated toward employment similar, if not identical, to that of their parents moved districts to begin the vocational experience in the early grades. The Arizona State Department of Education implemented early vocational curriculum because it found that "under present conditions" most Mexican children would enter unskilled or semiskilled positions, regardless of schooling; that being the case, vocational education was "to be introduced early and homemaking should be an important part of the elementary course for both boys and girls." One researcher who investigated the curriculum in Mexican schools throughout the Southwest found that the "sentiment of many teachers of Mexican children was known to favor an early introduction in the grades of these subjects [industrial education] for Mexicans."[28]

The degree and form of segregation did not end there, however. Vocational tracks absorbed the majority of children, but not all who were funneled into such classes attended the same course level. Some were judged to have an even lower mental ability than the majority of Mexican children and required a special vocational curriculum. An excessively large number of these children scored below .70, in the feeble-minded category. In Los Angeles, this group required a special education separate from their peers, which created a second level of segregation that funneled them en masse into schooling for the "mentally handicapped" (later "educationally mentally retarded") in sites named development centers and development rooms. These "less-capable" students could be trained for basic types of employment as unskilled and low-paid factory workers and workers in restaurants, hotels, laundries, private homes, agriculture, shoe-shine parlors, and the like. In 1929, some twenty-eight hundred children were assigned to ten development centers and thirty development rooms, located largely in work-

Development School agricultural training, Los Angeles City Schools, ca. 1930

ing-class sections of the city, a substantial distance in terms of space and curriculum from the "normal" schools in Los Angeles. According to district reports, space in the centers and rooms accommodated only one-quarter of the "subnormals"; many more waited for a transfer out of the normal classes.

By 1930, approximately one-fourth of the development schools and rooms were located in or near Los Angeles's Mexican colonia. One supervisor noted that "the subnormal child is apt to come from a low type home. . . . Often he comes from a foreign home," and thus the majority of recruits for the development centers and rooms attended near their neighborhoods.[29] By 1940 the population at these centers had increased to about five thousand, and throughout the era Mexican children composed approximately a quarter of the enrollees. As late as the 1960s, Chicano children still comprised one-quarter of students in the educationally mentally retarded classes, double their proportion of the school population.[30]

The Los Angeles City Schools, like most school districts administering Mexican schools, implemented a complex plan to adjust the subnormal child to the area's economic enterprises. District publications announced that at the Coronel Center, attended largely by Mexican children, courses were offered in "auto shop, tin shop, wood shop, paint shop, bakery, cookery, laundry work, power machine sewing, electric stitching, millinery, dressmaking, personal hygiene (including shampooing and manicuring), nursery maid training, cafeteria work, paper favor work, and trade ethics."[31] Every effort was made to correlate trade training with language instruction. Spelling and vocabulary words were selected from a list relating to words used in auto shops, laundries, cafeterias, and garment factories. Boys and girls received training suitable to their gender; for girls, employment in garment factories, laundries, bakeries, domestic service, and restaurants was determined adequate to their mental capacity. Beauty shop classes did not aim to prepare girls to become beauticians, but taught them grooming and personal hygiene—"to know how to keep themselves neat and clean"—which would make them more employable in their eventual search for work. Some girls were selected for training for day nursery work, not to care for children but to do the "unskilled tasks of cleaning, scrubbing, polishing, washing the dishes, etc." Particular emphasis was placed on laundry work for girls, training that, unlike beauty shop courses, had specific occupational objectives. The director of the elementary development centers reported in the 1929 *Yearbook* of the Division of Psychology and Educational Research that "several employers have told us that a dull girl makes a very much better operator on a mangle than does a normal girl. The job is purely routine and is irksome to persons of average intelligence, while subnormals seem to get actual satisfaction out of such a task. Fitting the person to the job reduces the turn over in industry and is, of course, desirable from an economic point of view."[32] Surrounded by agricultural fields, Los Angeles served as a harbor for many farmworkers, who migrated during some portion of the year. Not surprisingly, enrollment in the development centers rose and fell with the harvests. According to a district publication:

> Enrollment in the Development classes is far from constant. The children enter in late Fall, due to the seasonal employment in the countryside, where the children and their parents are employed picking fruits and nuts. The enrollment reaches the peak in the Spring when many centers and Rooms have to maintain waiting lists. The month of June usually brings an appreciable exodus when the children and their parents go out into the fields to harvest the onion crop.[33]

While IQ tests appeared to wear the mantel of infallibility, not all choices in the strict vocational regimen for Mexican children were based on testing. Some elements of Mexican culture were thought to be superior, and many a smiling educator theorized that these innate abilities redeemed Mexicans and demonstrated that not all was lost. It was believed that Mexicans enjoyed an artisanal dexterity that could turn almost anything into a work of art. Unfettered by the frenzied materialism of industrial society, Mexicans supposedly harbored a love of music, poetry, and philosophy. They did have something to offer, claimed many teachers, but nothing that was essential or of primary importance in the schooling enterprise. Moreover, in asserting that Mexicans were naturally gifted in handwork, were happy and carefree, if rather indolent despite (or perhaps because of) their poverty, educators offered more reasons for segregation and nonacademic schooling for Mexican children.

We should not be surprised that prevailing opinion among educators and employers considered Mexicans, as a group, culturally and genetically destined to perform manual labor. In 1932, the Texas Department of Education urged teachers to gauge the occupational future of Mexican children and to measure the curriculum against the findings. One Texas teacher's method was selected as a good example of an effective and appropriate approach for teaching Mexican children. In her English-language instruction, she placed "special emphasis upon the words the child will use in his work-a-day life as a tiller of the soil."[34] Later in the decade, the California State Board of Education *Bulletin* made a similar recommendation when it warned that growth in the minority population "would seem to present a problem of which educators must take cognizance, that a minority group . . . may receive appropriate instruction, *especially in reference to their probable* vocations" (emphasis added).[35] Whether by way of the IQ test or by determining "probable vocations," industrial education anchored the curriculum in Mexican schools across the Southwest. Not only did industrial course work follow the child from elementary school to junior high, but for the small minority fortunate enough to graduate from the eighth grade and enter secondary school, it also followed them. As a consequence, many Mexican students experienced at least twelve years of manual training linked with heavy doses of Americanization.

EXCLUSION AND THE MIGRATORY CHILD

Not all Mexican children were fortunate enough to attend school. Total and partial exclusion, a third level of segregation, affected Mexican children, principally in rural areas where migrant family labor predominated. In these cases, the opportunities for schooling were rare because the family relied on children's labor for income. In districts that depended heavily on the labor of the family, as in the cotton-growing region of Texas, the sugar beet fields of Colorado, and the farming areas of some California counties, school boards in effect hung signs on schoolhouse doors to warn "No Migrant Children Allowed." One study of Hidalgo County, Texas, reported a widespread "attitude that school attendance should not be allowed to interfere with the supply of cheap farm labor." A Texas school superintendent candidly justified the practice: "Most of our Mexicans are of the lower class. They transplant onions, harvest them, etc. The less they know about everything else the better contented they are. You have undoubtedly heard that ignorance is bliss; it seems that it is so when one has to transplant onions."[36] Economist Paul S. Taylor noted that in Dimmit County, Texas, not "more than 25 percent of the Mexican scholastics, i.e., children aged 7 to 17 inclusive" were enrolled in school and that "the average number in attendance [was] undoubtedly less."[37] In 1938, a study found that in Crystal City, Texas, "the average 18 year old [Mexican] youth has not completed the third grade of school." Carey McWilliams's observation that "so far as migratory children are concerned, the compulsory school attendance laws might just as well never have been enacted" came as no surprise to those in the Southwest's agricultural belts.[38] A Texas district superintendent said as much when he testified that "the compulsory school attendance law is a dead letter—there is no effort to enforce it. Nobody cares."[39] In Texas, as late as 1945, only half of all Mexican school-age children actually attended any school, although school districts received state funds for the nonattending group. In short, Anglo-American children and corporate growers benefited from the nonenforcement of attendance laws in relation to Mexican children; meanwhile, thousands of children were denied their basic Constitutional right to equal protection of the laws.

It was not uncommon for a school district to allow migrant children into segregated schools, but this did not imply an invariable full school day. School hours, in another variation on the exclusion policy, were shortened to accommodate family labor needs during harvests. For the rural Mexican child, admission policies and the length of the school day were determined by the corporate agricultural interests. Education for the Mexican child under these conditions was a rare privilege. Obstacles to their education generated by growers shaped public policy and forced them into a kind of "hands-on" vocational education in the fields alongside their parents. The 1924 biennial report of California's superintendent for public instruction lauded the value of the special dispensation for migrant children: "There should be an adjusted school day beginning not later than the field work. This provides for the whole family leaving the camp at the same time, the adults going to the field and the children to school. . . . It also means that the school day is over when the mid-day meal is ready. It provides also that the children may work in the afternoon."[40] In school districts across Southern California, even in districts in Los Angeles County, schedules were modified throughout the 1920s to meet the demands of growers for the cheapest of all labor, that of children. County Superintendent of Schools John R. Hunt advised that the absence of Mexican children during the harvests was handled through "special migratory classes in each district whenever necessary." He continued:

> Harvesting of [walnuts] is peculiarly adapted to the Mexican family. . . . It provides them with a fine vacation, a camping experience under ideal conditions. . . . The walnut ranchers are particularly anxious to have the Mexican family do this work because of their adaptability [and because their availability] provides the rancher with the cheapest method of harvesting the crop. No other kind of labor could possibly be secured that could compete in price, and so it is an economic factor that the rancher faces.[41]

Hunt noted that students were bused to school at 8:00 a.m. and returned at noon in time to go to work in the orchards.

Despite admission into flexibly scheduled schools, the educational success of thousands of children from the migratory camps and rural colonias was affected by severe nutritional and health problems. A Depression-era study of California's migrant labor camps reported miserable wages, poor housing, irregular employment, malnourishment, and "children . . . growing up without an opportunity for normal education and recreation. . . . Medical care which they need is unavailable to them."[42] A report by the National Child Labor Committee commented that migratory "children are apt to have no schooling at all, or schooling of so poor a character and given under such adverse circumstances that it can not be effective, and the children are badly retarded."[43] Public officials, like the growers, could wash their hands of responsibility because, presumably, migrant children needed no formal preparation for the arduous agricultural tasks they would assume as adults. And if there were any doubts, IQ scores and "expert" opinion could be called upon in support of educational policy.

TEACHERS AND PHYSICAL RESOURCES

Despite the widely held contention that the Mexican school was but a temporary measure to ensure equality of opportunity, vast differences divided these schools from those attended by Anglo-American children. Teachers assigned to Mexican schools bore the stigma of the social inferiority attached to the school. Beginning teachers, older teachers, or poor teachers were commonly placed in Mexican schools. For novice teachers, their initiation into the profession required some experience before promotion "up" to a nonsegregated school. In Los Angeles, young graduates from teachers' colleges could expect to be assigned to the less-desirable sections of the city; if they proved competent, a spot somewhere in the better part of the city would be their reward. The Los Angeles assistant superintendent of assignments casually remarked in 1928 that teachers should expect a period of breaking in to demonstrate worthiness for assignment to one of the popular schools: "After two years of probation in the valley or harbor districts, the teacher transfers to the city proper. It is usually necessary to place her in the foreign, semiforeign, or less convenient schools. After a few more years of satisfactory service, she may be placed in the more popular districts."[44] The all-Mexican Miguel Hidalgo School in Brawley, California, in the fertile Imperial Valley, rotated teachers every three years. One researcher wrote that "the best teachers from the Mexican school are 'promoted' to the American school in order to provide experienced teachers there." In 1935, for example, thirty teachers taught 1,551 students, over fifty per class, at Miguel Hidalgo, but only twenty-two classrooms were available. Seasonal harvests caused some classes to expand overnight to as many as eighty students.[45]

Ambition, or status consciousness, motivated teachers to leave the Mexican schools. Administrators regularly evaluated the teaching force by school assignment and level of classes taught. Teachers at Mexican schools were considered less qualified, found little respect from their peers across town, and earned considerably less for their efforts. The best teachers were assigned to the "best" schools and taught the "bright" students. Teachers of the superior or gifted classes not only earned the greatest respect, but also were rewarded with higher salaries.

Mexican school practice eventually became tradition, ingrained in a conventional wisdom that few educators challenged. The most visible signs of educational policy were found in the quality of the physical resources available to Mexican children compared to those of the Anglo-American child. Overcrowded, poorly designed and constructed buildings, insufficient recreational space, used and repaired furniture, and books handed down from the Anglo schools plagued the Mexican schools.

In conducting research for his master's thesis, Carlos Calderón studied a district in the Lower Rio Grande Valley of Texas in 1950 to gauge the differences between a Mexican school and an Anglo school. The distinctions stood out boldly. He found the pupil-to-teacher ratio to average 32 to 1 in the Anglo schools, but 47 to 1 in Mexican schools. In eight cases a Mexican classroom held over fifty pupils, and Calderón reported that one class held seventy pupils. Nearly five hundred Mexican children were taught in inferior facilities—old frame buildings that had once served as army barracks and were badly in need of paint and repair. Classrooms were illuminated by a single light bulb, or perhaps two, and ventilated by a screen door and two transom windows. A small wooden shack housed an outdoor restroom finished with a rough cement floor and two toilets without stalls. The boys and girls used identical back-to-back restroom facilities. Drinking fountains were outdoors and unprotected for use in inclement weather. Neither medical facilities nor a cafeteria was available. Calderon then described the school for the Anglo-American community: "a modern brick structure with rest rooms, drinking fountains, book rooms, principal's office and teacher's lounge." Restrooms were finished with tile floors and six toilet stalls with doors, and the school had an indoor water cooler. The only cafeteria in the district served the Anglo school.[46]

The investigations of reformer George I. Sánchez revealed that in district after district this pattern was repeated.[47] Mexican schools were inferior in every respect, from teachers to curriculum to physical plant. Board of education policies ensured that the inequalities would remain, despite pleas for a larger share of the budget. These pleas went unheard. The principal at both La Jolla elementary and junior high in Southern California (located on the same grounds) recalled:

> They moved all the old buildings, all the old wooden shacks that they could move in and although we did get a few of the portable bungalows . . . some of the other schools had them too, but not to the extent that we had them. And if they got rid of the furniture it was shipped down to us. After it didn't look good in the Anglo school, they would ship it down and we had no other say than to take what we were given. I was never glad to have it but we had to use it anyway.[48]

The board of education in La Jolla accepted the common belief that Mexican children were not capable of high school work and so curtailed instruction for them at tenth grade. The La Jolla school was considered a terminal school.

STRUGGLES TO DESEGREGATE
THE MEXICAN SCHOOLS

If oppression is never permanent, it is only so because the victims rise up against their oppressors, and in the Southwest the Mexican community engaged in a political struggle to dismantle segregation. Despite segregation, the educational institution held a valued place within the Mexican communities, which manifested itself as a strong belief in the power of education as a means for social betterment. Bitterness arose from within the community. One observer noted, in relation to Brawley's Miguel Hidalgo School, that "Mexicans resent the crowded condition of the school, the double session, and the dearth of conveniences." A teacher commented that parents and children understood the underlying racial motives of the board of education: "Many times . . . our youngsters would say to me 'The reason they do it is because we're Mexicans.' The parents felt that way too."[49]

Formal assaults came from organizations and community leaders. In Texas, the League of United Latin American Citizens battled long for school reform and desegregation. One member expressed a sentiment shared by many in the organization in proclaiming that "WE MUST BATTLE SEGREGATION BECAUSE OF RACE PREJUDICES!"[50] George I. Sánchez and labor leader Ernesto Galarza criticized segregation throughout the 1930s and 1940s, calling the practice arbitrary, capricious, and racially motivated. Sánchez's trenchant criticisms expressed the community's growing sentiment for reviewing the injustice of segregation. In an unprecedented legal action, incensed Mexican parents in Lemon Grove, California, boycotted their school in 1930 before suing the board of education in the first successful desegregation case in the nation's history.[51] Although the case had only local impact, the rebellion augured the resistance to come in the 1940s.

Despite the post-1920s transition to a culture-based interpretation of IQ, the curriculum remained as before; little changed in administrative procedure. The consequences of a nonhereditary theoretical basis for IQ proved meager for the Mexican community. Through the late 1930s and into the 1940s, the culture of the community was still used to explain the "Mexican problem." Gradually a philosophy, freed from scientific race theory, took shape. In the new pedagogical environment, the culture of the Mexican community was defined as the cause of the tangle of pathologies that were alleged to plague it. It was believed that nothing could be gained until there was a transformation, either coerced or voluntary, from Mexican cultural standards to American standards. Nothing appeared to indicate that segregated schooling required modification, and it remained the prescription of choice for "remedying" Mexican culture.

It is within this atmosphere that the Mexican American community engaged in its civil rights struggles of the 1940s to desegregate schools. The Mexican community joined a national political struggle to force the democratization of the nation's schools. The first round of the conflict that eventually led to the historic *Méndez v. Westminster*[52] case occurred in 1943 in Santa

Ana, California, the county seat of Orange County. The school board instituted segregated classes in 1913 and established the first Mexican school in 1919. Parents at the time opposed the move and appealed to the board, but without success. For two generations, the board, with few exceptions, directed Mexican children to attend one of three segregated schools. Throughout the county, fifteen Mexican schools were maintained and attended by nearly five thousand children. Chafing under decades of segregation, several Santa Ana parents appeared before the board of education in 1943 and vociferously demanded the right for their children to attend the school of their choice. An unbending board, upset at the strident tones of the petitioners, refused.

Officials were negotiating with the politically aware second generation, however, a generation more cognizant of the injustices and harm generated by segregation. Many members of that generation had served in the armed forces during the Second World War, and many had relatives who had served. Returning veterans had tasted equality in the armed forces and were restive under the segregationist codes now governing their conduct. Leaders began to emerge and organize to challenge segregation. In Orange County, veterans founded the Latin American Organization and resolved to reform schools to serve the needs of the Mexican community. Meanwhile, parents joined the movement throughout the county.

In rural Westminster, Gonzalo and Felicitas Méndez, who had only recently moved into the area, sent their youngsters to the closest elementary school. Unknown to them, the school restricted admission to Anglos. When school officials discovered the nationality of the Méndez children, they were refused admission. Unfazed, the Méndezes took an unheard-of step and refused to send their children to the segregated school and protested to the board. The board recommended a "special admission" for the Méndezes. The Mexican parents, calling the special admission a slap in the face, refused the board's offer and organized a boycott of all parents until all children were allowed to enroll in the school of their choice. Mrs. Méndez later recalled that she and her husband organized the boycott because they got "tired of being pushed around." That sentiment became more widespread.[53]

In Garden Grove, Ruth and Cruz Barrios defied the board, and Santa Ana parents had already confronted the board in 1943. The stage was set when, in 1945, a class action lawsuit filed by five parents on behalf of five thousand children was filed in federal court to demand the desegregation of the county's schools. Assisted by the newly formed Santa Ana chapter of the League of Latin American Citizens, the plaintiffs argued that the Fourteenth Amendment's equal protection clause had been violated, as there were no laws enabling the segregation of Mexican children. The defendants answered that segregation in this case passed legal muster under the *Plessy*[54] doctrine, that is, separate but equal, and that schools for Mexican children were as good as those for Anglo children. Furthermore, argued the defendants, Mexican children required special courses in Americanization, particularly English, to prepare them for the higher grades, and thus segregation involved strictly educational objectives.

In February 1946, U.S. District Court Judge Paul L. McCormick ruled that the school districts were guilty of violating the Fourteenth Amendment in forcing Mexican children to attend segregated schools. Judge McCormick found that a "paramount requisite in the American system of public education is social equality. It must be open to all children by unified school association regardless of lineage."[55] The judge clearly broke with *Plessy* by maintaining that separation implied inferiority, and that inferiority was obtained through arbitrary administrative practices. He wrote that the county's practices "foster[ed] antagonism in the children and [suggested] inferiority among them where none exist[ed]."[56] The county counsel appealed to the U.S. Circuit Court of Appeals, but the appeals judges upheld the lower court's ruling. The county was ordered to begin the process of dismantling segregation in the fall of 1948.

The class action suit, known by the legal title *Méndez v. Westminster,* reverberated throughout the nation, particularly in the Southwest, and led to successful challenges in Arizona and Texas. Legal analysts quickly focused on the case. An article in the *Columbia Law Review* argued that the case strongly suggested that the *Plessy* doctrine might be in for a constitutional test. The author noted that the "courts in the [*Méndez*] case breaks sharply with this approach and finds that the Fourteenth Amendment requires 'social equality' rather than 'equal facilities.'" A piece in the *Yale Law Journal* affirmed that the Méndez decision "questioned the basic assumption of the Plessy Doctrine. . . . A dual school system even if 'equal facilities' were provided does imply social inferiority."[57]

Civil rights activists understood the significance of *Méndez*. The NAACP legal defense team of Thurgood Marshall and Robert C. Carter followed the case closely and filed amicus curiae briefs during the appeals process. According to Carter, the briefs were a "dry run for the future" and contained every one of the key arguments later used in the *Brown v. Board of Education* case (which followed *Méndez* by eight years). All the documents filed by the plaintiffs' lawyer were handed over to Marshall and Carter, who read them with great interest. Clearly, the struggle to desegregate the United States has many points of origin, but one that we must not ignore is the *Méndez* case of 1947.

Many districts, particularly in rural areas, ignored the decision, and even districts that desegregated maintained many discriminatory practices. Segregation reappeared in the form of gerrymandered neighborhood school districts, and schools with a majority of Chicano students increased notably. Strong reliance on IQ testing, heavy tracking into industrial education, Americanization, English immersion, and the generally negative perception of Mexican culture continued to guide education. Continuity and change marked the transition from the era of the Mexican school to the era of integration shaped by the culture concept. Continuity, however, maintained the dominant position.

NOTES

1. Charles C. Teague, *Fifty Years a Rancher* (Los Angeles: Ward Ritchie Press, 1944), p. 143.
2. Gilbert G. González, *Labor and Community: Mexican Citrus Worker Villages in a Southern California County* (Urbana: University of Illinois Press, 1994), p. 28.
3. Susan B. Dorsey, "Problems of the Los Angeles School Board," *Los Angeles City Schools Journal*, 6 (1923), 59.
4. See Charles Clifford Carpenter, "Segregation vs. Non-Segregation of the Mexican Student," Master's thesis, University of Southern California, 1935; see also Gilbert G. González, "Educational Reform in Los Angeles and Its Effect Upon the Mexican Community, 1900-1930," *Explorations in Ethnic Studies, 1*, No. 2 (1978), 5–26.
5. Edward A. Ross, *Social Control: A Survey of the Foundations of Order* (New York: MacMillan, 1912,) p. 2; also, Charles Horton Cooley, *Social Process* (New York: Scribners, 1918).
6. See Samuel Bowles, "Unequal Education and the Reproduction of the Social Division of Labor," in *Schooling in a Corporate Society*, ed. Martin Carnoy (New York: David McKay, 1972), pp. 36–64; see also, Raymond E. Callahan, *Education and the Cult of Efficiency* (Chicago: University of Chicago Press, 1962); also, David Nasaw, *Schooled to Order: A Social History of Public Schooling in the United States* (New York: Oxford University Press, 1981).
7. In the early twentieth century the term "efficient" meant "scientific management," that is, Taylorisation in all spheres of society, the controlled utilization of all available resources, human and physical, for social and economic "uplift" or progress toward a harmonious society. In practice, efficiency meant that schools (and society) were to be managed by the same principles governing the large-scale business enterprise and employ the conveyorbelt system used in factories for processing students through their courses. Further, immigrants were a drag upon progress until Americanized and able to integrate into the bureaucratic social system. In this context, labor strikes were "inefficient" because they prevented the full and unfettered control of labor power in the production of commodities, and also because strikes "balkanized" society into classes, a great fear among adherents of efficiency.
8. See, for example, Samuel Bowles and Herbert Gintis, *Schooling in Capitalist America* (New York: Basic Books, 1976); see also, Martin Carnoy, *Education as Cultural Imperialism* (New York: David McKay, 1974).
9. Gilbert G. González, *Chicano Education in the Era of Segregation* (Philadelphia: Balch Institute, 1990), p. 37.
10. H. F. Bradford, "The Mexican Child in Our American Schools," *Arizona Teacher Parent, 27* (March 1939), 199.
11. Jessie Hayden, "The La Habra Experiment," Master's thesis, Claremont College, 1934.
12. Leonard John Vandenburgh, "The Mexican Problem in the Schools," *Los Angeles School Journal, 11*, No. 34 (1928), 15.
13. Susan B. Dorsey, "Mrs. Pierce and Mrs. Dorsey Discuss Matters Before the Principals Club," *Los Angeles School Journal, 6*, No. 25 (1925), 59.
14. González, *Labor and Community*, p. 101.
15. See Gilbert G. González, "The Americanization of Mexican Women and Family During the Era of De Jure Segregation," in *Ethnic and Gender Boundaries in the United States: Studies of Asian, Black, Mexican, and Native Americans*, ed. Sucheng Chan (Lewiston, NY: Edwin Mellon Press, 1989), pp. 55–79.
16. See González, *Labor and Community*, pp. 127–129.
17. See Gilbert G. González, "The Historical Development of the Concept Intelligence," *Review of Radical Political Economy, 11*, No. 2 (1979), 44–54.
18. See González, *Labor and Community*, pp. 127–129.
19. George K. Miller, "Birds of a Feather," *Los Angeles School Journal, 9*, No. 24 (1926), 17.
20. Ellen Alice McAnulty, "Achievement and Intelligence Test Results for Mexican Children Attending Los Angeles City Schools," *Los Angeles Educational Research Bulletin, 11*, No. 7 (1932), 89.
21. See Merton Hill, *The Development of an Americanization Program* (Ontario, CA: Board of Trustees of the Chaffey Union High School District and the Chaffey Junior College, 1928), p. 110.

22. Alma Leonhardy, "Slow-Learning Groups in High Schools," in *Third Yearbook,* ed. Los Angeles City School District (Los Angeles: Los Angeles City Schools, Division of Psychology and Educational Research, 1929), pp. 187–188.

23. Joseph M. Sniffen, "The Senior High School Problem Boy," *Los Angeles School Journal, 11,* No. 32 (1928), 14.

24. William John Cooper, "Character Education," *Los Angeles School Journal, 10,* No. 26 (1927), 18.

25. This observation is based on a selected number of master's theses written by students at the University of Southern California. I used the bibliographies to gauge the typical readings covered in the course work. In all the examples consulted, conventional distortions of Mexico, Mexican culture, and immigrants permeated the works. Teacher college training programs embraced and promulgated the scientific racism of day.

26. In this article, the terms "vocational" and "industrial" are used interchangeably; however, in the materials used to prepare this article, "trade" was sometimes synonymous with the two. In Los Angeles, the district Trade School carried out training for skilled trades, whereas industrial or vocational course work implied an unskilled or semi-skilled training curriculum. The distinctions were not always consistent. In relation to Mexican children, all job-oriented curriculum, whether termed trade, vocational, or industrial, meant training for the lower skilled categories of the work force.

27. González, *Chicano Education,* p. 87.

28. González, *Chicano Education,* pp. 87, 89.

29. Mary Florence Macredy, "The Mentally Handicapped Child for Wage-Earning and Citizenship," *Los Angeles Educational Research Bulletin, 9,* No. 6 (1930), 6.

30. James Vásquez, "Measurement of Intelligence and Language Differences," *Aztlán, 3,* No. 1 (1973), 155.

31. M. Frances Martin, "Development Centers and Rooms," *Third Yearbook,* ed. Los Angeles City School District (Los Angeles: Los Angeles City School District, Division of Psychology and Educational Research, 1929), pp. 84–85.

32. Martin, "Development Centers and Rooms," p. 87.

33. "Development Centers," *Fourth Yearbook,* ed. Los Angeles City School District (Los Angeles: Los Angeles City Schools, Department of Psychology and Educational Research, 1931), p. 116.

34. González, *Chicano Education,* p. 87.

35. González, *Chicano Education,* p. 88

36. Herschel Manuel, *The Education of Mexican and Spanish-Speaking Children in Texas* (Austin: University of Texas Press, 1930), pp. 76–77.

37. Paul S. Taylor, "Mexican Labor in the United States: Dimmit County, Winter Garden District, South Texas," *University of California Publications, 6,* No. 5 (1930), 372

38. Carey McWilliams, *Ill Fares the Land: Migrants and Migratory Labor in California* (New York: Barnes and Noble, 1942), p. 256.

39. McWilliams, *Ill Fares the Land,* p. 256.

40. State of California Superintendent of Public Instruction, *Biennial Report of the School Years Ending 30 June 1923 and 30 June 1924* (Sacramento: California State Printing Office, 1924), p. 35.

41. John R. Hunt, "The Problem of the Migratory School Child," *Los Angeles School Journal, 12,* No. 14 (1928), 24.

42. Bertha Underhill, "A Study of 132 Families in California Cotton Camps with Reference to Availability of Medical Care" (Sacramento: California Department of Social Welfare, Division of Child Welfare Services, 1936), p. 18.

43. González, *Chicano Education,* p. 105.

44. Jessie A. Tritt, "The Problem of Elementary Assignments," *Los Angeles School Journal, 12,* No. 1 (1928), 15.

45. Jay Newton Holliday, "A Study of Non-Attendance in Miguel Hidalgo School of Brawley, California," Master's thesis, University of Southern California, 1935.

46. Carlos Calderón, "The Education of Spanish-Speaking Children in Edcouch-Elsa, Texas," Master's thesis, University of Texas, 1950.

47. See, for example, Virgil E. Strickland and George I. Sánchez, "Spanish Name Spells Discrimination," *Nation's Schools, 41* (1948), 22–24.

48. Interview with Chester Whitten by Robin Rodarte and Richard Gutiérrez in *Harvest: A Compilation of Taped Interviews on the Minority Peoples of Orange County*, ed. Priscilla Oaks and Wacira Gethalga (Fullerton: California State University, Fullerton, 1974).

49. González, *Labor and Community*, p. 104.

50. Guadalupe San Miguel, Jr., *"Let Them All Take Heed": Mexican Americans and the Campaign for Educational Equality in Texas, 1910–1981* (Austin: University of Texas Press, 1987), p. 76.

51. Superior Court of the State of California, County of San Diego. *Roberto Alvarez v. the Board of Trustees of the Lemon Grove School District*. February 13, 1931.

52. *Méndez et al. v. Westminster School District of Orange County et al.* Civil Action Number 4292. District Court S. D., California. Central Division February 18, 1946. 64 F. Supp. 544 (S.D. California, 1946), (C.C.A., 9th April, 1947).

53. María Newman, "Tired of Being Pushed Around," *Celebrate, 3* (1989), 75.

54. *Plessy v. Ferguson*, 163 U.S. 537, 1896.

55. González, *Chicano Education*, p. 153; also, Gertrude Staughton, "In California's Orange County Mexican Americans Sue to End Bias in School Systems," *People's World, 16* (March 1945), 324; Mary M. Peters, "The Segregation of Mexican American Children in the Elementary Schools of California—Its Legal and Administrative Aspects," Master's thesis, University of California, Los Angeles, 1948.

56. González, *Chicano Education*, p. 153.

57. González, *Chicano Education*, p. 154.

CHICANA/O EDUCATION FROM THE CIVIL RIGHTS ERA TO THE PRESENT

DOLORES DELGADO BERNAL

pedagogy

The struggle of Chicanas/os for educational equity and the right to include their culture, history, and language in K-12 and higher education curricula predates the civil rights movements of the 1960s by decades.[1] Although Chicanas/os have made significant progress in terms of educational inclusion over the last five decades, since the late 1970s hard-won gains have eroded. Many of today's most hotly debated educational issues are very similar to those discussed in Mexican communities since before the turn of the century: improvement of inferior school facilities; removal of racist teachers and administrators; elimination of tracking; and inclusion of Mexican history, language, and culture in the curriculum. Today's conditions can be better understood within a contextual and historical analysis that connects the present to earlier periods, and links belief systems to our judicial system and social policies.

This chapter addresses educational policies and practices and judicial decisions that have affected Chicana/o education from the 1950s through the 1990s. This period encompasses the early civil rights era, including the Chicana/o Movement, which brought significant improvements in Chicana/o schooling, and the more recent neoconservative era in which we have seen the deterioration of Chicana/o educational rights. I have included several educational themes that were especially prominent throughout the Southwest from the 1950s through the 1990s: continued school segregation, bilingual education, and higher education. During this period, school segregation and desegregation efforts took on a new form, and differ greatly from the era of de jure segregation that officially ended in 1954 with the *Brown* decision.[2] The bilingual education movement is unique to this period, and Chicana/o participation in higher education was virtually nonexistent prior to the 1950s. Another common thread that weaves through this chapter (and the entire book) is the resistance and activism of Chicana/o communities, including their use of the judicial system in demanding educational equity. Though each of these themes was important throughout the Southwest, this chapter places an emphasis on California and Texas, where the majority of

Chicanas/os live and where much of the research on Chicana/o education has focused. In addition, the contemporary focus on California at the end of this chapter is purposeful, as California seems to be setting a national public policy standard in regards to legislation that negatively impacts the schooling of Chicanas/os.

Starting with the 1950s and early 1960s, I examine the continued school segregation of Mexican students even after numerous court decisions found de jure segregation of Mexican students illegal. Next I turn to the social activism and social policies that positively influenced Chicana/o schooling during the late 1960s and early 1970s. Then I address the conservative retrenchment that began in the mid-1970s, specifically the tension between desegregation and bilingual education, the educational inequity in K-12 education, and the myth of meritocracy in higher education. Finally, I assess where we are today, acknowledge progress in some aspects of Chicana/o schooling, and briefly analyze recent California legislation that has or will have a negative impact on Chicana/o education.

DE FACTO SCHOOL SEGREGATION: THE 1950S TO THE EARLY 1960S

In the 1950s and early 1960s, Mexicans saw the elimination of school segregation as the key to full economic and social mobility. Throughout the Southwest, however, judicial decisions outlawing the segregation of Mexican students were ignored; instead, school boards purposely overlooked desegregation, and de facto segregation of Mexican students actually increased (Bogardus, 1949; Rangel & Alcala, 1972; Salinas, 1971). Why were these judicial decisions ignored? I argue that the White social belief system about Mexicans helped support the many political and economic reasons for their continued segregation. Indeed, the images of Mexicans held by educators and the judicial system shared a common trait during this period: both were "premised upon political, scientific, and religious theories relying on racial characterizations and stereotypes about people of color that help support a legitimating ideology and specific political action" (Tate, 1997, p. 199). The ideologies of Anglo-Saxon superiority, capitalism, and scientific theories of intelligence provided the cornerstones of de jure segregated schooling for Mexicans throughout the Southwest during the first half of this century (González, 1990; Menchaca & Valencia, 1990). These theories, along with a belief system that viewed Mexicans as "culturally deficient" and characterized them as ignorant, backward, unclean, unambitious, and abnormal, were unaffected by major judicial decisions in California and Texas (see González, 1974; Taylor, 1934)

In California, the Méndez v. Westminster (1946) landmark case officially ended de jure segregation for Mexican students and cast doubt on the "separate but equal" doctrine. Five Mexican families, including Felicitas and Gonzalo Méndez, claimed that their children and other children of Mexican

Dolores Delgado Bernal

descent were victims of unconstitutional discrimination in the segregated schools of Orange County. U.S. District Court Judge Paul L. McCormick's 1946 ruling in favor of the plaintiffs, upheld in the Court of Appeals in 1947, found that the segregation of Mexican children could be considered arbitrary action taken without due process of the law (Wollenberg, 1974). In Texas, just one year later, Minerva Delgado and twenty other parents filed a suit against several Texas school districts in *Delgado v. Bastrop Independent School District* (1948). As in California, the court ruled that placing Mexican students in segregated schools was arbitrary and discriminatory, and in violation of constitutional rights guaranteed by the Fourteenth Amendment (San Miguel, 1987). However, these cases, which ended de jure racial segregation for Mexican students, did not change the existing American belief system that portrayed Mexicans as inferior.

In Texas, even after the *Méndez* and *Delgado* decisions found de jure segregation of Mexican students illegal, segregation continued to be widely practiced (Bogardus, 1949; Menchaca, 1995). When state school officials were confronted with evidence of continued school segregation, there was little interest in seriously addressing the problem. For example, representatives from the League of United Latin American Citizens (LULAC) and the American G.I. Forum found this to be true when they appeared before the State Board of Education in 1950 with a list of twenty Texas cities that were still practicing segregation in spite of the recent judicial decisions (San Miguel, 1987).[3] In response, the State Board of Education proposed a policy statement on the illegality of the segregation of Mexican schoolchildren, but allowed local districts to handle the complaints and grievances of discriminatory treatment. The Board's policy simply created a bureaucratic process that limited the number of grievances that could actually reach the state commissioner of education. As San Miguel stated, "Between 1950 and 1957 nine local school districts were brought to the commissioner of education for special hearings, although hundreds of school districts throughout the state were segregating Mexican American students" (p. 132).

Belief in the cultural deficiency of Mexicans remained in place and supported the political action that continued to segregate Mexican students. At the same time, school segregation itself perpetuated an ideology of inferiority. Critical race theorist Charles Lawrence (1993) argues that school segregation conveys an ideology of inferiority that denies equal citizenship based not just on the act of segregation (de jure or de facto), but also on the defamatory message it sends about students of color:

Brown held that segregation is unconstitutional not simply because the physical separation of Black and white children is bad or because resources were
distributed unequally among Black and white schools. *Brown* held that segregated schools were unconstitutional primarily because of the message segregation conveys—the message that Black children are an untouchable
caste, unfit to be educated with white children. Segregation serves its purpose by conveying an idea. It stamps a badge of inferiority upon Blacks, and
this badge communicates a message to others in the community, as well as to
Blacks wearing the badge, that is injurious to Blacks. (p. 59)

Following this line of reasoning, the injurious message behind Mexican
school segregation was that Mexican students were inferior and did not deserve society's investment in their education. For example, in the *Méndez* decision, Judge McCormick stated, "the methods of segregation prevalent in
the defendant school districts foster antagonisms in the children and suggest
inferiority among them where none exists" (64 Federal Supplement, 1946,
cited in Harders & Gómez, 1998, p. 8). In other words, school segregation itself suggested an inferiority that was greater than any attempt to provide
equal school facilities, making them inherently unequal. Thus, even after the
end of de jure segregation, Mexican students remained segregated in sub-
standard schools and were labeled as members of an inferior group. The
comments of a Los Angeles teacher in the 1960s reveal the cultural deficit beliefs many teachers held:

The attitudes of my colleagues are negative toward the Mexican American. I
have heard some remarks in the teachers' room made like, "I have never
had a Mexican who could think for himself." I have heard others say, "These
Mexican kids, why do they have to be here?" (Delgado Bernal, 1997, p. 83)

The historic devaluation of Spanish also promoted these beliefs. Prohibiting Spanish-language use among Mexican schoolchildren was a social
philosophy and a political tool used by local and state officials to justify
school segregation and to maintain a colonized relationship between Mexicans and the dominant society.4 Bilingualism was seen as "unAmerican" and
considered a deficit and an obstacle to learning. There were no formal bilingual programs for Spanish-speaking students prior to the late 1960s, and it
was routine to segregate Mexican students into "Mexican schools" or "Mexican classrooms," using their perceived language deficiency as justification.
Even after the end of de jure segregation, it was common to find Mexican students physically separated from other students within the same classroom.
Los Angeles Unified School District board member Vickie Castro, who went
through elementary school in the 1950s, recalls how she was physically separated from her peers:

I do recall my first day of school. And I did not speak English. . . . I just recall
being frightened and I recall not knowing what to do and I recall being told
to just sit over there in the corner. And there was one other little girl and we
were just scared out of our minds. (Castro, 1994, p. 2, 3)

It was also common to hold Mexican students back for several years while they learned English. This left them over age for their grade, and thereby more likely to quit school before graduating.[5] This "assimilationist" perspective viewed bilingualism as a cognitive disability that caused confusion and impeded academic development (Jensen, 1962). In other words, many educators believed that there was only so much room in the brain, and children would not be able to function if they were learning English and maintaining their native Spanish. In fact, during the 1950s and early 1960s, most educators, along with LULAC, strongly supported the idea of intensive English instruction without the maintenance of Spanish (Crawford, 1992). LULAC's motive in supporting this type of instruction was their desire for Mexican students to learn English as quickly as possible so they could be successful in the dominant society. Though the goal of LULAC leaders was not total assimilation of the Mexican population, they were drawn into the assimilationist language perspective, and only later recognized the damage this perspective had on Mexican students (San Miguel, 1987).

Some Mexican educators at the time also advocated for an English-only approach, prior to offering their support for bilingual education in the late 1960s. One interesting example is Joe Bernal, the Texas senator and former educator, who later sponsored the Bilingual Education Act of 1968. He grew up on the predominantly Mexican west side of San Antonio in the 1940s, and as a high school student leader helped enforce an English-only campus policy. Each student was given a ribbon that said, "I Am an American—I Speak English," and was urged to turn in classmates heard using Spanish. Those caught speaking Spanish faced corporal punishment, after-school detention, and other forms of discipline (Crawford, 1992). Later, as an elementary schoolteacher in the 1950s, Bernal fined his pupils a penny for each time they used Spanish, saving the proceeds for a class party. He remembers: "I used to collect a lot of money from these kids. The parents knew about it and they were very supportive" because they believed that their children must learn English, whatever the cost (Crawford, 1992, p. 79). Suppressing Spanish was a way to degrade and control an entire cultural group without explicitly using force or violence. It was one strategy for sustaining a colonized/colonizer relationship between Mexicans and the dominant White society. Many Mexicans internalized these negative views of Spanish—and therefore a negative view of themselves and their families—in order to assimilate into the dominant society.

Although the relationship between Mexicans and the dominant White society is complex and beyond pedagogical issues, it was clearly a part of Mexican school segregation. Mexican boys and girls continued to be tracked into vocational classes that served an economic function and supported the unequal division of power, wealth, and status, just as in the era of de jure segregation. Young Mexican women were tracked into home economics and clerical or secretarial classes, which prepared them for low-paying domestic and subservient work. Mexican women had an additional hurdle to jump, for even if they were able to move beyond paid domestic work, their families usually did not expect them to pursue an education beyond the domestic skills they would need in their homes (García, 1997; López, 1977; Nieto Gómez, 1974). The sexist attitudes of the wider society were manifested in the Mexican culture through such common sayings as, *¿Para que quieres educarte si de nada te va a servir cuando te cases?* (Why do you want to educate yourself if it will not be of any use to you when you get married?) (López, 1977).

Throughout the 1960s, the message that both Chicana and Chicano students were inferior continued to translate into overcrowded and underfinanced schools, low graduation rates, and the overrepresentation of Chicana/o students in special education classes, including classes for the mentally retarded and the emotionally disturbed (California State Advisory Committee, 1968). A 1967 Chicana high school graduate remembers the deplorable educational conditions at her urban high school:

> We had severely overcrowded classrooms. We didn't have sufficient books. We had buildings that were barrack type buildings that had been built as emergency, temporary buildings during World War II, and this was in the late 1960's, and we were still going to school in those buildings. (Delgado Bernal, in press)

Demographic factors such as the expanding Chicana/o school-age population, immigration, urbanization, and White flight also contributed to the increased de facto segregation of Chicana/o students. In cities such as Los Angeles, San Jose, Phoenix, Denver, San Antonio, and Houston, the picture was especially stark. By 1960, more than 80 percent of California's 1.4 million Spanish-surnamed people lived in urban areas, and the number of Spanish-surnamed children attending inferior segregated schools had increased (Wollenberg, 1974). Nearly half of all Chicana/o students in the Southwest attended elementary and secondary schools in which the Chicana/o enrollment was over 50 percent of the total student body (U.S. Commission on Civil Rights, 1971). As educational conditions worsened, tension and resentment increased, and Chicanas/os became disillusioned with the "American Dream." In response, many Chicanas/os in the 1960s embraced a nationalist perspective and a militancy to bring about educational, political, and social reform.

SOCIAL ACTIVISM AND SOCIAL POLICY OF THE LATE 1960S

The last half of the 1960s marked the first time that youth played a central role in the shaping of movements aimed against social institutions and those in power. Street politics and mass protests marked this period, and student movements helped shape larger struggles for social and political equality (Muñoz, 1989). During this period of social unrest, Chicana/o students were influenced by numerous social and political forces, such as the wider Chicana/o movement, the Black civil rights movement, the federal government's War on Poverty, anti–Vietnam War sentiments, the women's movement, and political struggles in Mexico and Latin America. At the same time, expanding economic opportunity for low-income citizens and people of color became the main focus of federal social policy, and education emerged as the fundamental mechanism for combating poverty and racial inequality (Wise, 1982).

Throughout the Southwest, Chicana/o students and their communities struggled to call attention to and improve the poor quality of public education offered to them. In March 1968, well over ten thousand Chicana/o students walked out of East Los Angeles high schools to protest inferior schooling conditions. The students boycotted classes and presented a list of grievances to the Los Angeles Board of Education. The list consisted of thirty-six demands, including smaller class sizes, bilingual education, an end to the vocational tracking of Chicana/o students, more emphasis on Chicano history, and community control of schools (McCurdy, 1968). The East L.A. walkouts focused national attention on the K-12 schooling of Chicanas/os and also set a precedent for school boycotts throughout the Southwest, including those in Crystal City and San Antonio, Texas; Denver, Colorado; and Phoenix, Arizona (Acuña, 1988).

Though their stories are often excluded in written historical accounts, Chicanas played crucial leadership roles in these mass demonstrations and were intimately involved in the struggles for educational justice. Celeste Baca, Vickie Castro, Paula Crisostomo, Mita Cuaron, Tanya Luna Mount, Rosalinda Méndez González, Rachael Ochoa Cervera, and Cassandra Zacarias were but a few of the women who made up the East L.A. student leadership. They engaged in networking, organizing, and developing consciousness; held elected and appointed offices; and acted as spokespersons (Delgado Bernal, 1997). For example, Paula Crisostomo and Rosalinda Méndez González both provided testimony to the U.S. Commission on Civil Rights regarding the education of Mexican American students. Méndez González described the racist curriculum and popular stereotypes of Chicanas/ os in this way:

> From the time we first begin attending school, we hear about how great and wonderful our United States is, about our democratic American heritage, but little about our splendid and magnificent Mexican heritage and culture. We look for others like ourselves in these history books, for something to be proud of for being a Mexican, and all we see in books and magazines, films, and T.V. shows are stereotypes of a dark, dirty, smelly man with a tequila bottle in one hand, a dripping taco in the other, a serape wrapped around him, and a big sombrero. (California State Advisory Committee, 1968)

Chicana students resisted both racist school policies and sexist educational practices. Artist Patssi Valdez, who participated in the East L.A. walkouts, remembers what her home economics teacher told her and other Chicanas: "She would say . . . 'You little Mexicans, you better learn and pay attention. This class is very important because . . . most of you are going to be cooking and cleaning for other people'" (Valdez, 1994). The teacher's comments illustrate the intersecting forms of subordination that have historically influenced the schooling of Chicanas.[6] Because they were female, Mexican, and working class, the teacher expected Chicana students to prepare themselves for domestic labor that met the needs of White middle- and upper-class families. Chicana students struggled against sexism not only in the wider society, but also within the Chicana/o community. Within the movement and various student organizations, Chicanas had to actively reject the traditional roles to which they were often relegated by their male peers. One Chicana stated, "My male friends at the time, in the organization, would try to put me in female roles. Like be the secretary, make the sandwiches, do that. But . . . I always challenged. And when I would see that there were no women involved, boom, I made myself right there" (Delgado Bernal, in press).

Chicana/o student activism also played a crucial role in gaining access to institutions of higher education. As Chicana/o students across the Southwest demanded equitable K-12 schooling, they likewise demanded their place in colleges and universities. Prior to this time, Mexican students were virtually absent from institutions of higher education. After World War II, the G.I. Bill gave a few Chicano servicemen access to college, and by 1958, "California enrolled nearly 36,000 college freshman of Mexican-American origin, several more than in Texas" (Weinberg, 1977, p. 341, cited in Webster, 1984, p. 42).[7] Less than a decade later, in 1967, one of the first Chicana/o college student organizations, the Mexican American Student Association (MASA), was formed at East Los Angeles Community College (Gómez-Quiñones, 1978). College student organizations rapidly formed in California and throughout the Southwest, including organizations such as United Mexican-American Students (UMAS) in California and the Mexican-American Youth Organization (MAYO) in Texas. The primary issue of these organizations was the lack of Chicana/o access to quality education, and their activities revolved around the institutionalization of Chicano Studies and support programs for Chicana/o students (López, 1977).

As a result of the development of Chicana/o student organizations, the East L.A. school walkouts in 1968, and Chicana/o student activism in general, there was a statewide student conference in Santa Barbara, California, in 1969. Rosalinda Méndez González remembers that she, like many young Chicanas, actively participated in the conference and that "the Santa Barbara conference . . . was like everybody coming together to reconceptualize the schools and higher education for our communities" (Méndez González, 1995, p. 37). At this conference, students, faculty, administrators, and community representatives produced a 150-page document called *El Plan de Santa Bárbara: A Chicano Plan for Higher Education* (Chicano Coordinating Council, 1970). *El Plan* provided the theoretical rationale for the development of Chicano Studies, a plan for recruitment and admission of Chicano students, support programs to aid in the retention of Chicano students, and the organization of Chicano Studies curricula and departments. Another significant result of the Santa Barbara conference and *El Plan* was the unification of Chicano student organizations and the creation of Movimiento Estudiantil Chicano de Aztlán (MEChA). MEChA's goal was to link all Chicano student groups throughout the Southwest and "to socialize and politicize Chicano students on their particular campus to the ideals of the [Chicano] movement" (Chicano Coordinating Council, 1970, p. 60).

El Plan offered a vision and course of action for Chicanos in higher education, one of the first of its kind among the Chicana/o community. However, it was confined in its scope, reflecting a limited consciousness by not including references to women, female liberation, or Chicana Studies (Pardo, 1984). Some have called it a *"manifesto"* for its grounding in traditional cultural nationalism, rather than an ideology that works toward the elimination of all forms of oppression (Orozco, 1986). In the early 1970s, in response to the absence of women in the curriculum, Chicana activists at a Chicano Studies/MEChA conference at California State University, Northridge, proposed five courses on La Chicana, including The Chicana in Education, The Chicana and the Law, and Religion and la Mujer. They also proposed a requirement that all Chicano Studies majors take at least one class on La Chicana (Nieto Gómez, 1973).

At the national level, Chicanas were also addressing the unique needs of Chicana students in attaining high school and/or higher education. At the National Women's Political Caucus Convention in 1973, the Chicana Caucus consisted of sixty women from seven states, including Texas, New Mexico, Illinois, and California. The Chicana Caucus submitted a resolution requesting that legislative efforts of the organization include: a) research on the educational needs of Chicanas; b) recruitment of Chicanas to higher education; c) financial support for the education of Chicanas; d) tutorial and counseling programs designed for Chicanas; e) incorporation of Chicana culture into educational systems and textbooks; and f) inclusion of Chicanas in all affirmative action activity (Chapa, 1973). In this way, the women of the Chicana Caucus attempted to address the unique problems that confronted Chicana students by shaping national social policy.

Throughout the 1960s and early 1970s, Chicana/o activism and Chicana feminist ideas merged with social policies to better address the needs of Chicana/o students and increase their access to institutions of higher education. During the Kennedy administration and President Johnson's War on Poverty, affirmative action attempted to equalize the playing field in the realm of higher education. Federal legislation helped facilitate Chicana/o participation in higher education. The Higher Education Act of 1965, among other things, authorized several financial aid programs, and Title VII extended the Civil Rights Act of 1964 to include all educational institutions. Federal and state programs were created, such as the Educational Opportunities Program (EOP), which played a critical role in recruiting and retaining Chicana/o students into universities and colleges. EOP and programs similar to it were the initial bridges that brought Chicana/o students into higher education in more visible numbers (Acuña, 1988). At the same time, as social activism and social policies were opening the doors to higher education, a number of social forces were also shaping bilingual education.

SOCIAL FORCES SHAPING BILINGUAL EDUCATION

The struggle by Chicanas/os to obtain bilingual education in public schools began with the social activism and policies of the 1960s. Historian Guadalupe San Miguel (1985) proposes that two views on bilingualism came into conflict and contributed to the formation of policies on bilingual education. The "assimilationist" perspective, discussed earlier, continued to uphold the post–World War II belief that bilingualism was divisive and un-American, a disability rather than an asset. Shared by associations of school administrators and their supporters, this view held that language and culture were incidental to the teaching and learning process. It did not recognize the value or utility of incorporating the language and culture of limited-English-speaking students into the public school curriculum. As discussed earlier in this chapter, prior to the late 1960s there were no bilingual programs for Mexican students, and it was routine to segregate Mexican students based on their perceived language deficiency. In fact, during the 1940s and 1950s, LULAC and Mexican educators such as Joe Bernal did not support bilingual instruction in public schools. The assimilationist ideology left students believing that speaking Spanish in school was an evil they had to avoid at all costs. Writer and poet José Antonio Burciaga (1993) articulates the pain experienced by students when their schooling was regulated by the assimilationist beliefs that devalued Spanish:

> Perhaps the most memorable experiences one has in school are those that come into direct conflict with one's family's beliefs and traditions. . . . No learning experience was more painful or damaging than the silence imposed on our Mexican culture, history and beautiful Spanish language. To speak Spanish was not only illegal but also a sin: "Bless me father, for I have sinned. I spoke Spanish in class and during recess. . . . *Mea culpa, Mea culpa, mea máxima culpa!*" (pp. 36, 40)

A second view on bilingualism in the 1960s, the "pluralist" perspective, accepted the plurality of languages as a necessary ingredient in U.S. education. This view was embraced by most Chicana/o communities and political allies (San Miguel, 1985). Pluralists viewed the first language and culture of the child as essential to the instructional and learning process. During the late 1960s, some educators, sociolinguists, and Chicana/o communities created a philosophical force that openly challenged the commonly held assimilationist perspective. Chicana/o student activism focused on poor educational conditions, racist school policies, and the implementation of bilingual education. Chicanas/os began to regard language as a matter of self-determination and language as a basic human right. Educator Reynaldo Macías has suggested that language rights can be based on "the right to freedom from discrimination on the basis of language" and "the right to use your language(s) in the activities of communal life" (1979, pp. 88–89). For many Chicanas/os, the right to maintain Spanish was a way of declaring some control over their lives and rejecting the colonized relationship between Chicanas/os and the dominant society. Whatever the justification, bilingual education offered some hope that Chicana/o schooling would be more meaningful and lead to educational equity.

With much political pressure from Chicana/o communities and liberal educators who held a pluralist perspective, the federal government, for the first time, funded bilingual education in 1968 through Title VII of the Elementary and Secondary Education Act of 1965 (Crawford, 1992). The 1968 Bilingual Education Act provided money to train teachers and aides, to develop instructional materials, and to establish parent-involvement projects (Loya, 1990). The Act was meant "to develop and carry out new and imaginative elementary and secondary school programs . . . [for] children of limited English-speaking ability" (Crawford, 1992, p. 85). However, the act did not impose teaching methods or even define the concept of bilingual education. In addition, the bill was viewed as a compensatory educational program in which linguistically "disadvantaged" children were assisted.

It is often argued that civil rights legislation has been very modest in its efforts to eliminate inequalities and often serves those in power as much if not more than those it is actually supposed to serve (Crenshaw, Gotanda, Peller, & Thomas, 1995; Matsuda, Lawrence, Delgado, & Crenshaw, 1993). For example, in most Chicana/o communities, bilingual education represented a way to maintain one's language and culture and was by definition a rejection of colonization. However, the official goals of bilingual education emanating from federal and state bilingual education guidelines from 1968 to the present have never included the maintenance of the student's first language. An early controversy in the House and Senate revolved around whether bilingual education was simply a better way to teach English or a means to preserve a student's first language, which might create unwanted ethnic pluralism. In fact, one of the sponsors of the original 1968 Bilingual Education Act was careful to state during the deliberation of the bill, "It is not the purpose of the bill to create pockets of different language throughout the country . . . not to stamp out the mother tongue and not to make their mother tongue the dominant language, but just to try to make these children fully literate in English, so that the children can move into the mainstream of American life" (Crawford, 1992, p. 84). Even during the mid-1970s, when bilingual education enjoyed its greatest level of support, native-language instruction was only seen as a necessary strategy that allowed a child to achieve competence in English (Roos, 1978). Never has federal or state legislation stated that bilingual education should help students maintain their first language to become bilingual and biliterate citizens. Yet, paradoxically, during the 1960s, the federal government spent millions of dollars trying to ensure a bilingual populace by calling for foreign-language requirements and well-funded foreign language departments in select high schools and most universities

(Crawford, 1992; Schaller, Scharff, & Schulzinger, 1992). These efforts, supported by the Cold War and the 1958 National Defense Education Act, certainly benefited middle-class Whites more than those Spanish-speaking students who started school already fluent in a "foreign" language.

In order to compel school officials to provide bilingual education, Chicanas/os have brought lawsuits under Title VI of the Civil Rights Act, which bans discrimination based "on the ground of race, color, or national origin" in "any program or activity receiving Federal financial assistance."[8] In the 1974 *Lau v. Nichols* case, non-English-speaking students of Chinese ancestry brought suit against the San Francisco Unified School District. The plaintiffs charged that where students were taught only in English, school officials had not taken significant action to provide a meaningful education. The U.S. Supreme Court unanimously found that by "failing to affirmatively overcome the English language deficiencies of national origin-minority group children with limited English-speaking ability, school officials had violated Title VI of the Civil Rights Act" (Roos, 1978, p. 116). The court handed down this decision even though the school district had made an effort to remedy language difficulties by providing supplemental English instruction to about one thousand of the 2,856 Chinese students who did not speak English. About 1,800 students, however did not receive any special instruction, which was a violation of Title VI of the Civil Rights Act. The decision helped to establish a precedent, though it did not provide a specific remedy to assist students with limited English proficiency.

Chicanas/os in New Mexico used the *Lau* decision in *Serna v. Portales Municipal Schools* (1974) to seek an order requiring the district to provide bilingual and bicultural education under Title VI. Chicanas/os in the New Mexico community felt that the school district's English as a Second Language (ESL) remedy was an inadequate response to the educational needs of Chicana/o students. And expert witnesses testified that when a child "goes to school where he finds no evidence of his language and culture and ethnic group represented [she/he] becomes withdrawn and nonparticipating" (cited in Roos, 1978, p. 129). Using *Lau* as a precedent, the court held that the district's failure to offer a bilingual and bicultural educational program that provided Chicana/o students with a meaningful education deprived them of their rights under Title VI (Martínez, 1994). It is significant that the court once again decided against the school district, even though the latter was making an effort to provide a limited ESL program.

Legal indeterminacy has led to various judicial interpretations. Policies and law regarding bilingual education are indeterminate in that courts often permit a judge to exercise discretion in rendering vague standards and justifying multiple outcomes to lawsuits (Martínez, 1994). Such was the case in decisions that ignored or interpreted *Lau* and *Serna* differently. For example, *Keyes v. School District Number 1* (1973), although often thought of as a desegregation case, was similar to the *Lau* and *Serna* cases.[9] The Chicana/o plaintiffs "alleged that the Denver school board's failure to adopt a bilingual and bicultural program constituted a violation of Title VI" (Martínez, 1994, p.

608). In 1975 the 10th Circuit Court of Appeals found that the district had implemented various programs to address the needs of students with limited English proficiency (as did the school districts in *Lau* and *Serna*), and therefore was not in violation of Title VI. The *Keyes* decision, made by the same circuit that affirmed the extensive bilingual and bicultural education programs in *Serna*, failed to discuss the *Serna* and *Lau* decisions and did not explain how its ruling was consistent or inconsistent with those cases (Martínez, 1994). The *Keyes* case demonstrates that courts can and have exercised discretion to limit access to bilingual and bicultural education.[10]

CONSERVATIVE RETRENCHMENT

The sociopolitically conservative era that began in the mid-1970s and that hit hard during the Reagan and Bush administrations had a negative impact on Chicana/o schooling conditions. A strong backlash against the social equity programs of President Johnson's War on Poverty was accompanied by increased military spending, reduced educational spending, and a growing recession. The conservatives regained a strong voice, which was reflected in social ideas, educational policy, and judicial decisions. As tension between desegregation and bilingual education intensified, the funding for bilingual education was drastically reduced and public school finance was restricted for Chicana/o schools. This left Chicana/o students in underfunded, segregated schools that failed to adequately prepare them for post-secondary education. At the same time, the myth of meritocracy in higher education and a growing attack on affirmative action programs also limited Chicana/o students' access to colleges and universities.

THE TENSION BETWEEN DESEGREGATION AND BILINGUAL EDUCATION

The desegregation process has usually been thought of as an issue pertinent only to African American communities, with Chicana/o students often being ignored in the process and in the educational literature. By the 1970s, more Chicana/o students attended second-rate segregated schools than at the time of the 1947 *Méndez* decision. In fact, many Chicana/o scholars and activists believe that the *Brown* decision had no effect on the schooling of Chicana/o students until the 1970s, when the courts were forced to decide how to treat Chicana/o students in the desegregation process (Acuña, 1988). *Cisneros v. Corpus Christi Independent School District* was filed in 1968 by Chicana/o labor activists in Corpus Christi, Texas, and was decided in 1970 at the federal district court level. The plaintiffs challenged the legal framework for future desegregation cases and the segregation of Chicana/o and African American school children in Corpus Christi. The court ruled that Chicanas/os were an identifiable ethnic minority and found them to be unconstitutionally segregated in the public schools. It also required that an appropriate desegregation plan that included Anglos, Chicanas/os, and African Americans be submitted (San Miguel, 1987). Prior to this case, the strategy employed in most successful school desegregation efforts was based on Chicanas/os' claim to "Whiteness."[11]

The U.S. Supreme Court reinforced how Chicana/o students were to be treated in the school desegregation process in the 1973 *Keyes v. School District Number 1* case. Before *Keyes*, Denver Public Schools, like many schools throughout the Southwest, integrated Chicana/o students with African American students and called it desegregation. The Court either had to define Chicana/o students as "Caucasians—and integrate them with African Americans or redefine their ethnic status (as a protected ethnic minority group)and integrate them with everyone else" (Donato, 1997, p. 124). In *Keyes,* the Supreme Court decided that Chicana/o students were an identifiable minority group and ruled that they had been denied their constitutional rights by the Denver Public Schools. The court authorized racial-balance remedies and required districts to integrate African Americans and Chicanas/os into White urban school districts.

It is important to note that after these decisions and throughout the 1970s, there was growing tension between the pursuit of bilingual education and school desegregation. During the 1930s and 1940s, Mexicans fought school segregation in the courts in such cases as *Alvarez v. Lemon Grove* (1931), *Del Rio Independent School District v. Salvatierra* (1931), *Méndez v. Westminster School District* (1947), and *Delgado et al. v. Bastrop* (1948). A few decades later, Chicanas/os began to see bilingual education as key to the quest for equal education, and judicial decisions such as those in *Lau* and *Serna* placed responsibility for meeting the needs of students with limited English proficiency on the schools. After a difficult struggle to obtain the right to bilingual instruction, many Chicana/o communities were suspicious of desegregation efforts that might disperse Chicana/o students without considering their need for bilingual education.[12] Parents and policymakers argued that bilingual education and desegregation might not be fully compatible. Desegregation usually meant "scattering Black students to provide instruction in 'racially balanced' settings. Bilingual education, on the other hand, has usually meant the clustering of Spanish-speaking students so they could receive instruction through their native language" (Zerkel, 1977, p. 181, cited in Donato, Menchaca, & Valencia, 1991). By the mid-1970s, enforcement of both the *Brown* and *Lau* decisions led to more complications than policymakers originally anticipated, as Chicana/o students were resegregated based on language within desegregated schools (Donato et al., 1991). This was an ironic result of desegregation and bilingual education efforts, and depending on one's educational philosophy, either desegregation or bilingual education could be openly supported. For example, education policymakers who opposed bilingual education could avoid it by scattering limited-English-proficient students throughout their districts in the name of desegregation. At the same time, someone who opposed mixing White and

Chicana/o students in the same classroom could use the opportunity to seg-regate Chicana/o students in bilingual classrooms, thus using the same old racially motivated rationale for separating Mexican children from White stu-dents based on their perceived language deficiency (see Donato, 1997).

By the early 1980s, the tension between desegregation and bilingual edu-cation was receiving increasingly more attention. Though some educators throughout the Southwest were optimistic that the two could work together, there was little time to successfully produce meaningful results in meeting the needs of Chicana/o students. During the 1980s, assimilationist educators and politicians gained the upper hand; bilingual education was under strong attack, and financial support for it was being drastically reduced. The 1980s provided a political climate in which community activism was difficult and bi-lingual education suffered many setbacks. In the words of Chicana feminist writer Ana Castillo:

> In 1980 when the Republicans and the Reagan administration came to of-fice, their tremendous repression quashed the achievements of the Chi-cano/Latino Movement. . . . Community projects and grassroots programs dependent on government funding—rehabilitation and training, child care, early education and alternative schooling, youth counseling, cultural projects that supported the arts and community artists, rehab-housing for low income families, and women's shelters—shut down. (1994, p. 31)

Under the Reagan administration, while the government spent billions of dollars on the military, Title VII bilingual education funding was cut from $167 million in 1980 to $133 million in 1986, representing more than a 20 percent reduction (Loya, 1990)—this at a time when the number of English learners was greatly increasing. In California alone, students with limited English proficiency increased nearly 75 percent, from 326,000 in 1980 to 568,000 in 1986 (California State Department of Education, 1993).

EDUCATIONAL INEQUITY IN THE 1970S AND BEYOND

At the same time that bilingual education was under attack and suffering re-duced financial support, the conservative retrenchment also attacked public school finance. In order to compel school officials to provide educational eq-uity, Chicanas/os brought lawsuits under the equal protection clause. In Col-orado, Josie Luján, one of the lead plaintiffs in *Luján et al. v. Colorado State Board of Education* (1979), along with a handful of parents charged that the Colorado school finance system violated the equal protection clause of the U.S. and Colorado Constitutions because of the extreme funding disparities among school districts in the state. Lower per-pupil expenditures existed in districts with high Chicana/o student enrollment. Though the district court ruled in favor of the plaintiffs, in 1982 the State Supreme Court of Colorado held that the financing system was constitutionally permissible, thus leaving the system virtually unchanged. Luján did, however, win a seat on the local school board and she became an education advocate for Chicana/o students (Espinosa, 1979).

In another key school finance case, *Serrano v. Priest* (1971), John Serrano sued the California state treasurer on the grounds that his son received an inferior education in East Los Angeles because the state school finance system was based on financing schools through local property taxes. He alleged that, due to the differential property values and resulting tax base, children were given unequal treatment and resources in poor districts that did not have as high a tax base and funding as wealthier districts (Acuña, 1988). In 1971, the California Supreme Court ruled in his favor, finding that "financing primarily through local property taxes failed to provide equal protection under the law" (Acuña, 1988, p. 389). The U.S. Supreme Court upheld the *Serrano* decision in 1976, but limited its decision to California, stating that the finance system violated the state's equal protection clause by denying equal access to education. *Serrano,* however, brought few changes to Chicana/o schools because wealthier districts still had better facilities, more experienced teachers, and less overcrowding. Soon after, in 1978, California's Proposition 13 applied a taxation cap that in effect restricted funding for all districts in California. By the late 1980s, California ranked eighth nationally in per capita income, but spent only 3.8 percent of its income on public education—placing it forty-sixth among the fifty states (Kozol, 1991). Although educators and researchers do not agree about whether there is a causal relationship between educational expenditures and the quality of education, there is widespread agreement that Chicanas/os are generally subjected to inferior educational conditions in poorly funded schools (De La Rosa & Maw, 1990; Valencia, 1991).

San Antonio Independent School District v. Rodríguez is a class-action suit filed in 1968 by Demetrio Rodríguez and other parents on behalf of their children who were students in the Edgewood School District, which was poor and 96 percent non-White. At the time, San Antonio had several school districts segregated along class and racial/ethnic lines. Edgewood was among the poorest, while Alamo Heights, with a predominately White student population, was the richest (Acuña, 1988). The Mexican American Legal Defense and Educational Fund (MALDEF) argued on behalf of the Edgewood parents that the Texas finance system taxed residents of the poor Edgewood district at a higher rate than it taxed residents of Alamo Heights. In addition, per-pupil spending was much lower in Edgewood than in the wealthier district. Even with the minimum provided by the state, Edgewood spent only $231 per pupil, while Alamo Heights was able to spend $543 on each pupil (Kozol, 1991). The state public school financing practices were challenged and presented as a violation of the federal equal protection clause of the U.S. Constitution. The district court ruled in favor of Rodríguez and the other parents, and found that Texas was in violation of the equal protection clause. However, the decision was overruled by the U.S. Supreme Court in 1973. The Court's five-to-four decision in *Rodríguez* is especially noteworthy because it signaled the end of an era of progressive change and set the tone for educational inequity during the 1980s and 1990s.

A number of other factors promoted the educational inequity of Chicana/o students in the 1980s and into the 1990s. For example, Chicana/o schools that were among the most severely underfunded were also the most overcrowded, offering a limited curriculum with few resources (Achievement Council, 1984; Assembly Office of Research, 1990). Chicana/o and other Latina/o students were disproportionately retained for at least one grade and were seldom exposed to enriched curricula or pedagogy (Achievement Council, 1984; Assembly Office of Research, 1985). There were few Chicana/o and other Latina/o teachers and administrators in California's schools (California State Department of Education, 1985, 1988). Throughout the Southwest, Chicana/o students were highly unlikely to have Chicana/o teachers to act as mentors, since Latinas/os made up only 2.9 percent of all public school teachers in the country (De La Rosa & Maw, 1990). Cassandra Zacarias, a high school counselor who went through school in the 1960s, remembers that as a student she too lacked role models in school:

> When I was in high school I never felt like there was anybody that was like me who was a teacher, or counselor, or principal. I mean there was, I don't know, maybe a couple of Latinos that were teachers and it always seemed really sad to me. (Delgado Bernal, 1997, p. 160)

Chicanas/os and other high school students of color continue to report that they feel their teachers, school staff, and peers neither like nor understand them, and many of their teachers admit to not always understanding ethnically diverse students (University of California, Latino Eligibility Task Force, 1995).

In addition, the continued school tracking of Chicana/o students into vocational programs and into special education programs for learning-disabled students has promoted educational, social, and economic inequities for such students and has limited their access to higher education (Aguirre, 1980; González, 1990; Mitchell, Powell, Scott, & McDaid, 1994; Oakes, 1985). Throughout the Southwest, Chicana/o students in K-12 schools have been systematically tracked into courses that do not provide an environment or curriculum that prepares them for the post-secondary level (Aguirre & Martínez, 1993; Oakes, 1985). Indeed, 75 percent of all Latina/o high school seniors in 1980 had been enrolled in a curricular program that made a college education improbable (Orum, 1986). For those Chicanas/os who enrolled in a post-secondary institution, half attended a community college instead of a four-year institution (Astin, 1982; Durán, 1983).

The use of a "counterstory" (Delgado, 1989) demonstrates how the secondary school context continues to promote the educational inequality of Chicana/o students and limits access to higher education.[13] Gloria Martínez, a Chicana and first-generation college student, compares her journey to higher education with the path of her White, middle-class roommate.[14] Her story describes the secondary experiences of most Chicanas/os:

One day during first semester of my freshman year, my roommate and I were sitting in our dorm room talking about our high schools. I already knew that we had very different life experiences, but I could barely believe the huge contrast between our two schools. She had attended a suburban upper middle-class high school and I went to an urban high school in a predominantly working-class Chicano community. During high school my roommate took two years of Japanese and had her choice of Spanish, French, Italian, German, and Chinese. I took Spanish in high school. I was already semi-bilingual in Spanish before I took it, but my only other choice was French, and I figured I wouldn't have much need for it. She said her high school's science department was chaired by a former NASA scientist and offered biology, chemistry, physics, geology, biochemistry, and astronomy. I was in the honors track and I was only offered biology and chemistry. Most of my friends were told to just take general science. The math department at my school was as limited as the science department, while hers offered algebra, geometry, algebra II, trigonometry, calculus, and statistics. Some of these were advanced placement [AP] courses so she was able to start our freshman year with several units of university credit. There were no AP classes at my high school, only honors courses that did not carry college credit. She enjoyed great electives like journalism and computer programming, because her school had up-to-date technology and lots of computers. They also had college counselors who helped students complete college and scholarship applications, enroll and take the college entrance exams, and get information materials from various in- and out-of-state colleges. The counselors at my high school had such a heavy student load that it was impossible to get an appointment with them, and college advising just wasn't their priority. My *tía* [aunt] who'd just started going to a local community college is the one who advised me and helped me apply for college.

After that conversation with my roommate, I remember feeling like I'd been shafted, not by my roommate, but by my high school or maybe the whole educational system. It seemed really unfair that my roommate came to the university so prepared and here I was struggling with the lower division courses. I knew I was a really smart person, did really well in high school, and was dedicated to my studies. But sometimes I doubted myself, and I wondered if I really belonged in this university. I used to wonder if the only people who could actually succeed in college were the ones who had backgrounds similar to my roommate. Sometimes I questioned whether or not I deserved my spot in the university and if in fact I could succeed.

The precollege experience of Chicanas/os continues to differ vastly from that of middle-class White students, and Gloria's experience illuminates what numerous studies have found: college access and successful college participation for Chicana/o students is severely limited by an inferior secondary school education.[15] By tracking Chicana/o middle and high school students into low-ability classes, they are not given enough exposure to the academic subjects, critical thinking skills, and writing skills that are needed to do well on college entrance exams or in a college classroom (Durán, 1983). Access to college by Chicana/o students today is also limited by the myth of meritocracy and the attack on affirmative action.

MERITOCRACY AND CHICANA/O
COLLEGE STUDENTS

In higher education, meritocratic values often contradict the fundamental educational mission of developing students' knowledge. Meritocracy is a system of rewards presumably based solely on ability and talent, so that rewards go to those who "perform the best." Meritocratic values drive a wide range of educational practices such as testing, grading, admissions, and ability tracking, all in the spirit of "equality." Higher education scholar Alexander Astin (1982) points out that advocates of a meritocratic higher education system often view education as an open competition, analogous to an intellectual footrace. All contestants are allowed to enter the race, and rewards go to the swiftest; however, he argues, certain realities about the competition are distorted. For example, Chicanas/os often never get to the starting line because of poor secondary school conditions. Limited school resources and tracking into vocational programs mean that Chicanas/os often fail to show up at the competition because they lack reliable information about the race. Many Chicanas/os who do start the race do not run well and struggle to remain in the race because of their inferior training and the fact that they were never given the complete rules of the game. And many Chicanas/os who participate and run well may still end up with a second-class award, since the race they have entered (community college) offers a very different trophy than the race in an Ivy League college (Astin, 1982).

It seems that most Americans do not question the myth of meritocracy in higher education, believing that admissions decisions are fair and based solely on comparing one's qualifications to a universal standard of excellence. An important and often overlooked reality in a meritocratic system, however, is the fact that "merit" is socially constructed and standards of competition are set by those in power. For example, in higher education, SAT/ACT scores and a student's high school grade point average have traditionally been the standard by which students are admitted to college. SAT/ACT scores have been used as a standard despite an abundance of research that shows that these scores are not good predictors of college success for Chicanas/os, and that standardized testing in general has had a negative impact on Chicana/o students (Aguirre, 1980; Durán, 1983; Goldman & Hewitt, 1975; Goldman & Richards, 1974; González, 1974; Valencia & Aburto, 1991). In fact, high school preparation and testing and admission standards have been cited as two of the largest barriers to higher education for Chicanas/os and other Latinas/os (Orum, 1986). In California, the SAT has been a barrier for eligibility and participation in the University of California for Chicanas/os since it was incorporated into UC admissions requirements in 1968 (University of California, Latino Eligibility Task Force, 1997). Yet, it seems that many people perceive the UC system to be a fair and meritocratic one, based on a universal standard of excellence (the SAT).

"Reverse discrimination" is only claimed by Whites and conservatives when they perceive that an allegedly fair and meritocratic system is being threatened. During the late 1970s, *Regents of the University of California v.*

Bakke (1978) popularized the discourse of "reverse discrimination" and the growing public opinion that higher education had overstepped its bounds in creating opportunities for women and students of color. After Alan Bakke, a 34-year-old White engineer, applied to and was rejected by thirteen medical schools, a White administrator at the University of California, Davis, suggested he sue, as presumably less qualified students of color had been admitted. Bakke challenged the special admissions program that set aside sixteen slots out of one hundred for "disadvantaged" students. The special admissions program had been initiated just six years before his lawsuit, and prior to the program only three students of color had been admitted (Acuña, 1988). In 1978, the U.S. Supreme Court issued a somewhat ambiguous opinion in the *Bakke* case. The university's set-aside program was found to be illegal, and the university was directed to admit Bakke. Yet, the Court also ruled that race could be used in admissions provided that it was not the sole selection factor. The *Bakke* decision reflected growing public opinion that higher education had "gone too far" in trying to accommodate the special needs of "minorities" and was a precursor of the discourse of "reverse discrimination" today (Astin, 1982).

 WHERE WE ARE TODAY

Today, there is evidence that points to modest progress. More Chicanas/os and other Latinas/os are going to college; most major universities in the Southwest offer some type of Chicana/o Studies courses; and more Chicana/o scholars are writing about and documenting the life experiences of Chicanas/os. In California, more Latina/o students are graduating from high schools, more are taking the SAT and ACT tests, and more are becoming eligible for the California community college and state university system (University of California, Latino Eligibility Task Force, 1995). These improvements are modest, however, particularly when contrasted with the proportional growth of the Chicana/o population over the last fifty years. Moreover, attacks continue on the educational opportunities of and the quality of education offered to Chicana/o students. Presently, Chicanas/os are still considered to be the most unlikely racial/ethnic group to finish high school, to attend college, and to graduate from college (Chapa, 1991; Gándara, 1994). From the civil rights era to the present, it is safe to say that public schools have continued to consistently fail Chicana/o students at every point in the educational pipeline. The current anti-Latino and anti-immigrant beliefs manifested in California's Propositions 187, 209, and 227 continue to shape public policy that directly affects Chicana/o communities' educational, economic, political, and social well-being. Although such legislation and policy initiatives seem to issue primarily from California, it is significant for all Latinas/os in the United States because California appears to be setting a national public policy standard (Brownstein, 1995; García, 1995).

AN EXTENDED FORM OF SCHOOL SEGREGATION:
CALIFORNIA'S PROPOSITION 187

Even the school segregation statistics of the late 1980s and the prediction that "the segregation of Chicano students will intensify in the years ahead" (Valencia, 1991, p. 7) did not prepare us for California's public referendum that attempted to push Chicana/o school segregation toward Chicana/o school exclusion. In the early 1990s, then Governor Pete Wilson and a group of "concerned" California residents tired of undocumented immigrants began the Save Our State (SOS) movement, which put Proposition 187 on the 1994 California ballot. Proponents of 187 argued that "illegal aliens" were unfairly benefiting from state resources and were crowding their children out of public schools. Proposition 187 attempted to extend the segregation of Chicana/o students by denying public education to anyone attending a public elementary, secondary, or post-secondary school who was "reasonably suspected" to be an "illegal alien" in the United States. In addition, Proposition 187 required teachers and other officials to report those who were suspected of being in this country without proper immigration documents. These educational sections of the initiative were in direct conflict with the U.S. Supreme Court's 1982 decision in *Plyler v. Doe,* which held that the state of Texas could not bar undocumented children from public elementary schools because doing so violates the Equal Protection Clause of the Fourteenth Amendment. The authors of Proposition 187 put forth the initiative knowing *Plyler* was a legal precedent that provided protection for undocumented students to attend public schools. In fact, one of the goals of the proposition's authors was to call on a more politically conservative Supreme Court to overturn the *Plyler* decision (Prince, 1994).

Supporters of Proposition 187 also contended that the measure had nothing to do with race/ethnicity, arguing that it was merely an attempt to save scarce state resources. However, opponents viewed the initiative as an attack on racial and cultural minorities, and saw it as part of a historical continuum of race-based immigration and education policies (García, 1995). For example, using the term "illegal alien" demonizes undocumented immigrants as criminals. Just as de jure segregation conveyed an idea of the inferiority of Mexican students, Proposition 187 criminalized undocumented immigrants and those who are suspected of being "illegal aliens": "If we assume that undocumented immigrants are a criminal element, then we are automatically accepting that the existing . . . laws are just and fair" (Bosco, 1994, cited in García, 1995, p. 118). Indeed, Proposition 187 was not a race-neutral law and would have disproportionately affected Chicanas/os, Latinas/os, and other people of color who are stereotyped as "illegal aliens."

Though the initiative passed by a margin of 59 percent to 41 percent, there was a tremendous amount of community action and mobilization against it. Students all over the state engaged in demonstrations, walkouts, and protests. Lilian Ramírez, a student who protested at San Francisco's city hall shortly after the passage of Proposition 187, believes that the proposition provided an "open season for racism" (Gutekunst, 1994). The 1994 student resistance to Proposition 187 was similar to the student resistance of the 1960s I have chronicled earlier in this chapter. In both cases, students were motivated to transform existing conditions (or a law) that devalued their sociocultural experiences and limited their access to quality education.

In fact, California's passage of Proposition 187 was the epitome of the educational segregation that Chicanas/os have historically resisted in their efforts to gain their constitutional right to an equal public education. The passage of Proposition 187 brought to the forefront a racist state law that attempted to dehumanize all Latina/o students and exclude them from public education. Similar measures followed in other states, as did calls for reduction in funding for bilingual education and the implementation of English-only policies (García, 1995). In California, MALDEF and the American Civil Liberties Union (ACLU) were key in pursuing legal action against the proposition, and the five lawsuits filed against the state were consolidated into one federal action. U.S. District Judge Mariana Pfaelzer recently ruled that the proposition was "unconstitutional from top to bottom" because the state has no power to regulate immigration ("Judge dumps," 1998). The 1994 student walkouts and assemblies in protest of Proposition 187 and the state and federal lawsuits filed against its passage illustrate the various actions taken by Chicanas/os to obtain equal access to public education. Certainly the legal challenges to Proposition 187, and its defeat in the courts, indicates that these grassroots and legal strategies can be successful and continue to be crucial in Chicanas/os pursuit for educational equity.

LIMITED ACCESS TO HIGHER EDUCATION:
CALIFORNIA'S PROPOSITION 209

Today, the discourse of "reverse discrimination" is as strong as ever, and California leads the national movement to dismantle affirmative action programs. In 1996, California voters passed Proposition 209, the California Civil Rights Initiative. Proposition 209 appropriates the language of early civil rights legislation to, in essence, eliminate all affirmative action in California, including that in higher education. It states that California shall not use "race, sex, color, ethnicity, or national origin as criterion for either discriminating against, or granting preferential treatment to any individual or group." While the legislation outlaws considerations of race/ethnicity in university admissions, outreach, and recruitment, it also ignores current societal inequalities. The anti-affirmative action legislation and its proponents adopted a narrow interpretation of the equal protection clause, embracing a colorblind constitution and the myth of meritocracy. Therefore, supporters are able to argue simultaneously that they strongly support equal opportunity for people of all color and that affirmative action policies violate a White man's right to equal protection, resulting in "reverse discrimination."

Proposition 209 legislates restricted access for Chicanas/os and other students of color at a time when college campuses remain racially stratified. Few middle- and upper-class Whites complain that throughout the Southwest at least 50 percent of all Chicanas/os who go to college go to a community college rather than a four-year institution (Astin, 1982; Olívas, 1986; Villalpando, 1996). The proposition is a specific political action supported by the meritocracy myth, and it validates a subjective and highly selective admissions process that tracks Chicanas/os into community colleges and keeps the gate to four-year campuses guarded. The admission policies at the "gate-keeper" schools, such as the University of California system, exert a powerful and controlling influence over who enters certain professions and who has access to positions of influence and economic and social reward.

Proposition 209's attack on affirmative action policies applies to the state's system of public employment, public education, or public contracting. Astin (1982, 1995) warns, however, that we should not confuse college admissions with employment and must acknowledge that discrimination in college admissions is often based on something other than a racial/ethnic classification:

> The employer seeks to exploit talent by hiring the best applicants; the public university seeks to develop the talents of the students it admits. University admissions are inherently discriminatory anyway, simply because there are not enough places for all applicants. . . . More than 95% of the 21,445 freshman admitted to the UC system last fall met . . . eligibility requirements. The 953 who did not meet them included athletes; students with artistic, musical, or other special talents; students with disabilities, and members of underrepresented minority groups. There were just as many white students among these 953 "special action" admits. (Astin, 1995, p. B5)

Proposition 209 limits access to education just as an increasing number of Chicana/o students are attending K-12 schools. In 1995, California's Latina/o student population was 2.3 million, and it is projected to reach 3.1 million by the year 2005 (University of California, Latino Eligibility Task Force, 1997). Yet only 3.9 percent of all Latina/o high school graduates were fully eligible for admission to the University of California, and the proportion of those admitted to four-year colleges appears to be declining nationally (Kerr, 1994; University of California, Latino Eligibility Task Force, 1997). These factors combine with the passage of Proposition 209 to create a great need for an overhaul in admission standards.

Legal scholar Richard Delgado (1995) argues for "an overhaul of the admissions process and a rethinking of the criteria that make a person a deserving . . . student" (p. 51). He and many others have argued for admission standards that would result in an increased number of women and students of color gaining admission, yet he points out that these recommendations are often ignored and never instituted. In fact, the University of California Latino Eligibility Task Force (1997) recently recommended that the university system simply eliminate the SAT in determining eligibility without reducing overall admissions standards. The Task Force argued that the eligibility of Latina/o students could be greatly increased by eliminating the SAT and relying only on grade point average. Without the SAT, the proportion of Latina/o high school graduates achieving full eligibility to the University of California would rise by 59 percent (from 3.9 to 6.2 percent). So far the University system has not acted on the Task Force's recommendation, but throughout public policy, university, and community circles, additional recommendations focusing on bringing in "educationally and economically disadvantaged" students are being proposed.

THE LATEST THREAT TO BILINGUAL EDUCATION: CALIFORNIA'S PROPOSITION 227

Even with a growing number of students with limited English proficiency and expanding global borders that call for multilingual abilities, the threat to bilingual education is as strong as ever. In June 1998, California voters passed Proposition 227, the "English Language Education for Immigrant Children" initiative. The proposition was cosponsored by Ron Unz, a wealthy Silicon Valley businessman who unsuccessfully ran for governor of California in 1994, and Gloria Matta Tuchman, who failed in her first attempt to be elected State Superintendent of Public Instruction.[16] The proposition espouses the values of a just society while calling for the elimination all bilingual education in the state of California. The proposition mandates that within sixty days of its passage, 1.38 million limited-English-speaking students be put into separate classrooms—regardless of age, language background, and/or academic ability (Citizens for an Educated America, 1997). In these separate classrooms, these students will be taught English by a teacher who will be restricted, under the threat of a lawsuit, from speaking to them in their primary language.

Supporters of the proposition claim to have in mind the best interests of children "regardless of their ethnicity or national origins" (Article I: b, c, f). However, Article 2, the crux of the proposition, requires a 180-day English-only approach and states that "all children in California public schools shall be taught English by being taught in English during a temporary transition period not normally intended to exceed one year." This requirement counters educational research that demonstrates that English immersion is one of the least effective ways to teach children with limited English proficiency (Cummins, 1981; Gándara, 1997; Krashen, 1981; Wong Fillmore, 1991). The initiative does away with all bilingual education and English-language development programs that do not meet its rigid 180-day English-only approach. It also allows local schools "to place in the same classroom English learners of different ages but whose degree of English proficiency is similar" (Article 2). This means that twelve-year-old boys and six-year-old girls of any language group, for example, can be placed in the same classroom for a full year (180 days) to study English, without any instruction in content areas such as math, science, and social studies. Chicanas/os know from experience that placing all English-language learners into a separate classroom, regardless of age and academic abilities, and using rote memorization to teach English without academic instruction will fail because it was the standard process that failed miserably in the era of de jure segregation. Indeed, its failure was the reason why the federal Bilingual Education Act was passed just thirty years ago.

Today, Proposition 227 represents a distinct cultural attack on Chicanas/os and other Latinas/os, and creates yet another educational barrier imposed on Chicana/o students. For example, although Ron Unz and many other Proposition 227 supporters presented themselves as the voices of Latinos, arguing that Latinos supported the measure by an overwhelming majority, the actual Latino vote on the proposition was 63 percent "No" and 37 percent "Yes" (Pyle, McDonnell, & Tobar, 1998). The proposition was carried by a two-to-one vote among Whites in an electorate in which Whites represent a larger percentage than they represent in the general population. The victory of Proposition 227 will be a victory imposed on Latinos despite their opposition. In fact, Latino students will be disproportionately affected if the new law goes into effect because 80 percent of California's K-12 limited-English-proficient students are Spanish speakers (Gándara, 1997). There is, however, hope that the new law will not be enforced, as a coalition of schoolchildren and civil rights groups filed a lawsuit in federal court to challenge Proposition 227 the day after it was passed by voters. Three of the civil rights groups participating in the lawsuit are the California Latino Civil Rights Network, Mujeres Unidas y Activas, and the National Council of La Raza. Their lawsuit, which contends that Proposition 227 violates the U.S. Equal Educational Opportunities Act of 1974, Title VI of the Civil Rights Act of 1964, and the constitutional right to equal protection (Colvin & Smith, 1998), continues the historic tradition of Chicana/o community resistance and activism in their pursuit of an equitable and just educational system.

CONCLUSION

I have provided an overview of Chicana/o education from the 1950s through the 1990s and demonstrated a relationship between popular belief systems, judicial decisions, and educational policies and practices. Bilingual education, access to higher education, K-12 school equity, and continued school segregation have all been at the forefront during this period. Schooling for Chicanas/os has indeed improved since the era of de jure segregation, yet since the late 1970s there has been a deterioration of educational gains. Many of today's most important educational issues are similar to those voiced in Mexican communities before the 1950s. In fact, Jonathon Kozol states that in the realm of public schooling, "social policy has been turned back almost one hundred years" (1991, p. 4). In reality, the improvements in Chicana/o schooling have been modest and have not really kept pace with the demographic growth of the Chicana/o population.

Chicanas/os have a rich historical legacy that includes active struggles to gain equal access to quality education. A focus of the Chicana/o student movement was improving the quality of education at various points in the educational pipeline, and Chicanas were actively involved in and offered leadership to this movement. Over the past five decades, Chicano families have used the judicial system to fight educational practices that have limited the education of their children. They have utilized the courts to fight for bilingual education and school access and to fight against school segregation and schooling inequities. Today, Chicana/o students and their families have remained active in the pursuit of quality education through grassroots resistance and legal recourse. History is repeating itself, and exclusionary laws such as California's Propositions 187, 209, and 227 contribute to an antagonistic sociopolitical climate that fosters the racist practices of the de jure segregation era. Inasmuch as the education of all Latina/o students is threatened, it is crucial that educators, policymakers, and Chicana/o communities continue to engage in strategies that combat this antagonistic sociopolitical climate and work toward educational equity.

REFERENCES

Achievement Council. (1984). *Excellence for whom?* Oakland, CA: Author.

Acuña, R. (1988). *Occupied America: A history of Chicanos.* New York: Harper Collins.

Aguirre, A. (1980). *Intelligence testing education and Chicanos* (ERIC/TM Report No. 76). Princeton, NJ: ERIC Clearing House on Tests, Measurement, and Evaluation, Educational Testing Service.

Aguirre, A., & Martínez, R. O. (1993). *Chicanos in higher education: Issues and dilemmas for the 21st century* (ASHE-ERIC Higher Education Report No. 3). Washington, DC: George Washington University, School of Education and Human Development.

Allsup, C. (1982). *The American G.I. Forum: Origins and evolution.* Austin: University of Texas, Center for Mexican American Studies.

Alvarez v. Lemon Grove School District (1931) Superior Court of the State of California, County of San Diego, Petition for Writ of Mandate, No. 66625.

Assembly Office of Research. (1985). *Dropping out, losing out: The high cost for California.* Sacramento, CA: Author.

Assembly Office of Research. (1990). *Education minority students in California: Descriptive analysis and policy implications.* Sacramento, CA: Author.

Astin, A. W. (1982). *Minorities in American higher education.* San Francisco: Jossey-Bass.

Astin, A. W. (1995, May 1). Perspective on affirmative action: Replace sound bites with discourse. *Los Angeles Times,* p. B5.

Barrera, M. (1979). *Race and class in the Southwest: A theory of racial inequality.* Notre Dame, IN: University of Notre Dame Press.

Biegel, S. (1994). Bilingual education and language rights: The parameters of the bilingual education debate in California twenty years after *Lau v. Nichols. Chicano-Latino Law Review, 14,* 48–60.

Bogardus, E. S. (1949, April). *School inspection report on fourteen schools* (American G.I. Forum Archives). Corpus Christi, TX: American G.I. Forum.

Brownstein, R. (1995, May 14). Immigration debate roils GOP presidential contest. *Los Angeles Times,* pp. A1, A18.

Burciaga, J. A. (1993). *Drink cultura: Chicanismo.* Santa Barbara, CA: Joshua Odell Editions.

California State Advisory Committee to the U.S. Commission on Civil Rights. (1968, April). *Education and the Mexican American community in Los Angeles county* (CR 1.2: Ed 8/3). Los Angeles: Author,

California State Department of Education. (1981). *Schooling and language minority students: A theoretical framework.* Los Angeles: California State University, Los Angeles, Evaluation, Dissemination and Assessment Center.

California State Department of Education. (1985). *Racial or ethnic distribution of staff and students in California public schools, 1984–85.* Sacramento, CA: Author.

California State Department of Education. (1988). *Racial or ethnic distribution of staff and students in California public schools, 1987–88.* Sacramento, CA: Author.

California State Department of Education. (1993). *R30-LC language census report.* Sacramento, CA: Author.

Castañeda v. Pickard, 648 F.2d 989 (5th Cir. 1981).

Castillo, A. (1994). *Massacre of the dreamers: Essays on Xicanisma.* New York: Plume.

Castro, V. (1994, December). [Transcribed interview conducted by Susan Racho with Vickie Castro]. Unpublished data.

Chapa, E. (1973). Report from the National Women's Political Caucus. *Magazín, 1*(9), 37–39.

Chapa, J. (1991). Special focus: Hispanic demographic and educational trends. In D. J. Carter & R. Wilson (Eds.), *Minorities in higher education:. Ninth annual status report* (pp. 11–17). Washington, DC: American Council on Education.

Chicano Coordinating Council on Higher Education. (1970). *El plan de Santa Bárbara: A Chicana/o plan for higher education.* Santa Barbara, CA: La Causa.

Citizens for an Educated America: No on Unz. (1997). Los Angeles: Citizens for an Educated America.

Cisneros v. Corpus Christi Independent School District, 324 F. Supp. 599 (S.D. Tex. 1970), appeal docketed, No. 71-2397 (5th Cir. July 16, 1971).

Colvin, R. L., & Smith, D. (1998, June 4). Prop. 227 foes vow to block it despite wide vote margin. *Los Angeles Times,* p. A1.

Crawford, J. (1992). *Hold your tongue: Bilingualism and the politics of English only.* Reading, MA: Addison Wesley.

Crenshaw, K. W., Gotanda, N., Peller, G., & Thomas, K. (Eds.). (1995). *Critical race theory: The key writings that formed the movement.* New York: New Press.

Cummins, J. (1981). The role of primary language development in promoting educational success for language minority students. In California State Department of Education (Ed.), *Schooling and language minority students: A theoretical framework* (pp. 4–49). Los Angeles: California State University, Los Angles, Evaluation, Dissemination and Assessment Center.

De La Rosa, D., & Maw, C. E. (1990). *Hispanic education: A statistical portrait 1990.* Washington, DC: National Council of La Raza.

Delgado Bernal, D. (1997). *Chicana school resistance and grassroots leadership: Providing an alternative history of the 1968 East Los Angeles blowouts.* Unpublished doctoral dissertation, University of California, Los Angeles.

Delgado Bernal, D. (in press). Grassroots leadership reconceptualized: Chicana oral histories and the 1968 East Los Angeles school blowouts. *Frontier: A Journal of Women Studies.*

Delgado, R. (1989). Storytelling for oppositionists and others: A plea for narrative. *Michigan Law Review, 87,* 2411–2441.

Delgado, R. (1995). The imperial scholar: Reflections on a review of civil rights literature. In K. W. Crenshaw, N. Gotanda, G. Peller, & K. Thomas (Eds.), *Critical race theory: The key writings that formed the movement* (pp. 46–57). New York: New Press.

Delgado et al. v. Bastrop Independent School District of Bastrop County et al., docketed, No. 388 (W.D. Tex. June 15, 1948).

Del Rio Independent School District v. Salvatierra, 33 S.W.2d 790 (Tex. Civ. App., San Antonio 1930), cert. denied, 284 U.S. 580 (1931).

Donato, R. (1997). *The other struggle for equal schools: Mexican Americans during the civil rights era.* Albany: State University of New York Press.

Donato, R., Menchaca, M., & Valencia, R. R. (1991). Segregation, desegregation, and integration of Chicano students: Problems and prospects. In R. R. Valencia (Ed.), *Chicano school failure and success: Research and policy agendas for the 1990's* (pp. 27–63). London: Falmer Press.

Durán, R. P. (1983). *Hispanics' education and background: Predictors of college achievement.* New York: College Entrance Examination Board.

Espinosa, A. L. (1979). Hispanas: Our resources for the eighties. *La Luz, 8*(4), 10–13.

Gándara, P. (1982). Passing through the eye of the needle: High-achieving Chicanas. *Hispanic Journal of Behavioral Sciences, 4,* 167–179.

Gándara, P. (1994). Choosing higher education: Educationally ambitious Chicanos and the path to social mobility. *Education Policy Analysis Archives, 2*(8).

Gándara, P. (1997). *Review of the research on instruction of limited English proficient students: A report to the California Legislature.* Davis: University of California, Linguistic Minority Research Institute, Education Policy Center.

García, R. J. (1995). Critical race theory and Proposition 187: The racial politics of immigration law. *Chicano-Latino Law Review, 17,* 118–154.

García, A. (Ed.). (1997). *Chicana feminist thought: The basic historical writings.* New York: Routledge.

Goldman, R. D., & Hewitt, B. N. (1975). An investigation of test bias for Mexican-American college students. *Journal of Educational Measurement, 12,* 187–196.

Goldman, R. D., & Richards, R. (1974). The SAT prediction of grades for Mexican-American versus Anglo-American students at the University of California, Riverside. *Journal of Educational Measurement, 11,* 129–135.

Gómez-Quiñones, J. (1978). *Mexican students por La Raza: The Chicano student movement in Southern California 1967–1977.* Santa Barbara, CA: Editorial La Causa.

González, G. G. (1974). *The system of public education and its function within the Chicano communities, 1910–1950.* Unpublished doctoral dissertation, University of California, Los Angeles.

González, G. G. (1990). *Chicano education in the era of segregation.* Cranbury, NJ: Associated University Presses.

Guadalupe Organization v. Tempe Elementary School District, 587 F.2d 1022 (9th Cir. 1978).

Gutekunst, L. (1994, November 21). Students protest passage of Prop. 187. *The Lowell,* p. 1.

Harders, R., & Gómez, M. N. (1998). Separate and unequal: *Méndez v. Westminster* and desegregation in California schools. In M. DeMartino (Ed.), *A family changes history: Méndez v. Westminster* (pp. 3–12). Irvine: University of California.

Jensen, V. J. (1962, February). Effects of childhood bilingualism, I. *Elementary English, 39,* 132–143.

Judge dumps rest of Proposition 187. (1998, March 19). *San Francisco Chronicle,* p. A15.

Kerr, C. (1994). *Troubled times for American higher education: The 1990s and beyond.* Albany: State University of New York Press.

Keyes v. School District Number 1 Denver Colorado, 413 U.S. 189 (1973), 521 F.2d 465 (10th Cir. 1975).

Kozol, J. (1991). *Savage inequalities: Children in America's schools.* New York: HarperCollins.

Krashen, S. D. (1981). Bilingual education and second language acquisition theory. In California State Department of Education, *Schooling and language minority students: A theoretical framework* (pp. 51–79). Los Angeles: California State University, Los Angles, Evaluation, Dissemination and Assessment Center.

Lau v. Nichols, 414 U.S. 563 (1974).

Lawrence, C. R. (1993). If he hollers let him go: Regulating racist speech on campus. In M. J. Matsuda, C. R. Lawrence, R. Delgado, & K. W. Crenshaw (Eds.), *Words that wound: Critical race theory, assaultive speech, and the First Amendment* (pp. 53–88). Boulder, CO: Westview Press.

López, S. (1977). The role of the Chicana within the student movement. In R. Sánchez & R. Martínez Cruz (Eds.), *Essays on la mujer* (pp. 16–19). Los Angeles: University of California, Chicano Studies Research Center.

Loya, A. C. (1990). Chicanos, law, and educational reform. *La Raza Law Journal, 3,* 28–50.

Luján et al. v. Colorado State Board of Education, 649 P.2d 1005 (Co. 1982).

Macías, R. (1979). Language choice and human rights in the United States. In J. E. Alatis (Ed.), *Georgetown University round table on languages and linguistics, 1979* (pp. 86–101). Washington, DC: Georgetown University Press.

Martínez, G. A. (1994). Legal indeterminacy, judicial discretion and the Mexican-American litigation experience: 1930–1980. *U.C. Davis Law Review, 27,* 555–618.

Matsuda, M. J., Lawrence, C. R., Delgado, R., & Crenshaw, K. W. (1993). *Words that wound: Critical race theory, assaultive speech, and the First Amendment.* Boulder, CO: Westview Press.

McCurdy, J. (1968, March 17). Frivolous to fundamental: Demands made by east side high school students listed. *Los Angeles Times,* pp. 1, 4–5.

Menchaca M., & Valencia, R. R. (1990). Anglo-Saxon ideologies and their impact on the segregation of Mexican students in California, the 1920s–1930s. *Anthropology and Education Quarterly, 21,* 222–249.

Menchaca, M. (1995). *The Mexican outsiders: A community history of marginalization and discrimination in California.* Austin: University of Texas Press.

Méndez González, R. (1995, October). [Transcribed interview conducted by Dolores Delgado Bernal with Rosalinda Méndez González]. Unpublished data.

Méndez v. Westminster, 64 F. Supp. 544 (S.D. Cal. 1946), 161 F. 2d 774 (9th Cir. 1947).

Mitchell, D. E., Powell, R. J., Scott, L. D., & McDaid, J. L. (1994). *The impact of California's special education pre-referral intervention activities and alternative assessments on ethnolinguistically diverse students: Final report of a federal-state joint agreement evaluation feasibility study.* Riverside: University of California, California Educational Research Cooperative.

Morin, R. (1963). *Among the valiant: Mexican Americans in WWII and Korea.* Los Angeles: Borden.

Muñoz, C., Jr. (1989). *Youth, identity, power: The Chicano movement.* New York: Verso.

Nieto Gómez, A. (1973). The Chicana: Perspectives for education. *Encuentro Femenil, 1,* 34–61.

Nieto Gómez, A. (1974). La feminista. *Encuentro Feminil, 1,* 34–47.

Oakes, J. (1985). *Keeping track: How schools structure inequality.* New Haven, CT: Yale University Press.

Olivas, M. (Ed.). (1986). *Latino college students.* New York: Teachers College Press.

Orozco, C. (1986). Sexism in Chicano studies and the community. In T. Córdova, N. Cantu, G. Cárdenas, J. García, & C. M. Sierra (Eds.), *Chicana voices: Intersections of class, race, and gender* (pp. 11–18). Austin, TX: Center for Mexican American Studies.

Orozco, C. (1992). *The origins of the League of United Latin American Citizens (LULAC) and the Mexican American Civil Rights Movement in Texas with an analysis of women's political participation in a gendered context, 1910–1929.* Unpublished doctoral dissertation, University of California, Los Angeles.

Orum, L. S. (1986). *The education of Hispanics: Status and implications.* Washington, DC: National Council of La Raza.

Otero v. Mesa County Valley School District Number 51, 408 F. Supp. 162 (D. Colo. 1975).

Pardo, M. (1984, March/April). A selective evaluation of El Plan de Santa Bárbara. *La Gente,* 14–15.

Plyler v. Doe, 457 U.S. 202 (1982).

Prince, R. (1994, September 6). Americans want illegal immigrants out. *Los Angeles Times,* p. B7.

Pyle, A., McDonnell P. J., & Tobar, H. (1998, June 4). Latino voter participation doubled since '94 primary. *Los Angeles Times,* p. A1.

Rangel, J. C., & Alcalá, C. M. (1972). Project report: De jure segregation of Chicanos in Texas schools. *Harvard Civil Rights-Civil Liberties Review, 7,* 348–359.

Regents of the University of California v. Bakke, 438 U.S. 265 (1978).

Roos, P. (1978). Bilingual education: The Hispanic response to unequal educational opportunity. *Law and Contemporary Problems, 42,* 111–140.

Salinas, F. (1971). Mexican-Americans and the desegregation of schools in the Southwest: A supplement. *El Grito, 4*(4), 36–69.

San Antonio Independent School District et al. v. Rodríguez et al., 337 F. Supp. 280 W.D. Tex. (1971), 36 L. Ed. 2d 16, 411 U.S. 1 (1973).

San Miguel, G., Jr. (1985). Conflict and controversy in the evolution of bilingual education in the United States: An interpretation. *Social Science Quarterly, 65,* 505–518.

San Miguel, G., Jr. (1987). *Let all of them take heed: Mexican Americans and the campaign for educational equality in Texas, 1910–1981.* Austin: University of Texas Press.

Sandoval, M. (1979). *Our legacy: The first fifty years.* Washington, DC: League of United Latin American Citizens.

Schaller, M., Scharff, V., & Schulzinger, R. D. (1992). *Present tense: The United States since 1945.* Boston: Houghton Mifflin.

Segura, D. (1993). Slipping through the cracks: Dilemmas in Chicana education. In A. de la Torre & B. Pesquera (Eds.), *Building with our hands: New directions in Chicana studies* (pp. 199–216). Berkeley: University of California Press.

Serna v. Portales Municipal Schools, 499 F.2d 1147 (10th Cir. 1974).

Serrano et al. v. Ivy Baker Priest, 487 P.2d 1241 (Cal. 1971).

Solorzano, D. G., & Delgado Bernal, D. (1998). *Critical race theory and transformational resistance: Chicana/o students in an urban context.* Unpublished manuscript.

Solorzano, D. G., & Villalpando, O. (in press). Critical race theory: Marginality, and the experiences of students of color in higher education. In C. A. Torres & T. R. Mitchell (Eds.), *Sociology of education: Emerging perspectives.* Albany: State University of New York Press.

Swarts, D. (1977). Pierre Bourdieu: The cultural transmission of social inequality. *Harvard Educational Review, 47,* 545–555.

Tate, W. F. (1997). Critical race theory and education: History, theory, and implications. *Review of Research in Education, 22,* 195–247.

Taylor, P. S. (1934). *An American-Mexican frontier: Nueces County, Texas.* Chapel Hill: University of North Carolina Press.

University of California, Latino Eligibility Task Force. (1995, March). *History of responses to Latino under-achievement* (Report No. 4). Berkeley, CA: Chicana/o/Latino Policy Project.

University of California, Latino Eligibility Task Force. (1997, July). *Latino student eligibility and participation in the University of California: Ya basta!* (Report No. 5). Berkeley, CA: Chicana/o/Latino Policy Project

U.S. Commission on Civil Rights. (1971). *Mexican American education study, report 1: Ethnic isolation of Mexican Americans in the public schools of the Southwest.* Washington: DC: Government Printing Office.

Valdez, P. (1994, December). [Transcribed interview conducted by Susan Racho with Vickie Patssi Valdez]. Unpublished data.

Valencia, R. R. (1991). The plight of Chicano students: An overview of schooling conditions and outcomes. In R. R. Valencia (Ed.), *Chicano school failure and success: Research and policy agendas for the 1990's* (pp. 3–26). London: Falmer Press.

Valencia, R. R., & Aburto, S. (1991). The uses and abuses of educational testing; Chicanos as a case in point. In Valencia, R. R. (Ed.), *Chicano school failure and success: Research and policy agendas for the 1990's* (pp. 203–251). London: Falmer Press.

Vásquez, M. (1982). Confronting barriers to the participation of Mexican American women in higher education. *Hispanic Journal of Behavioral Sciences, 4,* 147–165.

Villalpando, O. (1996). *The long term effects of college on Chicano and Chicana students: "Other oriented" values, service careers, and community involvement.* Unpublished doctoral dissertation, University of California, Los Angeles.

Webster, D. S. (1984). Chicano students in American higher education. *Integration Education, 22*(1-3), 42–52.

Wise, A. E. (1982). *Legislated learning: The bureaucratization of the American classroom.* Berkeley: University of California Press.

Wollenberg, C. (1974). *Westminster v. Méndez:* Race, nationality, and segregation in California schools. *California Historical Quarterly, 53,* 317–332.

Wong-Fillmore, L. (1991). Language and cultural issues in early education. In S. L. Kagan (Ed.), *The care and education of America's young children: Obstacles and opportunities, the 90th yearbook of the National Society for the Study of Education* (pp. 39–50). Chicago: University of Chicago Press.

Zambrana, R. (1994). Toward understanding the educational trajectory and socialization of Latina women. In L. Stone & G. M. Boldt (Eds.), *The education feminism reader* (pp. 135–145). New York: Routledge.

Zavella, P. (1991). Reflections on diversity among Chicanas. *Frontiers: A Journal of Women Studies, 12,* 73–85.

NOTES

1. "Chicana/o" is used when referring to both females and males of Mexican origin living in the United States, irrespective of immigration or generation status. Chicana/o is meant to be inclusive of females and males, rather than using the Spanish masculine gender, Chicano, to refer to both genders. Terms of identification vary according to context, and Chicana/o is used here as a political term of self-determination and solidarity that was popularized during the Chicano Movement of the 1960s. The terms Chicana and Chicano were not prominent prior to the late 1960s, and are used interchangeably with "Mexican" when referring to pre-1960s history. "Latina/o" is sometimes used when referring to contemporary issues in order to be more inclusive of all mestizo peoples whose families might originate in Central America, South America, the Caribbean, and Mexico, and who share geographic and sociopolitical space with Chicanas/os. Latina/o is also used when data on "Hispanics" has not been disaggregated specifically for Chicanas/os.
2. "De jure" segregation refers to that which is supported by official policy or law, while "de facto" segregation refers to that which exists in reality, but without lawful authority.
3. LULAC was founded in Texas in 1929 by middle-class English-speaking Mexican Americans who stressed American patriotism. As a civil rights organization, LULAC led the fight for school desegregation in the 1930s and 1940s (see Sandoval, 1979; San Miguel, 1987; Orozco, 1992). In 1948, the American G.I. Forum was founded in Texas as a Mexican American veteran's organization that was interested in the welfare of veterans and their families. The organization became interested in fighting discriminatory practices in all public institutions, and educational issues were of primary importance (see Allsup, 1982; San Miguel, 1987). Today, LULAC and the G.I. Forum are national organizations that have often joined forces in their struggles for educational and social equity.
4. A colonized relationship in general is one of economic, political, and cultural domination and subordination of one group by another. The dominant and subordinate groups are defined along ethnic and/or racial lines, and the relationship is established to serve the interests of the dominant group. See Mario Barrera (1979) for a theoretical discussion of Chicanas/os and internal colonialism—a form of colonialism in which the dominant and subordinate groups are within a single society and there are no clear geographic boundaries of a "colony."
5. For historical and contemporary discussions of Chicana/o grade retention and risk factors for dropping out, see California State Advisory Committee (1968), Assembly Office of Research (1985), and De La Rosa and Maw (1990).
6. See Segura (1993), Gándara (1982), and Vásquez (1982) for studies that examine barriers to education experienced by various groups of Chicanas.
7. The Servicemen's Readjustment Act of 1944, or the G.I. Bill, provided veterans and their families with various employment, health, economic, and educational benefits until the program ended in 1956. Veterans pursuing a college education received $110 a month, plus allowance for dependents and payment of tuition, fees, and books. Nationally, the G.I. Bill opened up a selective higher education system to working-class people by assisting over two million new students. Chicano servicemen also took advantage of the G.I. Bill's educational benefits (see Morin, 1963). However, because of the relatively small number of women who had served in the military and of active discrimination (i.e., women did not receive full benefits), Chicanas and other women received few direct educational benefits (see also Schaller, Scharff, & Schulzinger, 1992).
8. These lawsuits include Serna v. Portales Municipal Schools (1974); *Otero v. Mesa County Valley School District* (1975); *Guadalupe Organization v. Tempe Elementary School District* (1978). For more on these cases see, Martínez (1994).
9. In *Keyes v. School District Number 1*, plaintiffs alleged that the school board was practicing de jure segregation. The U.S. Supreme Court ruled that the school board had an unconstitutional policy of deliberately segregating Park Hill schools, one segment of the Denver school district, and mandated a desegregation plan. The Keyes case did not address the issue of de facto segregation (see Martínez, 1994; San Miguel, 1987).
10. Later in 1981, the *Castañeda v. Pickard* case put forth a three-pronged test that the federal courts continue to follow today when evaluating a school districts' actions in overcoming the language barriers of students. In *Castañeda*, a group of Chicana/o children and their

parents challenged the practices of a Texas school district under the Fourteenth Amendment, Title VI, and the Equal Educational Opportunity Act. The plaintiffs charged that the district failed to offer adequate bilingual education to overcome the linguistic barriers of students. The court ruled in favor of the plaintiffs and set forth the three-pronged analysis for courts to follow: 1)Êa court must determine whether the district is pursuing a program that is based on sound educational theory; 2) the court must establish whether or not the programs and practices effectively implement the educational theory adopted; and 3) the court must determine if the school's program actually results in overcoming language barriers of students (see Biegel, 1994).

11. In other words, since federal and state policies prior to 1954 had allowed for the segregation of Blacks and Whites and had not referenced Mexicans, the strategy had been to have Mexicans classified as part of the White race. If Mexicans were declared White, then segregating Mexican students from White students in the absence of a law allowing for their separation would be illegal. The Cisneros case was the first time a court officially recognized Mexicans as an identifiable minority group, thereby allowing them to use the equal protection strategy used in Black desegregation cases, rather than the claim to "Whiteness" strategy (see San Miguel, 1987).

12. See Donato (1997) for documentation of the tension between bilingual education and desegregation.

13. Critical race theorist Richard Delgado (1989) describes "counterstorytelling" as both a method of telling the story of those experiences not often told, and a tool for analyzing and challenging the dominant discourse and the stories of those in power.

14. Gloria Martínez is a composite character based on data from focus group interviews, individual conversations, and personal experiences. She was first introduced as an undergraduate student in an article by Daniel G. Solorzano and Octavio Villalpando (in press) and also appears in an article by Solorzano and Dolores Delgado Bernal (1998). In these articles, Gloria facilitates a technique of counterstorytelling.

15. The complex relationship between race/ethnicity, class, and gender, and how each of these categories contributes to the marginalization of Chicana/o students, cannot be fully dealt with here. However, it should be noted that even middle-class Chicana/o college students often experience a sense of marginalization, particularly when they are first-generation college students. These students may lack the kind of "cultural capital" valued by higher education systems. As Bourdieu has stated, "academic performance is linked to cultural background . . . and is more strongly related to parents' educational history than to parents' occupational status" (Swarts, 1977, p. 547). See Gándara, this volume, for a discussion of class, gender, and Chicana/o college students, and see Zavella (1991), Castillo (1994), Zambrana (1994), and García (1997) for a general discussion on how institutional and cultural differences based on sexism, racism, and classism create a different range of choices and options for Chicanas in particular.

16. In California's June 1998 primary election, Gloria Matta Tuchman once again ran for the position of State Superintendent of Public Instruction. She came in second with 25.5 percent of the votes, behind the incumbent Delaine Eastin with 43.3 percent of the votes. The two will face a run-off in the November 1998 state election.

I would like to express my sincere appreciation to Octavio Villalpando, who offered me invaluable input, criticism, and support in conceptualizing and writing this chapter. I am also grateful to the *Harvard Educational Review* Editorial Board, especially José Moreno, who patiently provided me with insightful feedback and editorial assistance.

PART TWO

CHICANO/CHICANA EDUCATION IN THE CONTEMPORARY ERA

Politics Matters:
Educational Policy and
Chicano Students

GARY ORFIELD

Contemporary education policy analysts rarely deal explicitly with politics, and almost never with racial politics. The absence of discussion occurs in part because both the Democratic and Republican parties have embraced the essentials of the "excellence reforms" of the early 1980s that assume schools can be reformed and that they should be judged without reference to social crises.[1] From such a perspective, education is something that any school staff can provide, regardless of external problems and unequal resources. In such a system, race and poverty are irrelevant.

Race and poverty are, however, related to school opportunity, and what we do about them is deeply related to politics. Since the Civil War, racial policy in the United States has dramatically changed direction four times, with enormous consequences for both minority students and society. After the Civil War, Reconstruction forced racial changes on the South, making education possible for American Blacks in states where educating slaves had been illegal and most Whites had chosen not to educate freedmen. Reconstruction led to the second shift in policy, the political and legal reaction codified in the 1896 *Plessy v. Ferguson* "separate but equal" U.S. Supreme Court decision, which entrenched White dominance and the idea of Black inequality so deeply into the sociopolitical educational structure that virtually no policy attention was given to this educational scandal for sixty years. The third shift in racial policy began when the Supreme Court reopened these issues in the 1954 *Brown v. Board of Education* decision, which held that the entire system of apartheid laws in southern schools violated the Constitution. Though the *Brown* decision was not seriously enforced for years, it helped set the stage for the emergence of the civil rights movement and sweeping social and political change. The judicial and policy revolution of the 1960s and early 1970s sparked civil rights legislation and court decisions that overthrew the previous racial system and created, for the first time in U.S. history, a national goal of fair interracial schooling.[2]

We are now living through the fourth major change in racial policy, a counterrevolutionary reaction to the racial policies that have so dominated U.S.

politics for nearly thirty years, so long that their consequences are now usually simply accepted as obvious starting points in school policy. This reaction took shape after the election of President Richard Nixon, whose "Southern Strategy" called for civil rights cutbacks and set the model for GOP campaigns for the rest of the century by creating a coalition combining Southern and suburban voters with the traditional Republican electorate.[3] The system of racial separation between city schools and suburban schools and the radical differences in school quality between suburban and city districts have not generated any significant legislative policy initiative for more than three decades.[4] Just as post-Reconstruction policymakers simply ignored the fact that "separate but equal" was a lie, most policymakers now ignore the obvious differences between ghetto and barrio and suburban White schools. Policymakers' fundamental assumption has shifted from a belief that policy must continually address deep forces of inequality that arise from our history to an assumption that historic racial problems have been solved and can be ignored.

The resulting conservative educational and social policy assumes that earlier civil rights policies, such as the 1964 Civil Rights Act, have solved racial issues and have now become counterproductive and disruptive. Operating from this assumption, critics claim, for example, that affirmative action subjects all minority students to negative attitudes and merely admits students who cannot succeed. The conservative shift has resulted in the reversal of desegregation and bilingual education and sparked the federal courts' retreat on many equity issues. Three major Supreme Court decisions in the 1990s authorized a return to segregated schools.[5] Bilingual education was attacked by the Reagan administration and was drastically curtailed by a statewide referendum in California in 1998. Playing on fears of racial change and immigration, this new conservative shift has also reversed college policies designed to recruit and support minority students on campuses. These changes have had dramatic impact on Chicano students[6] and profoundly affected their community, which was already experiencing inequalities ineffectively addressed during the previous civil rights era.

This chapter concerns the ways in which that fourth shift—a reaction against civil rights and poverty programs—is affecting these students and their communities. It analyzes the consequences of political changes for Chicano education, focusing particularly on California, which is the epicenter of the conservative counterrevolution that is currently reshaping national policy. It also shows that in this reconstruction of national policy, politics matter. Not dealing with politics may be ignoring the most important explanations of why California and even the nation have made major educational gains, as well as serious reversals of these gains.

HOW CALIFORNIA POLITICS MATTERS

With more than one-ninth of the nation's population, California is likely to be a fulcrum in devising models for reacting to the demographic tidal wave of La-

Gary Orfield

tinos that will spread across the country in the coming century. Within a half century, California will have a Mexican-origin population bigger than the entire U.S. Black population in 1990.[7] It is therefore likely that California will define many of the most important issues of the coming century in the United States. As the powerful center of mass media, California spins off political and cultural trends that reverberate broadly. It also has a strange blend of progressive and discriminatory traditions that reflects all the ambiguities of dramatic social transformation. For example, in the second half of this century, California created the tax-cutting movement and produced Ronald Reagan, the most important leader of the conservative movement.

After World War II, California was at the forefront of the progressive movement and the creation of a huge world-class educational system. Its schools were among the best financed in the nation, and the University of California system became the model for development of public research universities that were internationally competitive. Public investments made the desert bloom, created an infrastructure for international trade and powerful communications links, and made the state a great center of technology and research, just as the post-industrial age opened and international trade mushroomed. Paradoxically, the very success of the state's development strategy created the vast demand for labor that drew in Chicanos/as and other immigrants and thus generated many of today's social tensions. In effect, California's current economic and financial growth is unimaginable without the immigration that is driving change in the state and, at the same time, producing profound unease and resistance among parts of its population.

In 1964, that progressive political climate in California changed. The conservative takeover of the state's Republican party machinery in 1964 and the 1966 election of Ronald Reagan as governor signified the conservative ascendancy. These events also signaled the development of a populist anti-government, anti–civil rights style of governing that polarized the state along racial lines. Essentially, Reagan's gubernatorial term redefined not only California politics, but national politics as well. In 1964, Reagan strongly endorsed a national ticket headed by Senator Barry Goldwater, the only Republican senator outside the South to oppose the 1964 Civil Rights Act. Reagan also supported a successful referendum campaign to prohibit fair housing legislation, which was later overturned by the U.S. Supreme Court. Two years later, after a bitter series of riots in Los Angeles's Black community, Reagan became governor following a campaign that included attacks on civil rights. As governor, he opposed any lawsuits brought by legal services for the state's illegal actions against the Farmworkers Union and other groups. Reagan was also famous for his efforts to turn the leadership of the University of California in a more conservative direction by his appointment of conservative regents and attacks on student activists.

In the increasingly conservative social and political climate, California's referenda attacked both the independence of the state judiciary and the state's tax base. These referenda helped limit civil rights and cut public support for education. The California Supreme Court, for example, had ruled that the state constitution had created broader desegregation rights than the federal Constitution, making it much easier to win a court order and permitting urban students access to suburban schools. Conservatives led a successful effort to amend the state constitution and restrict this possibility through Proposition 1, and the California Supreme Court and U.S. Supreme Court eventually accepted the validity of that referendum. The state high court, threatened by a conservative recall campaign, accepted the termination of the desegregation order in the Los Angeles school district, allowing Los Angeles to become the first major district in the United States to end its desegregation order.[8]

While the state courts successfully dismantled federal civil rights requirements, the California state government, in the 1990s, tried to cope with its first serious recession since the early 1930s. Huge cuts in state tax resources had resulted from the 1978 adoption of Proposition 13, the anti-tax referendum that drastically curtailed local taxes.[9] That victory set the stage for an orgy of tax cuts at the state and national levels and opened an era in which control of California state policy by referenda campaigns enabled interest groups with sufficient resources to bypass normal politics and the concomitant system of negotiation and compromise. It allowed powerful and usually wealthy groups to force choices on issues posed in terms most favorable to their side. With the reduction of tax resources dictated by a succession of referenda, California plummeted from its position as one of the states contributing the largest share of its wealth to education to one of those contributing the least.[10] This change came as the state's school enrollment was shifting from a White to a non-White majority.

As student enrollment soared and tax support declined, the state did not build new schools, as it had done in the postwar baby boom. Instead, hundreds of schools went on year-round sessions in areas such as Los Angeles, where migration was concentrated. As the state population grew, the University of California system stopped adding new campuses or expanding enrollment significantly in the old ones, thus reducing access to the flagship state university and increasing racial conflict over an increasingly scarce resource. From 1964 to 1970, for example, total University of California enrollment grew by more than a third in just six years. In the next five years, UC enrollment grew by another 20 percent. From 1975 to today, enrollment has grown by only one-fourth. In the 1990s, enrollment rates became virtually flat, with slightly fewer students in 1996 than 1990.[11] At the same time, there was massive growth in the state's population and in the number of high school graduates. There was clearly a need for many new university campuses to preserve the previous level of access. These policies limited the opportunities for Latino students, but they also limited the opportunities for Whites who, caught in this state-created bind, often blamed immigrants for the problems they encountered in the restrictive university system.

When the Reagan administration drastically cut federal resources through tax cuts, state governments suddenly faced ever larger cuts that necessitated further limiting of state services. Among the casualties was California's tradition of very low-cost public higher education and free community colleges.[12] Conservatives who had promised no negative impact from tax cutting shifted blame away from themselves by scapegoating immigrants' use of public services. For example, the media campaign for Proposition 187—a referendum that sought to limit public services to undocumented immigrants—used television ads filled with images of schools overcrowded with non-White students. Non-Anglo immigrants who were not yet citizens were easy targets because they were very visible and could not vote to protect their interests. This political strategy of blaming immigrants continues in California and has greatly increased the difficulty of developing coherent policies for the success of immigrant children in schools.

The California GOP targeted the nativist fear of an immigrant-dominated society to win elections in the early 1990s. Governor Pete Wilson used this issue as a "wedge" in a 1994 anti-immigrant referendum that helped him overcome a Democratic lead in the polls. Focusing on the growing immigrant population as a threat to the economic, political, and social welfare of California, Wilson spent over $2 million dollars on television commercials that promoted Proposition 187 and promised to turn immigrants away from schools and hospitals.[13]

The proposition served its political purpose, sparking what the *Los Angeles Times* called "one of the most dramatic comebacks in California political history."[14] The GOP learned its lessons well, and two years later took over as the key financial supporter of the Proposition 209 referendum campaign against affirmative action in employment and higher education. This time, the proposed proposition shifted its target from illegal residents who had already been excluded from such programs to "legal" Latinos and African Americans who were the principal beneficiaries of affirmative action.

The conservative climate indicated by the successful referendum movement in California soon expanded into national politics. The national Republican tickets reflected the conservative strategy of the California GOP to try to break the Democratic party coalition that had been dominant in Congress since 1930. In the 1990s, Congressional Republicans led by Newt Gingrich pushed for radical cuts in welfare programs and passed particularly harsh cutbacks for legal resident aliens who did not have citizenship. Implementation of the law rapidly produced severe problems, including hunger among families losing benefits.[15] Another restriction prohibited higher education for welfare recipients. Clearly, it was a time of serious polarization against the poor, particularly against immigrants and minorities.

In California, the state's agenda was also shaped by referenda that imposed cuts in taxes and state expenditures. Political power of elected officials was further weakened by the imposition of term limits through referendum. Under the referenda system, representative government in California gave way, to a considerable extent, to government by plebiscite, a method of government ill-suited to the management of complex issues and often ideal for demagogues with apparently simple solutions to deep emotional problems and fears. The referenda system moved California politics to the right and against civil rights. With at least $1 million needed to gather enough signatures to put a measure on the ballot, the California referenda campaigns are only accessible to groups with major financial resources. In 1996, for example, contributors supporting California referenda campaigns spent $141 million.[16] Since the 1960s, Californians have enacted a series of referenda that have affected minority opportunity, including:

1) banning fair housing laws (1964);
2) limiting taxes (1978 and 1979);
3) cutting back on school desegregation rights (1980);
4) recalling three liberal members of the state supreme court (1986);
5) ending services for undocumented immigrants (1994);
6) banning affirmative action (1996);
7) banning bilingual education (1998).

Had the decisions been left to the elected branches of government, most of these provisions would not have been enacted. In fact, following California's referendum against affirmative action, many states and a national Congress controlled by conservatives raised the issue, but they all failed.

WHY POLITICS MATTERS TO THE CHICANO COMMUNITY

The 1990s are a time of maximum vulnerability for the Chicano community. As a huge young population without the power to protect itself politically, the Chicano community is an easy target for demagogic attacks by those holding and maintaining a power that depends on polarizing the declining White majority against Chicanos. The community's relative youth and poverty, together with its members' status as legal residents without citizenship, mean that the proportion of Latino voters is very small in comparison with the proportion of Latino children enrolled in public schools. In the late 1990s, nearly one-fifth of the children born in the United States were Latino, but in the 1996 election only 5 percent of the U.S. electorate was Latino.[17] As presently constructed, the community lacks the internal political power to achieve its needs. In fact, those needs and the community's limited political representation create a serious temptation for conservative politicians to use the fear of change to hold power through ethnic polarization.

California's conservative reversals have come at a dangerous time for the Chicano community. It is a community with low levels of educational achievement in a world in which educational credentials are essential for success in a competitive job market in which rewards go to those with post-secondary education.[18] On average, Chicano adults have low education levels, and young Chicanos continue to lag behind in achievement levels and high school completion rates. In 1994, for example, 46.7 percent of Chicanos over the age of twenty-five had high school diplomas, compared to 82.0 percent of Whites and 72.9 percent of African Americans. Only 6.3 percent of Chicanos over twenty-five years of age had completed college.[19] Among young adults ages twenty-five to twenty-nine, 62.9 percent of Latinos reported graduating or getting a GED in 1996, compared to 92.6 percent of Whites and 86.0 percent of Blacks.[20]

These statistics translate into lower economic levels and, therefore, lower political leverage for the Chicano community. Latinos often take on very difficult burdens, such as poor housing, bad jobs, and health risks, to create better opportunities for their families. Mexican Americans, like African Americans, tend to earn wages more than one-fifth lower than European Americans, but one recent study found that "more than three-quarters of the wage gap is attributable to their relative youth, English language deficiencies, and especially their lower educational attainment."[21] If a family fails to have the needed access to education for its children, the intergenerational prospects are grim. For example, for the first generation, having a job is progress. Yet for the second generation, unless they get a post-secondary education, they will be isolated with no chance of mobility.

The risk is that, as a result of this fourth shift in racial policy, Chicano communities will be cut off from the economic and social mobility that drew them to the United States. Increasing numbers of Chicanos face the possibility—some would argue the probability—of growing up without the necessary skills for and connections to the economic system, and will thus face further isolation. Without the traditional structures that sustained their families through poverty in Mexico and with only limited access to middle-class opportunity in American life, the Chicano community is trapped on the periphery. They will know what they are missing, but will lack the educational opportunity to achieve it. As the economy becomes more and more stratified by education, and as programs to help minority students are terminated, the consequences become even more severe.

POLITICS MATTERS TO EDUCATION

Most Chicanos are either immigrants or descendants of recent immigrants, but they understand the importance of education in U.S. society and give high priority to educational opportunity for their children. Although Chicano parents share the dream of other parents in the United States about educational mobility, the worst schools are typically provided for the most isolated and powerless families. Segregated Black and Latino schools are sixteen times as likely as segregated White schools to have a majority of poor children.[22] Such schools have more children in special education, more rapid turnover of students and teachers, more teachers not qualified in the subject they are teaching, many fewer honors and Advanced Placement courses, more violence, much lower graduation and college-going rates, and many other forms of inequality. Latino students face higher levels of segregation by both race and poverty than African Americans. That dream has been made more unattainable by the current political climate that Chicanos face: the combined force of a White backlash against the Black civil rights movement; the ongoing backlash against government spending and taxation; and a systematic campaign of demagogic racial polarization against immigrants and Latinos led by the Republican party in California.

Today, Chicanos represent 41 percent of students in California's public schools. Yet, an increasing number of Chicano students attend low-achieving, high-poverty schools where few students are prepared competitively for college. They attend schools where overcrowding is often severe and where teachers often teach key courses in subjects they did not major in, and who cannot communicate with students or parents due to language barriers.[23] As of June 1998, these are also schools in which transitional bilingual programs of the sort most likely to succeed are illegal, as a result of a successful campaign to outlaw bilingual education through statewide referendum, Proposition 227.

In addition, the combination of high-stakes tests and rising college admissions standards threaten to decrease further access to post-secondary education at the same time that affirmative action for college admissions has been declared illegal as a result of Proposition 209. To make matters worse, these changes, part of the civil rights counterrevolution, come at a time when education is a prerequisite for most jobs offering real mobility. This shift to the right in California politics, and therefore in California post-secondary education, has not reached its apex. Almost immediately after the Proposition 227 victory, some of its leaders announced that the next policy target would be university ethnic studies programs. Regent Ward Connerly, famous as the leader of the 1996 anti-affirmative action referendum, announced that he was going to attack programs studying African Americans, Latinos, or other groups that he labeled as practicing "self-imposed segregation."[24]

Eventually, the sheer force of demographic change is likely to produce policy change. If the existing long-term trends continue, California will become a Chicano-majority society. Politics will eventually shift, but that change may be far in the future, given the relative youth, citizenship problems, and lower electoral participation of the Chicano community. Most civil rights battles by Chicanos during the past two decades have been defensive attempts to protect policies and programs that arose in the 1960s. It is important to think about two dimensions of this situation: first, that the movements in the 1960s succeeded only when they could build an interracial coalition; and second, that the sociopolitical context has changed since the 1960s. These dimensions require new research and creative thought to move the United States toward a multiracial civil rights and educational policy agenda that fits the needs of a society in transition.

As the changes unfold, scholars and policymakers have special responsibilities. We are in the midst of change in U.S. education and U.S. society—a time in which there has been little effective leadership by policymakers or politicians. The evidence suggests that much of the public is not acting vindictively, but out of ignorance. For example, in a 1998 California survey, only 9 percent of California White parents thought that Latinos were treated worse than Whites in the California schools, and 10 percent actually thought that they were treated better. Fifty-two percent of Latino parents and 61 percent of Asian parents thought that there were no differences in treatment of students by race.[25] The insensitivity to differences in school conditions, teacher qualifications, curriculum and level of instruction, levels of completion and graduation rates, and many other inequities tends to place the blame on parents, the lack of education standards, and teachers.

Such lack of awareness directs no attention to the overarching civil rights dimensions of these issues. Only 3 percent of Californians and less than 1 percent of White parents saw racism as the state's deepest problem. Less than 1 percent saw poverty as the basic reason for school problems, although research indicates that socioeconomic status is always very powerfully related to school outcomes and that only minority children tend to be isolated in high-poverty schools.[26]

CONCLUSION

The bleak experience of the attack on Chicano rights in the 1990s helped mobilize California's Latino community in the 1998 election, as seen in increased citizenship rates, rapidly growing voter registration, and a strong voter turnout. These changes signal an increased sense of community responsibility that might presage a welcome fifth shift in racial policy in the United States. In this situation, it is vital that the public receive better information if it is to make informed decisions on the direction this shift will take. More importantly, it is vital that policymakers and the general public care enough to do so.

NOTES

1. National Commission on Excellence in Education, *A Nation at Risk* (Washington, DC: Government Printing Office, 1983); Bill Clinton and Al Gore, "Education," in *Putting People First: How We Can All Change America* (New York: Times Books, 1992), pp. 84–89.
2. Gary Orfield, *The Reconstruction of Southern Education: The Schools and the 1964 Civil Rights Act* (New York: John Wiley, 1969).
3. Harry S. Dent, *The Prodigal South Returns to Power* (New York: John Wiley, 1978); Leon Panetta and Peter Gall, *Bring Us Together: The Nixon Team and the Civil Rights Retreat* (Philadelphia: Lippincott, 1971).

4. The U.S. Supreme Court blocked city-suburban desegregation in the 1974 decision, *Milliken v. Bradley*, 418 U.S. 717, and rejected the effort to equalize school spending in *San Antonio Independent School District v. Rodríguez*, 411 U.S. 1(1973). Both of these historic 5-4 decisions were deeply influenced by President Nixon's appointment of four justices who voted to limit rights.

5. *Board of Education of Oklahoma City v. Dowell*, 498 U.S. 237 (1991); *Freeman v. Pitts*, 503 U.S. 467 (1992); and *Missouri v. Jenkins*, 115 S. Ct. 2038 (1995).

6. Jerome Karabel, "No Alternative: The Effects of Color-Blind Admissions in California," in *Chilling Admissions: The Affirmative Action Crisis and the Search for Alternatives*, ed. Gary Orfield and Edward Miller (Cambridge, MA: Harvard Civil Rights Project and Harvard Educational Publishing Group, 1998), pp. 33–50.

7. By 1996, 47 percent of the children being born in California were Latino. By 2010, the state is expected have nearly 14 million Latinos in a population projected to reach 41 million. It is projected that by 2050 the state will have a population of more than 60 million, with more than 30 million Latinos, if the existing trends continue. In 1990, there were 30 million Blacks in the United States. U.S. Census Bureau, *Statistical Abstract of the United States, 1995* (Washington, DC: Government Printing Office, 1995), pp. 20, 37.

8. Gary Orfield, "Lessons of the Los Angeles School Desegregation Case," *Education and Urban Society* (May 1984); "Exclusion of the Majority: Shrinking College Access and Public Policy in Metropolitan Los Angeles," *Urban Review, 20*, No. 3 (Fall 1988), 147–163.

9. David O. Sears and Jack Citrin, *Tax Revolt: Something for Nothing in California* (Cambridge, MA: Harvard University Press, 1985); Terry Schwadron, ed., *California and the American Tax Revolt: Proposition 13 Five Years Later* (Berkeley: University of California Press, 1984).

10. Between 1980 and 1992, for example, the growth in California's per pupil spending was 20.1 percent, compared to 37.0 percent for the national average, in spite of the state's exceptional wealth. In 1992, California was spending $3.73 per $100 of personal income on schools, compared to a national average of $4.36 (William J. Fowler, Jr., ed., *Developments in School Finance* [Washington, DC: National Center for Education Statistics, 1995], pp. 41, 47). In 1997, the Governor's Office reported that the state was 37th in the country in school spending, rising to 28th only in 1998. State Superintendent Delaine Eastin reported that California was still spending about $1,000 less per student than the other large industrial states (Julian Guthrie, "School Spending Ranking Gets Boost," *San Francisco Examiner*, June 11, 1998).

11. FTE enrollment from University of California "Afteweb," the web site of the UC Office of the President, updated August 20, 1997.

12. California traditionally had no tuition and modest fees for its public colleges and universities. In 1973–1974, for example, the total tuition and fees for the University of California system was $664 a year and the total for the California State University system was $168. Community college courses were free. The costs of the system rose rapidly in two key periods—following the tax cuts in the late 1970s and federal aid cuts in the early 1980s, and during the recession of the early 1990s. By 1986 the costs of four-year universities in California were $5300; by 1996 the costs had reached $8300 (Carnegie Commission on Higher Education, *Tuition* [New York: Carnegie Commission, 1974], p. 53; National Center for Education Statistics, *Digest of Education Statistics 1988*, Table 219; *Digest of Education Statistics 1997*, Table 253.

13. Lydia Chávez, *The Color Bind: California's Battle to End Affirmative Action* (Berkeley: University of California Press, 1998), p. 37.

14. Chávez, *The Color Bind*, p. 38.

15. Virginia Ellis, "Study Shows More Immigrants Are Going Hungry," *Los Angeles Times*, May 27, 1998.

16. David S. Broder, "Taking the Initiative on Petitions: Signatures for a Price," *Washington Post Weekly Edition*, April 20, 1998, p. 11.

17. "Presidential Election Exit Poll Results," CNN/TIME All Politics Web Site.

18. In 1996 a Latino adult who was a high school dropout earned $13,287 on average, compared to $32,955 for a college graduate. Jennifer Day and Andrea Curry, *Educational Attainment in the United States, March 1997* [Current Population Reports] (Washington, DC: U.S. Bureau of the Census, May 1998), p. 5.

19. U.S. Bureau of the Census, *Statistical Abstract of the United States 1995*, Table 238.

20. National Center for Education Statistics, *The Condition of Education 1997, Supplemental and Standard Error Tables*, p. 99.
21. Stephen Trejo, "Why Do Mexican Americans Earn Low Wages?" *Journal of Political Economy*, *105* (1997), 1235–1268.
22. See Gary Orfield, with Mark D. Bachmeier, David R. James, and Tamela Eitle, "Deepening Segregation in American Public Schools: A Special Report from the Harvard Project on School Desegregation," *Equity and Excellence in Education, 30,* No. 2 (September, 1997), 8–12; Reuben Espinosa and Alberto Ochoa, "Concentration of California Hispanic Students in Schools with Low Achievement: A Research Note," *American Journal of Education, 77,* No. 1 (1986), 77–95; Paul E. Barton, Richard J. Coley, and Harold Wenglinsky, *Order in the Classroom Violence, Discipline, and Student Achievement* (Princeton, NJ: Educational Testing Service, 1998), pp. 21, 25, 32.
23. Jeannie Oakes, *Multiplying Inequalities: The Effects of Race, Class and Tracking in Opportunities to Learn Math and Science* (Santa Monica, CA: Rand, 1990).
24. Frank Bruni, "California Regent's New Focus: Ethnic Studies," *New York Times,* June 18, 1998, p. A22.
25. Los Angeles Times Poll, November 18–December 12, 1997, questions 58, 59.
26. Los Angeles Times Poll, November 18–December 12, 1997, questions 9, 22.

EDUCATIONAL TESTING AND
MEXICAN AMERICAN STUDENTS:
PROBLEMS AND PROSPECTS

RICHARD R. VALENCIA

The field of educational testing—which includes, for example, norm-referenced standardized intelligence, achievement, personality, and adaptive behavior tests—is an enormous enterprise. Most of the national public school student population, which currently numbers more than 46 million students (U.S. Department of Education, 1997), takes at least one group-administered standardized test each year. Given that standardized educational tests are imperfect measures of samples of behaviors and are based on the shaky assumption that such tests can be uniformly administered across groups (e.g., different racial/ethnic groups, groups by differing socio-economic levels), it is not surprising that problems abound.

In this chapter, my focus is on a number of testing concerns vis-à-vis Mexican American students: cultural bias in tests; problems in the assessment of students with limited English proficiency; underrepresentation of Mexican American students in gifted and talented programs; the disparate, negative impact of high-stakes testing; inequalities of curriculum differentiation; and the adverse impact of testing on admissions to institutions of higher education. I also discuss how these testing issues can be addressed in ways that could lead to nondiscriminatory assessment and greater access to equal educational opportunities for Mexican American students.

First, I provide historical context for educational testing and Mexican American students, followed by a discussion of the emergence of contemporary testing issues. In the chapter's core, I offer brief discussions of the six testing issues named in the previous paragraph, and then provide an overview of a number of testing ideas that could lead to fairer practices and more inclusive outcomes for the rapidly growing Mexican American student population. I close with a comment on the importance of linking test reform with school reform.

HISTORICAL CONTEXT

Several decades after the signing of the Treaty of Guadalupe Hidalgo in 1848, the testing movement—which is frequently attributed to English biologist Sir Francis Galton (Anastasi, 1988)—was launched. In his 1883 book, *Inquiries into Human Faculty and Its Development,* Galton (who was Charles Darwin's cousin) discussed a number of techniques (e.g., visual discrimination and reaction time) to measure a human's psychological processes. In his 1870 book, *Hereditary Genius,* he was not shy about discussing his racial views in the chapter entitled, "The Comparative Worth of Different Races" (see Valencia, 1997a). Undoubtedly a brilliant scientist, Galton was also a racist and a classist in his ideology and in his work (see, e.g., Galton, 1870). Galton, a firm believer in hereditarianism—the theory that individual and group differences in behavior (e.g., intelligence) can primarily be accounted for on the basis of genetics—was a key player in the eugenics movement. His pronouncements about racial differences in intelligence and societal stratification had indirect but significant influence on how American psychologists viewed the practice of testing Mexican American children, and on how these behavioral scientists attempted to explain the differences in intellectual performance between Whites and Mexican Americans.

Although the testing movement was launched by Galton, it was the team of Frenchmen Alfred Binet and Théodore Simon that, in 1905, provided the fuel that actually ignited the movement. The Binet-Simon scale, the first cognitively based intelligence test, was subsequently imported, culturally appropriated, translated, psychometrically modified, and normed by U.S. psychologists such as Henry H. Goddard and Lewis Terman (see Valencia, 1997a). By 1916, the individually administered Stanford-Binet Intelligence Test had been developed. Lewis Terman, the test's designer, intentionally sought to obtain a standardization group that was White and middle class (Terman, 1916). His flagrant disregard of Mexican Americans and other children of color in creating the norm group would be an issue for decades.

By the time the Stanford-Binet Intelligence Test was developed, over two hundred group-administered achievement tests were available for use in the schools (Chapman, 1988), but no group-administered intelligence test had been developed. This problem would be addressed, however, with the development of the National Intelligence Tests (NIT) in 1920.[1] With respect to norming, the NIT was just as exclusive as the Stanford-Binet: no Mexican American, African American, Asian American, or American Indian children were part of the standardization sample (Valencia, 1997a). Soon after the publication of the NIT, "other group-administered intelligence tests were developed and ready for consumption by a very hungry and receptive public school system bent on promoting efficiency" (Valencia, 1997a, p. 56). Group-administered intelligence (and achievement) tests were used frequently by the mid-1920s. In a response to differentiated intellectual abilities observed among students, some researchers and educators argued that there was a need for differentiated curriculum (see, e.g., Dickson, 1923; Terman, 1919). Intelligence tests served this sorting function quite well.

Richard R. Valencia

Three points regarding Mexican American students in the 1920s are particularly noteworthy (Valencia, 1997a). First, "race psychology" studies of the 1920s were unanimous and uniform in their conclusions (implicit or explicit) about Mexican American-White differences in intelligence: the lower intellectual performance of Mexican American students was genetically based.[2] Second, given their typically low performance on intelligence tests, Mexican American students were frequently placed in classes for "slow learners." Third, the criticisms directed at intelligence tests (i.e., their questionable validity and reliability, questionable measures of innate ability, exclusive norming, cultural bias, and the fallibility of using such tests for curriculum differentiation) would reverberate for decades.

In sum, it is not at all surprising that during the advent of the testing movement in the 1920s, Mexican American students were deemed to be intellectually inferior and only minimally educable. By the mid-1920s, state governments became interested in the education of Mexican American students. The prevalent racial animus toward Mexican Americans and the subsequent inferior education they were provided were "in part shaped by the legacy of hate engendered by the Texas Revolution and the Mexican American War" (San Miguel, 1987, p. 33). Furthermore, the intellectual assessment of Mexican American students must be understood within the ideological context of the intelligence testing movement of the 1920s. Chapman (1988) has commented that this ideological framework can be reduced to several essential components:

> Intelligence could be measured by tests and expressed in a single, numerical ratio. This ability was largely constant and determined by heredity. Class and racial inequality could be explained in large part by differences in intelligence. Used in schools, intelligence tests could be used to identify ability, prescribe curricula and determine students' futures. (p. 92)

THE EMERGENCE OF CONTEMPORARY TESTING ISSUES

Beginning in the 1920s and until the early 1970s, standardized group-administered achievement and intelligence tests were routinely given to elementary and secondary school students, and test results were used, in part, to make curricular assignments. The civil rights movement of the late 1950s and early 1960s made the rights of racial and ethnic minorities focal points of national concern. Included in this debate was the role of group-administered IQ tests in the classification of minority students within the educational mainstream and its special education tributary. Speaking of those years, Anastasi (1988) commented, "A common criticism of intelligence tests is that they encourage a rigid, inflexible, and permanent classification of pupils" (p. 67). So deep were these concerns that the use of group IQ tests was discontinued, for example, in 1964 in the New York City public schools (Gilbert, 1966).

As the allegations of discriminatory assessment mounted, three influences shaped the discourse that would eventually lead to nondiscriminatory assessment mandates: professional associations, litigation, and legislation (Henderson & Valencia, 1985). For Mexican Americans and reform in testing, litigation was particularly salient. Mexican American students and parents (as plaintiffs in litigation) were highly instrumental in raising discriminatory assessment issues (e.g., failure to assess a child's dominant language and the use of culturally biased tests) and promoting nondiscriminatory practices (e.g., greater use of nonverbal and performance IQ tests).[3] One of the most profound changes resulting from the anti-discriminatory-assessment campaign of the late 1960s and the early 1970s was the widespread ban on group-administered IQ tests, largely implemented under the auspices of local school districts. As we shall see in the next section, however, individually administered IQ tests—along with a host of other issues—continued to be of concern for Mexican Americans.

CURRENT TESTING ISSUES

Suffice it to say, testing concerns vis-à-vis Mexican Americans have been long-standing. It is important to be aware that many concerns are ongoing. I have identified six testing issues that are germane to Mexican American students: 1) cultural bias in tests; 2) problems in the assessment of students with limited English proficiency; 3) underrepresentation of Mexican American students in gifted and talented programs; 4) the disparate, negative impact of high-stakes testing; 5) inequalities of curriculum differentiation; and 6) the adverse impact of testing on admissions to institutions of higher education.

CULTURAL BIAS IN TESTS

Although the routine use of group-administered intelligence tests has been banned for nearly three decades, individually administered intelligence tests used in special education diagnoses (e.g., of learning disabilities or mental retardation) and classifications remain an issue. The concern is whether such intelligence tests are culturally biased against Mexican American and other minority students, especially African Americans. I define test bias, as does Reynolds (1982), as a "systematic error in the estimation of some 'true' value for a group of individuals" (p. 186).

In our analysis of research on cultural bias on individually administered intelligence tests, Suzuki and I (Valencia & Suzuki, 1998) reviewed seventy-six studies published between 1966 and 1997. We drew two major conclusions from this review of the literature. First, although there are some exceptions (e.g., Valencia & Rankin, 1988; Valencia, Rankin, & Livingston, 1995), researchers have consistently found that these tests are *not* biased against minority populations. Second, there appears to be a waning of research on cultural bias; that is, the peak of research activity was between 1974 and 1988 (when 65, or 86%, of the 76 studies were published). This rapid decline in research on cultural bias is likely related to the rather consistent finding of nonbias.

Notwithstanding the fairly strong finding of nonbias, Suzuki and I (1997) assert that research on cultural bias on individually administered intelligence tests should continue. For example, most of the studies Suzuki and I reviewed (Valencia & Suzuki, 1998) used "normal" children—not children referred for special education assessment or placed in special education. Also, some of the prominently used tests have been vastly underexamined (e.g., Stanford-Binet; see Terman & Merrill, 1973). These and other reasons led us (Suzuki & Valencia, 1997) to conclude that "a strong case can be made that test publishers and measurement specialists have an obligation to engage in expanded research on cultural bias in intelligence tests. Such research appears even more pressing to undertake given the dramatic growth of culturally/linguistically diverse school-age populations occurring presently in the United States" (p. 1109).

PROBLEMS IN THE ASSESSMENT OF STUDENTS WITH LIMITED ENGLISH PROFICIENCY

Historically, a major assessment problem vis-à-vis Mexican American students has been the failure of assessment personnel and researchers to assess language dominance, fluency, and proficiency *prior* to the assessment of academic or intellectual abilities on English-language tests (Klineberg, 1935; Sánchez, 1934). Furthermore, many researchers who have measured the intellectual performance of Mexican American youngsters have been negligent in even *mentioning* the language status of their participants.[4]

Currently, the reliable and valid assessment of the language status of limited-English-proficient (LEP) Mexican American students is particularly critical in identifying children for enrollment in, and exit from, bilingual education programs and enrollment in bilingual special education. Without accurate language assessment, a Mexican American child may be prematurely exited from a bilingual program to a mainstream English class. For the potential bilingual special education LEP Mexican American child, faulty language assessment may result in a diagnosis of a language disorder when, in reality, a language difference may be the accurate diagnosis.

The standardized tests used for language assessment of LEP Mexican American children are typically referred to as "oral language proficiency tests."[5] Such tests can be problematic in that they vary in difficulty level, have low predictive validity for academic achievement, and have poor intertest reliability (Langdon, 1992). In sum, the psychometric integrity of oral language proficiency tests is in dire need of development. This is urgent, given the rapid growth of the LEP Mexican American school-age population (Macías, 1993).

UNDERREPRESENTATION OF MEXICAN AMERICAN STUDENTS IN GIFTED AND TALENTED PROGRAMS

Beginning with the work of Terman (1925), researchers and educators have shown considerable interest in the identification and cultivation of intellectually gifted and talented students (see, e.g., Winner, 1996, 1997).[6] Unfortunately, Mexican American students—compared with their White peers—have not been a focal group, as evidenced by rates of underrepresentation. Data on the underrepresentation of gifted Mexican American children in gifted and talented programs have been available since the early 1970s. For example, Moreno (1973) reported that in the fall of 1971, Mexican American K-12 public school students in California comprised 16 percent of the total K-12 population, but only 3.8 percent of the total K-12 gifted population —a disparity of 76.3 percent. On the other hand, White students comprised 71 percent of the total K-12 enrollment, yet they were 87.5 percent of the gifted population—a disparity of 23.2 percent.[7] More recent data show similar patterns. According to a report by the U.S. Department of Education's Office of Civil Rights (1991) based on 40,020 schools nationwide, Mexican American and other Latino K-12 students were underrepresented by 46.2 percent in gifted and talented programs.[8]

Why has the educational enterprise been only partially successful in identifying and serving Mexican American gifted and talented students at levels commensurate with their representation in the school population? Nationwide, the vast majority of elementary school districts use high IQ scores or some other type of aptitude or achievement test to identify gifted students; teacher recommendations and checklists are also used in some circumstances (Winner, 1997). In light of the issues surrounding the use of intelligence tests with Mexican American students and problems in language assessment, as well as educators' perceptions of Mexican American students' educability (see Valencia, 1997b), the underrepresentation of these children and youths in gifted and talented programs is not at all surprising (see Valencia, 1997c, p. 5).

Nonetheless, the core issue remains: Many extremely bright Mexican American students go undetected and intellectually unchallenged, and are deprived access to the highest levels of knowledge. Certainly, this does not need to be the case. There are a number of suggested guidelines and strategies available that, if judiciously implemented, can dramatically increase the percentage of Mexican American and other minority youngsters in gifted and talented programs (see, e.g., Bernal, 1973, 1976; Mercer, 1977; Renzulli, 1978; Renzulli & Reis, 1991).

THE DISPARATE, NEGATIVE IMPACT OF HIGH-STAKES TESTING

What is high-stakes testing? A colleague and I (Valencia & Guadarrama, 1996) have defined high-stakes testing as

> the exclusive or near-exclusive use of a test score to make significant educational decisions about students, teachers (prospective and incumbent), and schools. Such decisions can have desirable or undesirable consequences for students, teachers, and schools. That is, a great deal rides on the results of certain tests. A significant gain or loss can result from test score outcomes (hence the notion of high-stakes). (p. 562)

The negative contingencies associated with high-stakes testing can be quite severe. They may result, for example, in students being denied the opportunity to participate in extracurricular activities (e.g., organized athletics), in grade retention for individual students, and even in the denial of a high school diploma. Furthermore, in some states (e.g., Texas), low-achieving schools may be taken over by the state government, which is the most extreme sanction.

As I argue elsewhere (see Valencia, 1997d, pp. 30–31), high-stakes testing constitutes test abuse. For Texas and other states that utilize such practices, high-stakes testing violates a major principle of measurement, which holds that test scores represent a very small sample of behavior and thus should always be used in conjunction with other sources of assessment. Furthermore, the use of high-stakes testing, which is a significant tool in the school-accountability movement, constitutes school reform via top-down, remote-control reformation in which threats are directed to virtually powerless schools. For example, in Texas, the Texas Education Agency (TEA), in a form of "institutionalized bullyism," uses the Texas Assessment of Academic Skills test as the basis for its school rating system (Valencia & Guadarrama, 1996). Guadarrama and I contend that

> the TEA campus rating policy ignores the systemic educational problems that abound in Texas (for example, massive school segregation, inequities in school financing, and underserving of the limited-English-proficient student population). For the TEA to sidestep these issues and to place the burden of school reform solely on the local campus is an indefensible policy. (1996, p. 593)

For Mexican American students in Texas, who are already forced to tread an educational path mired in obstacles, high-stakes testing exacerbates the difficulties of attaining school success.

INEQUALITIES OF CURRICULUM DIFFERENTIATION

I conceptualize "curriculum differentiation" as "the sorting of students into instructional groups based on perceived and/or measured educability" (Valencia, 1997a, p. 71). As discussed earlier, curriculum differentiation is a long-standing educational practice. Today it is typically referred to as "ability grouping" at the elementary school level and "tracking" at the middle and high school levels (Valencia, 1997d).[9]

There is ample evidence from the 1920s (e.g., González, 1990), from approximately a quarter of a century ago (e.g., U.S. Commission on Civil Rights, 1974), and from the present (e.g., San Miguel & Valencia, 1998) that Mexican American students (particularly from low socioeconomic backgrounds) have suffered the inequalities of curriculum differentiation. Although curriculum differentiation may lead to increased teaching efficiency, such instructional means do not justify the ends (Oakes, 1985). That is, tracking at the secondary level, for example, of Mexican American and other students of color into low-status, unchallenging curricular channels can lead to depressed self-esteem, limited interethnic and interracial contact, and, perhaps most important, very limited access to "high-status knowledge," the prerequisite knowledge for college matriculation and success (see, e.g., Oakes, 1985, 1990, 1992; Page & Valli, 1990; Wheelock, 1992). The available literature is inconclusive about the relative weights of standardized test results, grade point average, student choice, parental guidance, and teacher/counselor recommendations in shaping curricular assignments; it is clear, though, that test scores do play an important role. In any event, the evidence shows that curriculum differentiation as a routine practice is not supportable, and the current movement to "untrack" schools is justifiable (Slavin, 1997).

THE ADVERSE IMPACT OF TESTING ON ADMISSIONS TO INSTITUTIONS OF HIGHER EDUCATION

The Scholastic Aptitude Test (SAT) is widely used by college admissions officers in their decisions about who does and who does not get admitted at the undergraduate level. Of course, most admissions personnel also consider the student's high school grade point average, college preparatory courses, and perhaps other factors such as extracurricular activities or a relationship to an alumnus of the institution.

How do Mexican American students perform, on average, on the SAT? It has consistently been found that Mexican American students perform lower than their White peers on both the verbal and mathematics portions of the SAT. The College Board (sponsors of the SAT) reports, for example, that for the high school class of 1996, the average math scores on the SAT for Mexican American males and females were 480 and 442, respectively. The average math scores for White males and females were considerably higher—542 and 507, respectively (Rigol, 1997). These White/Mexican American average differences have remained relatively constant over time (e.g., see Durán, 1983).

The implication is clear. With the current dismantling of affirmative action in college admissions, particularly in California and Texas (see San Miguel & Valencia, 1998), Mexican American students will face higher hurdles in the admissions process if colleges and universities choose to place more emphasis on SAT scores than they previously have, especially now that they cannot use race or ethnicity in admissions decisionmaking.

How well does the SAT predict first-year undergraduate grade point average (UGPA) for Mexican American and other Latino students, in comparison to their White peers?[10] The research by Durán (1983) and Pennock-Roman (1990, 1992) is very informative in addressing this question. Their analyses are quite comprehensive; thus, I only offer highlights (see Valencia, 1997c, pp. 8–9).

Durán (1983) reviewed sixteen studies of Latino students in U.S. colleges.[11] The SAT was the primary (although not sole) predictor in the various investigations. The median correlations between predictor variables and UGPA were verbal test scores (.25), quantitative test scores (.23), high school record (.30), and combined high school record and admissions test scores (.38). These predictor variables, Durán found, were not as good for the prediction of Latinos' UGPA as they were for their White peers' UGPA. Durán's conclusions and recommendations, offered fifteen years ago, are still immensely relevant today:

> The evidence on prediction of Hispanics' college grades from high school grades and admissions test scores suggests that the latter information should be used with extreme caution in the admissions process. . . .The evidence reviewed in this study supports the positive value of high school grades and college admissions test scores in aiding decisions about Hispanics' college admissions. However, the results suggest that admissions officers ought to rely critically on the overall profile of Hispanic students in making admissions decisions. . . . Admissions personnel need to be provided with a broader range of information on Hispanics' background, language, and culture in weighing admissions decisions. (p. 105, emphasis added)

Pennock-Roman's empirical investigation (1990)—which analyzed a host of background variables—included Latino students at six universities (two in California, and one each in Texas, Florida, New York, and Massachusetts). She found that correlations between SAT verbal scores and UGPA ranged from .13 to .37, and correlations between SAT math scores and UGPA ranged from .13 to .30 (these were observed in California, Texas, and Florida; lower values were found in New York and Massachusetts). In all, the observed correlations were of low predictive validity, corroborating the conclusions drawn by Durán (1983). Pennock-Roman's (1992) major conclusion is, "In general, we are on fairly safe ground when making inferences about short-term predictions of academic performance . . . for students at moderate to high levels of English proficiency" (p. 130). She presents caveats, however, about making inferences from the test performance of bilingual students for whom English is not their strongest language, and of Latino students who lack prerequisite course work or experience in test-taking.

PROSPECTS FOR REFORM IN TESTING

Although testing problems faced by Mexican American students are very serious and may appear to be unsolvable, they can be addressed. On the bright side, there has been considerable attention paid to testing concerns vis-à-vis Mexican American and other minority students (e.g., see Cummins, 1984; Dana, 1993; Geisinger, 1992; Hamayan & Damico, 1991; Jones, 1988; Suzuki, Meller, & Ponterotto, 1996). In this section, I offer six suggestions I think are particularly important for how the educational testing of Mexican Americans could be improved: 1) the establishment of the psychometric integrity of tests; 2) the use of alternative forms of assessment of intelligence; 3) emphasis on the importance of language assessment of students with limited English proficiency; 4) greater emphasis on the monitoring role of tests; 5) the use of multiple data sources in assessment; and 6) the unification of science and ethics of assessment.

THE ESTABLISHMENT OF THE PSYCHOMETRIC INTEGRITY OF TESTS

As mentioned earlier, there appears to be a waning of research interest in cultural bias in tests. Such research needs to be reactivated, especially in light of the fact that new tests are always being developed.[12] I advocate continued research into the subject of the cultural bias of various tests (particularly those measuring intelligence). These investigations need to be creatively designed to cover the complexities of the testing situation, such as the actual item under study, test instructions, the examiner, and aspects of the examinee (e.g., motivation, cultural background, and schooling experiences). More attention also needs to be paid to the finer-grained mental processes, such as memory and information processing (see Scheuneman, 1984).

THE USE OF ALTERNATIVE FORMS OF ASSESSMENT OF INTELLIGENCE

In addition to improving traditional testing approaches, much more research should be devoted to developing and evaluating alternative methods of assessment (see Suzuki & Valencia, 1997, p. 1110). A case in point is the Learning Potential Assessment Device (LPAD) (Feuerstein, Rand, & Hoffman, 1979). The goal of the LPAD, a dynamic assessment procedure, is to assess a student's potential for learning by modifying basic cognitive structures and teaching problem-solving principles and strategies to apply to new situations. "The best predictor of learning is learning, not knowledge that one presumes to have accumulated in situations that examiners do not know and could not control" (Feuerstein et al., 1979, p. 44). According to test developers, the LPAD has been used successfully with thousands of children from a range of cultural backgrounds who have demonstrated depressed performance according to other measures (Feuerstein, Rand, &

Rynders, 1988). The LPAD is a clinical procedure and does not yield a particular score.[13]

EMPHASIS ON THE IMPORTANCE OF LANGUAGE ASSESSMENT OF STUDENTS WITH LIMITED ENGLISH PROFICIENCY

I cannot emphasize enough the importance of ascertaining the language status of Mexican American students with limited English proficiency prior to undertaking any intellectual or academic achievement assessments. One of the most critical issues in the assessment of these students is to be able to reliably "distinguish between temporary difficulties that students face in learning to function in a nonproficient language and more permanent perceptual and cognitive deficiencies that interfere with learning" (Hamayan & Damico, 1991, p. viii). Conducting appropriate language assessments can help avoid misdiagnoses among limited-English-proficient students.

GREATER EMPHASIS ON THE MONITORING ROLE OF TESTS

One important function of educational testing is the "management of instruction" (Resnick, 1979). Here, educational tests serve several purposes—the "sorting," "monitoring," and "grading" functions. When tests serve as a mechanism for sorting, they are administered before instruction to assist in the assignment of students to curricular groups (either in the educational mainstream or in its tributary of special education). With respect to the monitoring function, tests are administered *during* the course of instruction in order to provide the teacher with feedback on the student's strengths and weaknesses. The focus is on making curricular adjustments so as to improve student learning and achievement, as well as for teachers to monitor their own effectiveness at communicating curricular material to students. The grading function of tests is perhaps the most familiar. Here, tests are given *after* a unit of instruction to provide an evaluation of a student's academic performance.

As we have seen, the sorting role of testing has created the most controversy regarding the assessment of Mexican American students. One way to improve the assessment of Mexican American students is to place much less emphasis on the sorting (and subsequent labeling) role of tests and to place much more emphasis on the monitoring function. On this, Anastasi (1988) has commented:

> Intelligence tests, as well as any other kind of tests, should be used not to label individuals but to help in understanding them. . . . To bring persons to their maximum functioning level we need to start where they are at the time; we need to assess their strengths and weaknesses and plan accordingly. If a reading test indicates that a child is retarded in reading, we do not label the child as a nonreader and stop. Nor do we administer a nonverbal test to conceal the handicap. Instead we concentrate on teaching the child to read. (p. 363)

THE USE OF MULTIPLE DATA SOURCES IN ASSESSMENT

"In all . . . educational decisions, test scores provide just one type of information and should always be supplemented by past records of achievement and other types of assessment data. No major educational decision should ever be based on test scores alone" (Gronlund, 1985, p. 480). It should be kept in mind that testing is only one component of three types of information that may be collected during the process of educational assessment. The other two sources of diagnostic information are "observations" and "judgments" (Salvia & Ysseldyke, 1988). Each of the three types can be collected by a diagnostician or another person, whom Salvia and Ysseldyke refer to as "direct information" and "indirect information" sources, respectively. In sum, according to Salvia and Ysseldyke, tests, observations, and judgments (i.e., evaluative statements) ideally form the basis of assessment. A best-case practice would use all three sources in the process of data collection.

Conceptualizing educational assessment as a tripartite structure and process would greatly enhance the gathering of data, the diagnosis of strengths and weaknesses within an individual student based on these multiple sources, and decisions on how to improve schooling (see Valencia & Aburto, 1991, p. 238). The use of multiple, informed data sources (e.g., tests, parent and teacher informants, classroom observations, and medical records) has the potential to provide a rich data base and also to improve the credibility of the various sources (Valencia, 1982). I strongly encourage multimeasurement efforts in the educational assessment of Mexican American students.

THE UNIFICATION OF SCIENCE AND ETHICS OF ASSESSMENT

Tests do not exist in a vacuum; rather, they have social consequences. As such, one goal of educational assessment must be a unified view of test validity that integrates both the science and the *ethics* of assessment (see Valencia & Aburto, 1991, p. 239). Messick (1989) has written a thoughtful paper on the importance and necessity of the integration of science and ethics. In brief, Messick contends that test validity and values are one imperative, not two. Thus, test validation implicates both science and ethics. This unified conceptualization of validity integrates both the scientific and the ethical underpinnings of how tests are interpreted and used. The following quotation, I believe, gets to the fundamental nature of this inherent tie between meaning and values in test validation: "It is simply not the case that values are being added to validity in the unified view. Rather, values are intrinsic to the meaning and outcomes of the testing. . . .This makes explicit what has been latent all along, namely, that validity judgments *are* value judgments" (Messick, 1989, p. 10).

It is easy to see that in the case of Mexican Americans—and other groups who have at times been victimized by abusive testing practices—such a unified view of test validity, if universally accepted, would certainly help to promote nondiscriminatory assessment.

CONCLUSIONS

As a colleague and I have discussed elsewhere (Valencia & Aburto, 1991), any reform efforts in educational testing need to be placed in the broader context of school reform. One can argue that the typically lower performance of Mexican American students on standardized intelligence and achievement tests, for example, is one manifestation of the poor schooling Mexican American students receive. Given the persistent and pervasive negative schooling conditions and outcomes experienced by many Mexican American children and youth (e.g., segregation and high dropout rates; see Valencia, 1991), it is not at all surprising that their test performance is generally below that of their White peers.

One way to understand the linkage between schooling inequality and low test performance is to examine the construct of "opportunity to learn" (see Valencia, 1992). The notion of opportunity to learn is concerned with the fit—or lack of fit—between test content (i.e., those samples of behavior that are measured) and the formal curriculum (i.e., that which is taught, how effectively it is taught, and what is learned in school). For Mexican American students, the implication is clear: if Mexican Americans are not given the opportunity to learn the test material on which they later will be tested, then it is not unexpected that their test scores will be low. As such, there are increasing instances in which claims like the following are being voiced: "Testing children on what they have not been taught and then stigmatizing their 'failure to learn' is a fundamental form of discrimination" (Hanson, Schutz, & Bailey, 1980, p. 21).

REFERENCES

Anastasi, A. (1988). *Psychological testing* (6th ed.). New York: Macmillan.

Ballard, W. S., & Tighe, P. L. (Eds.). (1980, 1982, 1983, 1987). *Idea Language Proficiency Test (Level I, II)*. Brea, CA: Ballard & Tighe.

Bernal, E. M. (1973). Gifted Mexican American children: An ethnoscientific perspective. *California Journal of Educational Research, 25,* 261–273.

Bernal, E. M. (1976). Gifted programs for the culturally different. *National Association of Secondary School Principals Bulletin, 60,* 67–76.

Burt, M., Dulay, H., & Hernández-Chávez, E. (1975, 1980). *Bilingual Syntax Measure (Level I, II)*. San Antonio, TX: Psychological Corporation.

Chapman, P. D. (1988). *Schools as sorters: Lewis M. Terman, applied psychology, and the intelligence testing movement, 1890–1930.* New York: New York University Press.

Covarrubias v. San Diego Unified School District, Civil Action No. 70-30d (S.D. Cal. 1971).

Cummins, J. (1984). *Bilingualism and special education: Issues in assessment and pedagogy.* San Diego, CA: College-Hill Press.

Dana, R. H. (1993). *Multicultural assessment perspectives for professional psychology.* Boston: Allyn & Bacon.

De Avila, E., & Duncan, S. E. (1977, 1979, 1983). *Language Assessment Scales.* Monterey, CA: McGraw-Hill.

Diana v. Board of Education, Civil Action No. C-70-37 (N.D. Cal. 1970).

Dickson, V. E. (1923). *Mental tests and the classroom teacher.* Yonkers-on-Hudson, NY: World Book.

Donlon, T. F. (Ed.). (1984). *The College Board technical handbook for the Scholastic Aptitude Test and achievement tests.* New York: College Entrance Examination Board.

Durán, R. P. (1983). *Hispanics' education and background: Predictors of college achievement.* New York: College Entrance Examination Board.

Feuerstein, R., Rand, Y., & Hoffman, M. (1979). *The dynamic assessment of retarded performers: The Learning Potential Assessment Device, theory, instruments, and techniques.* Baltimore, MD: University Park Press.

Feuerstein, R., Rand, Y., & Rynders, J. E. (1988). *Don't accept me as I am: Helping "retarded" people to excel.* New York: Plenum Press.

Ford, S. F., & Campos, S. (1977). *Summary of validity data from Admissions Program Validity Study Service.* Princeton, NJ: College Entrance Examination Board.

Galton, F. (1870). *Hereditary genius: An inquiry into its laws and consequences.* London: Macmillan.

Galton, F. (1883). *Inquiries into human faculty and its development.* London: Macmillan.

Garth, T. R. (1925). A review of race psychology. *Psychological Bulletin, 22,* 343–364.

Geisinger, K. F. (Ed.). (1992). *Psychological testing of Hispanics.* Washington, DC: American Psychological Association.

Gilbert, H. B. (1966). On the IQ ban. *Teachers College Record, 67,* 282–285.

González, G. G. (1990). *Chicano education in the era of segregation.* Philadelphia, PA: Balch Institute Press.

Gould, S. J. (1981). *The mismeasure of man.* New York: W. W. Norton.

Gronlund, N. E. (1985). *Measurement and evaluation in teaching* (5th ed.). New York: Macmillan.

Guadalupe v. Tempe Elementary School District, No. 3, Civ. No. 71-435 (D. Ariz., 1972).

Hamayan, E. V., & Damico, J. S. (1991). Preface. In E. V. Hamayan & J. S. Damico (Eds.), *Limiting bias in the assessment of bilingual students* (pp. v–xi). Austin, TX: PRO-ED.

Hanson, R. A., Schutz, R. E., & Bailey, J. D. (1980). *What makes achievement tick: Investigation of alternative instrumentation for instructional program evaluation.* Los Alamitos, CA: Southwest Regional Laboratory for Educational Research and Development.

Henderson, R. W., & Valencia, R. R. (1985). Nondiscriminatory school psychological services: Beyond nonbiased assessment. In J. R. Bergan (Ed.), *School psychology in contemporary society* (pp. 340–377). Columbus, OH: Charles E. Merrill.

Jones, R. L. (1988). *Psychoeducational assessment of minority group children.* Berkeley, CA: Cobb and Henry.

Klineberg, O. (1935). *Race differences.* New York: Harper & Brothers.

Langdon, H. W. (1992). Speech and language assessment of LEP/bilingual Hispanic students. In H. W. Langdon (Ed., with L. L . Cheng), *Hispanic children and adults with communication disorders* (pp. 201–227). Gaithersburg, MD: Aspen.

Macías, R. F. (1993). Language and ethnic classification of language minorities: Chicano and Latino students in the 1990s. *Hispanic Journal of Behavioral Sciences, 15,* 230–257.

Mercer, J. R. (1977). Identifying the gifted Chicano child. In J. R. Martínez (Ed.), *Chicano psychology* (pp. 155–173). New York: Academic Press.

Messick, S. (1989). Meaning and values in test validation: The science and ethics of assessment. *Educational Researcher, 18,* 5–11.

Moreno, S. (1973). [White, Chicano, and Black rates of representation in gifted programs in California public schools.] Unpublished data.

Oakes, J. (1985). *Keeping track: How schools structure inequality.* New Haven, CT: Yale University Press.

Oakes, J. (1990). *Multiplying inequalities: The effects of race, social class, and tracking on opportunities to learn mathematics and science.* Santa Monica, CA: Rand.

Oakes, J. (1992). Foreword. In A. Wheelock, *Crossing the tracks: How "untracking" can save America's schools* (pp. IX–XV). New York: New Press.

Page, R., & Valli, L. (Eds.). (1990). *Curriculum differentiation: Interpretive studies in U.S. secondary schools.* Albany: State University of New York Press.

Pennock-Román, M. (1990). *Test validity and language background: Hispanic American students at six universities.* New York: College Entrance Examination Board.

Pennock-Roman, M. (1992). Interpreting test performance in selective admissions for Hispanic students. In K. F. Geisinger (Ed.), *Psychological testing of Hispanics* (pp. 99–135). Washington, DC: American Psychological Association.

Ramist, L., Lewis, C., & McCamley-Jenkins, L. (1994). *Student group differences in predicting college grades: Sex, language, and ethnic groups* (Report No. 93-1). New York: College Entrance Examination Board.

Renzulli, J. S. (1978). What makes giftedness? Reexamining a definition. *Phi Delta Kappan, 60*, 180–184, 261.

Renzulli, J. S., & Reis, S. M. (1991). The reform movement and the quiet crisis in gifted education. *Gifted Child Quarterly, 35*, 26–35.

Reschly, D. J. (1984). Beyond IQ test bias: The National Academy Panel's analysis of minority EMR overrepresentation. *Educational Researcher, 13*, 15–19.

Resnick, L. B. (1979). The future of IQ testing in education. *Intelligence, 3*, 241–253.

Reynolds, C. R. (1982). The problem of bias in psychological assessment. In C. R. Reynolds & T. B. Gutkin (Eds.), *The handbook of school psychology* (pp. 178–209). New York: Wiley.

Rigol, G. W. (1997, June). *Research notes: Common sense about SAT score differences and test validity* (College Board Report No. RN-01). New York: College Entrance Examination Board.

Salvia, J., & Ysseldyke, J. E. (1988). *Assessment in special and remedial education* (4th ed.). Boston: Houghton Mifflin.

Sánchez, G. I. (1934). Bilingualism and mental measures. *Journal of Applied Psychology, 18*, 765–772.

San Miguel, G., Jr. (1987). *"Let all of them take heed": Mexican Americans and the campaign for educational equality in Texas, 1910–1981*. Austin: University of Texas Press.

San Miguel, G., Jr., & Valencia, R. R. (1998). From the Treaty of Guadalupe Hidalgo to Hopwood: The educational plight and struggle of Mexican Americans in the Southwest. *Harvard Educational Review, 68*, 353–412.

Scheuneman, J. D. (1984). A theoretical framework for the exploration of causes and effects of bias in testing. *Educational Psychologist, 19*, 219–225.

Slack, W. V., & Porter, D. (1980). The Scholastic Aptitude Test: A critical appraisal. *Harvard Educational Review, 50*, 154–175.

Slavin, R. E. (1997). *Educational psychology: Theory and practice* (5th ed.). Boston: Allyn & Bacon.

Suzuki, L. A., Meller, P. J., & Ponterotto, J. G. (Eds.). (1996). *Handbook of multicultural assessment: Clinical, psychological, and educational applications*. San Francisco: Jossey-Bass.

Suzuki, L. A., & Valencia, R. R. (1997). Race-ethnicity and measured intelligence: Educational implications. *American Psychologist, 52*, 1103–1114.

Terman, L. M. (1916). *The measurement of intelligence: An explanation of and a complete guide for the use of the Stanford revision and extension of the Binet-Simon scales*. Boston, MA: Houghton Mifflin.

Terman, L. M. (1919). *The intelligence of school children: How children differ in ability, the use of mental tests in school grading and the proper education of exceptional children*. Boston: Houghton Mifflin.

Terman, L. M. (1925). *Genetic studies of genius: Vol. 1. Mental and physical traits of a thousand gifted children*. Stanford, CA: Stanford University Press.

Terman, L. M., & Merrill, M. A. (1973). *Stanford-Binet intelligence scale: 1972 norms edition*. Boston: Houghton Mifflin.

U.S. Commission on Civil Rights. (1974). *Mexican American education study, report 6: Toward quality education for Mexican Americans*. Washington, DC: Government Printing Office.

U.S. Department of Education, Office of Civil Rights. (1991). *1988 elementary and secondary school civil rights survey: State and national summaries* (Report No. ASI 4804-33). Washington, DC: Author.

U.S. Department of Education. (1997). *Common core of data surveys and projection of education statistics to 2007*. Washington, DC: National Center for Education Statistics.

Valencia, R. R. (1982). Psychoeducational needs of minority children: The Mexican American child, a case in point. In S. Hill & B. J. Barnes (Eds.), *Young children and their families: Needs of the 90s* (pp. 73–87). Lexington, MA: D.C. Heath.

Valencia, R. R. (1985). *Chicanos and intelligence testing research: A descriptive state of the art.* Unpublished manuscript.

Valencia, R. R. (1991). The plight of Chicano students: An overview of schooling conditions and outcomes. In R. R. Valencia (Ed.), *Chicano school failure and success: Research and policy agendas for the 1990s* (pp. 3–26). London: Falmer Press.

Valencia, R. R. (1992). Explaining cultural bias in educational tests: How important is "Opportunity to Learn"? *Child Assessment News, 2*(1), 8–11.

Valencia, R. R. (1997a). Genetic pathology model of deficit thinking. In R. R. Valencia (Ed.), *The evolution of deficit thinking: Educational thought and practice* (pp. 41–112). London: Falmer Press.

Valencia, R. R. (Ed.) (1997b). *The evolution of deficit thinking: Educational thought and practice.* London: Falmer Press.

Valencia, R. R. (1997c, December). *Latino students and testing issues: Perspectives on the great gatekeeper.* Paper presented at the Harvard University Civil Rights Project Research Conference on the Latino Civil Rights Crisis, Los Angeles, CA, and Washington, DC.

Valencia, R. R. (1997d). Latinos and education: An overview of sociodemographic characteristics and schooling conditions. In M. Yepes-Baraya (Ed.), *ETS invitational conference on Latino educational issues* (pp. 13–37). Princeton, NJ: Educational Testing Service.

Valencia, R. R., & Aburto, S. (1991). The uses and abuses of educational testing: Chicanos as a case in point. In R. R. Valencia (Ed.), *Chicano school failure and success: Research and policy agendas for the 1990s* (pp. 203–251). London: Falmer Press.

Valencia, R. R., & Guadarrama, I. N. (1996). High-stakes testing and its impact on racial and ethnic minority students. In L. A. Suzuki, P. J. Meller, & J. G. Ponterotto (Eds.), *Multicultural assessment: Clinical, psychological, and educational applications* (pp. 561–610). San Francisco: Jossey-Bass.

Valencia, R. R., & Rankin, R. J. (1988). Evidence of bias in predictive validity on the Kaufman Assessment Battery for Children in samples of Anglo and Mexican American children. *Psychology in the Schools, 25,* 257–263.

Valencia, R. R., Rankin, R. J., & Livingston, R. (1995). K-ABC content bias: Comparisons between Mexican American and White children. *Psychology in the Schools, 32,* 153–168.

Valencia, R. R., & Suzuki, L. A. (1998). *Intelligence testing and minority students: Foundations, performance correlates, and assessment issues.* Manuscript submitted for publication.

Weschler, D. (1974). *Manual for the Weschler Intelligence Scale for Children* (rev.). New York: Psychological Corporation.

Weschler, D. (1991). *Manual for the Weschler Intelligence Scale for Children* (3rd ed.). New York: Psychological Corporation.

Wheelock, A. (1992). *Crossing the tracks: How "untracking" can save America's schools.* New York: New Press.

Winner, E. (1996). *Gifted children: Myths and realities.* New York: Basic Books.

Winner, E. (1997). Exceptionally high intelligence and schooling. *American Psychologist, 52,* 1070–1081.

NOTES

1. The NIT stemmed from the development of the Army Alpha and Beta mental tests used to assess the intellectual ability of recruits during World War I. As Gould (1981) has noted, "These [NIT] tests are the direct result of the application of the army testing methods to school needs" (p. 178).

2. "Race psychology" (apparently coined by scholars such as Garth, 1925) was the study of racial differences (Whites and people of color), particularly in terms of intellectual performance. Of the many groups studied, African Americans were the most frequently tested, followed by American Indians, followed by Mexican Americans. Race psychologists of this era used race in a biological sense and confused race with national origin and ethnicity. Most scholars today assert that race is best understood as a social concept.

3. Mexican American plaintiffs (and coplaintiffs) brought forth their charges in *Diana v. Board of Education* (1970), *Covarrubias v. San Diego Unified* (1971), and *Guadalupe v. Tempe* (1972). See Henderson and Valencia (1985) for a brief discussion of these cases.

4. For example, in a review of intelligence testing research in which Mexican American children were participants, I found that, in 124 intelligence testing instances in 106 studies spanning six decades, the language status of the children *was not even reported* in sixty-three (51%) instances (Valencia, 1985).

5. Examples of prominent tests are the Bilingual Syntax Measure (Burt, Dulay, & Hernández-Chávez, 1975, 1980); the Idea Oral Language Proficiency Test (Ballard & Tighe, 1980, 1982, 1983, 1987); and the Language Assessment Scales (De Avila & Duncan, 1977, 1979, 1983).

6. Notwithstanding the interest in and dramatic growth of gifted and talented programs, little money is spent on these programs; there is also a growing effort, based, for example, on charges that they are elitist, to disband existing programs (see Winner, 1997).

7. These data are from a one-page mimeograph developed by Moreno (1973; archived in the current author's files).

8. Nationwide, 13 percent of the total K-12 population was Latino, and 7 percent of the total gifted and talented population was Latino.

9. Another framework for understanding curriculum differentiation is offered by Slavin (1997). According to Slavin, *tracking* refers to assignments in high school (e.g., college preparatory or general); *between-class ability grouping* refers to the grouping of students by ability level in separate classes in junior high and middle schools; *within-class ability grouping* refers to the grouping of students (e.g., in reading) of similar ability levels in elementary school classes.

10. Space limitations do not permit a review of the literature on the predictive validity of the SAT in general. For pertinent reviews, see Donlon (1984); Ford and Campos (1977); Ramist, Lewis, and McCamley-Jenkins (1994); Slack and Porter (1980). Also see Valencia (1997c) for a brief summary of some of these works.

11. In Durán (1983) and Pennock-Roman (1990, 1992), the data are presented for Latinos, but not disaggregated by Latino subgroups.

12. A case in point is the Weschler Intelligence Scale for Children, Third Edition (Weschler, 1991), which successfully replaced its predecessor, the Weschler Intelligence Scale for Children, Revised Edition (Weschler, 1974).

13. Two criticisms apply to the LPAD. First, the administration time for the LPAD is four to eight hours, considerably longer than traditional measures. Second, the actual success of the LPAD as an alternative assessment measure remains to be seen, especially its link to effective educational programming (Reschly, 1984).

CHICANOS/AS IN THE UNITED STATES: LANGUAGE, BILINGUAL EDUCATION, AND ACHIEVEMENT

EUGENE E. GARCÍA

I was trained as a behavioral psychologist. My brand of theoretical "behaviorism" put great stock on the environmental influences of what we do (Skinner, 1957). Through this theoretical lens, I focused on a set of environmental stimuli that, if arranged in a specific manner, would significantly affect learning—that is, effect a change in behavior. That theoretical tenure guided how I tried to make sense of the world—what questions to ask, how to ask them, where to ask them, and how to assess the effects of any interventions I might try. It called for precision and relied on the scientific world.

New theories of human development and learning seem more applicable to understanding my work, which is why I must admit that professionally I am no longer a "behaviorist." I am, however, still guided by theories. I am not without a conceptual framework that guides my present professional task of understanding the world, particularly issues of development, learning, teaching, and schooling. In a study I completed in 1991, I found that teachers also have theories of how children develop and learn, and their own teaching role in such processes. In short, whether we articulate them or not, we all have theories that guide us in making meaning of the world we live in. That's why theories are important to all of us, not just to "scientists" who more often are linked to the use of theories.

Within my own professional sphere, whether at the local, state, or national level, I have also confronted a cohort of policies that govern the education of Chicanos/as as much as if not more than theories. These policies are not always guided by our theories; in fact, in many cases they are not. Yet they are important determiners of student expectations, instructional practices, and resource distribution that significantly affect the type of education provided to students. This has been particularly true for the Spanish/English bilingual student in the United States. Although I emphasize in this chapter the workings of our theories of human development, learning, and schooling, I also attempt to address the intersections among theory, policy, and practice.

Similarly, in an effort to realize how theory and policy come together in classrooms, I have tried to document instructional practices that have important effects on Chicanos/as as they experience the schooling process (Garcia, 1994). Such practices are sometimes linked directly or indirectly to theories of learning and development, and also to conceptual frameworks related to language acquisition (August & Garcia, 1988). Therefore, in this chapter, I attempt to expand on my own perceived linkages of theory, policy, and practice as they relate to the educational treatment of Chicano/a students. I focus on the foundations related to the schooling initiatives targeted at bilingual Chicano/a students in the United States, and also include an expanded discussion of the issues that bring together research, theory, and educational policy and practice that are significant to these students. More specifically, I address educationally related conceptual/theoretical pursuits that attempt to explain and therefore lay the foundation for educational action.

It seems appropriate to indicate that our understanding of population diversity as it relates to educational endeavors continues to expand in its utilization of diverse theories of language, learning, thinking, teaching, socialization, and culture (August & García, 1988). What was once considered the study of values and behavior (Mead, 1939; Skinner, 1957) has become an interlocking study of linguistic, psychological, and social domains. While each is significant alone, they converge in the attempt to reconstruct the nature of the cultural experience at the micro (smallest unit of social analysis, such as a speech event) and macro (larger unit of social analysis, such as social class) levels. It is this complex set of understandings upon which an educator must depend when addressing teaching and learning in today's classrooms. For the educator of culturally and linguistically diverse students, and of Chicanos/as in particular, the issue of culture—what it is and how it directly and indirectly influences academic learning—becomes particularly important. Within the last few years, educational policy approaches related to culture and education have shifted from a focus on "Americanization," to educational equity, to multicultural education, and, more recently, to the "effective" instruction of children from diverse cultural and linguistic groups (García, 1997).

UNDERSTANDING LANGUAGE, CULTURE, AND EDUCATION

In the following four subsections, I will introduce the theoretical and empirical knowledge bases related to an understanding of language, culture, and education, and the broader understanding of cultural diversity as it relates to schooling. In doing so, I will address teaching and learning as it relates to linguistic, cognitive, social, and educational research and theory that have developed over the last two decades. Such contributions have dramatically reshaped our view of cultural "difference" in education, particularly for Chicanos/as.

Eugene E. García

AMERICANIZATION

Historically, Americanization has been a prime institutional education objective for culturally diverse children, particularly for those children who came to school with a language and culture not represented in the U.S. English-language schooling process (Elam, 1972; González, 1990). Americanization schooling practices were adopted whenever the population of these students rose to significant numbers in a community. The desired effect of "Americanizing" students was to socialize and acculturate the diverse community. This adaptation established special programs and was applied to both children and adults in urban and rural schools and communities. In essence, the theory was that if schools could teach these students the English language and "American" values, then presumably educational failure could be averted. Ironically, social economists have argued that this effort was coupled with systematic efforts to maintain disparate conditions between Anglos and "minority" populations. Indeed, more than anything else, past attempts at addressing the "Black, Chicano/a, Native American, Asian, etc., educational problem" have actually preserved the political and economic subordination of these communities (Spener, 1988).

Coming from a sociological theory of assimilation, Americanization has traditionally been recognized as a solution to the problem of immigrants and ethnicity in the modern industrialized United States. It was intended to merge small ethnic and linguistically diverse communities into a single dominant national institutional structure and culture. Thomas and Park (1921) argued that the immigrants' "Old World" consciousness would eventually be overcome by "modern" American values. Although I will not provide here a detailed review of the literature regarding the historical circumstances of the many immigrant populations that came to the United States, I will rely on recent analyses by González (1990) and Spener (1988).

Coupled with the sociological theory of assimilation, Americanization as it was articulated for Chicanos/as was also supported by the general psychological theory related to development of intelligence and its relationship to bilingualism (García, 1983). In essence, early studies comparing IQ test scores for Spanish/English bilinguals with monolingual English students and army recruits reported a consistently lower IQ for bilinguals (Cummins, 1986). These reports theoretically supported the policy of eliminating any bilingual attributes and moving students toward a monolingual experience in schools. At the practice level, these policy and theoretical foundations often resulted in teachers being told to speak only English to Spanish-speaking students, to punish the use of Spanish in school, and to encourage parents—many of them limited in English proficiency—to speak/teach their Spanish-speaking children English. This link of theory-to-policy-to-practice was experienced extensively by most new immigrants who did not speak English as their primary language. It was also experienced by indigenous populations who were inhabitants of territories annexed by the United States, such as those individuals residing in U.S. Southwest, annexed through the Treaty of Guadalupe Hidalgo, which ended the Mexican American War in 1848.

It can be argued that Americanization is still the goal of many programs aimed at non-White and non-English-proficient students (Nieto, 1992; Rodríguez, 1989; Weis, 1988). For these students, Americanization unfortunately still means the elimination not only of linguistic and cultural differences, but also of a culture deemed undesirable. Americanization programs assume a single premodern homogeneous culture considered ethnic that is in contact with a single homogeneous culture considered modern, with the relationship between the two being unequal. The dominant community, which enjoys greater wealth, power, and privileges, claims its position by virtue of cultural superiority (Ogbu, 1987). In one way or another, nearly every culturally diverse Chicano/a child, whether born in the United States or elsewhere, is likely to be treated as a foreigner, an alien, or an intruder. The Los Angeles school superintendent voiced a common complaint in a 1923 address to district principals: "We have the [Mexican] immigrants to live with, and if we Americanize them, we can live with them" (August & García, 1988, p. 37). Unfortunately, even today the objective is to transform the diversity in our communities into a monolithic English-speaking and American-thinking-and-acting community.

In June 1998, California voters approved a return to the policies of Americanization when they adopted Proposition 227. This proposition mandates that all non-English-speaking children be taught in English, prohibiting the use or development of languages other than English for these students. It does provide for a one-year instructional intervention intended to help non-English-speaking students learn English, then mandates their inclusion into regular English-instruction classrooms. It also provides for funding of non-school community activities that can assist adults and children in acquiring English. In doing so, this new policy closely mirrors the goals and practices of previous Americanization era efforts that were quite clear in regard to homogenization activities concerning language and culture. Proposition 227, however, does not directly address issues of culture, only issues of language, and therefore can be considered a revised Americanization policy.

The Americanization solution has not worked (García, 1994). Moreover, it depends on the flawed notion of group cultural and linguistic deficiency, even in its most recent iterations. The Americanization solution presumes that culturally and linguistically different Chicano/a children as a group are flawed. To fix them individually, we must act on the individual as a member of a cultural and linguistic group. Americanizing agents believe they have arrived at the solution to the educational underachievement of students who represent culturally different groups by changing the values, language, and other behaviors associated with these groups. In essence, the groups should "melt" into one large and more beneficial American culture. New theory, policy, and practice suggest that the challenge facing educators with regard to Chicano/a students is not to Americanize them, but to recognize and work with cultural and linguistic diversities as a way to increase the participation in citizenship and improve educational conditions for this community. Proposition 227 will need to be tested in the courts prior to its implementation, for it is in the courts that new policy regarding equity has been articulated with regard to these issues.

EDUCATIONAL EQUITY

No one argues about the significance of education in this country. We are all quite convinced that an educated society is beneficial in sustaining and enhancing individual well-being, our standard of living, and in maintaining a democratic society (Dewey, 1921). Education is perceived as a vehicle for achieving our "American Dream." It is, therefore, not surprising that numerous social institutions have attempted to initiate and maintain their educational endeavors in conjunction with efforts in the public schools. In fact, today's adult will have been exposed to more formal educational experiences (courses, workshops, seminars, and conferences) outside the usual kindergarten-high school process than within it. Education in U.S. society, from cradle to grave, is important to all inhabitants of the country.

If education is important, then equal access to educational opportunities is a corollary to this basic assumption. This was clearly brought home by the U.S. Supreme Court decision of 1954 in *Brown v. Board of Education*—a landmark case that concluded that separate/segregated education for African Americans was unequal to that education provided for White Americans. In essence, the court argued that every effort must be made to guarantee equal access to education regardless of race. This decision was reinforced for Latinos, Asian Americans, Native Americans, and women in the significant U.S. congressional activity during the War on Poverty era of the 1960s and 1970s. In 1964, Title IV of the Civil Rights Act banned discrimination on the grounds of race, color, or national origin in any program receiving federal financial assistance (Title VII of that act addressed educational equity across gender). Not coincidentally, the Elementary and Secondary Act of 1965 began to provide millions of federal dollars in assistance to state and local school systems. To receive these increased federal funds, school systems had to meet the mandated standards of nondiscrimination.

This legislation banned recipients of federal resources from "restricting an individual in any way in the enjoyment of any advantage or privilege enjoyed by others receiving any service, financial aid or benefit under the (federally) funded program" (Equal Education Opportunities and Transportation Act, 1974). Moreover, recipients of federal funds were prohibited from using criteria or methods that would impede the accomplishment of the objectives of the federally funded program with respect to individuals of a particular race, color, or national origin. Significantly, other provisions of this legislation included the possibility of a private cause of action (a lawsuit) against federally funded institutions to rectify issues of discrimination. This meant that Chicano/a students and their parents need not wait for the federal government to find funded programs out of compliance; they could independently move the courts to seek relief. And they did. A barrage of legal action aimed at addressing education inequities soon followed.

In addition to legal action, further administrative and legislative activity resulted from this initial legislative attention to equal educational opportunity. In 1970, the Department of Health, Education and Welfare issued a memorandum, later referred to as the May 25 Memorandum, which clarified the mandate of the 1964 Civil Rights Act with respect to the non-English-speaking student populations: "Where a liability to speak and understand the English language excludes national origin minority group children from effective participation in the educational program offered by a school district, the district must take affirmative steps to rectify the language deficiency in order to open instructional programs to these students" (May 25 Memorandum, 1970, p. 3). The 1974 Equal Educational Opportunities and Transportation Act made this administrative protection for language-diverse students into formal law. The act makes "the failure by an educational agency to make appropriate action to overcome language barriers that impede equal participation by its students in its educational programs" an unlawful denial of equal educational opportunities.

Taken together, these legal and legislative initiatives placed the societal values regarding the importance of education into a form that was of direct relevance to Chicanos/as. In essence, any child, regardless of race, color, national origin, and language, was entitled equally to the benefits of educational endeavors. This equal education approach to the growing number of culturally diverse students pervaded our schools for over two decades and was reinforced by related adjudication in *Lau v. Nichols* (1974) and *Castañeda v. Pickard* (1981). Equal access is still a part of what drives many educational initiatives for students who arrive at the schoolhouse door speaking a language other than English.

It is important to note that these policies had important theoretical foundations and related practice implications. At a theoretical level, children who came to school not speaking English were perceived to have particular deficiencies that required particular instructional attention. In the 1968 Bilingual Education Act, such theory supported the use of the child's native language, when deemed necessary, as a tool for the instruction of English (August & García, 1988). Using a child's native language as a tool for the instruction of English led to a greater understanding of the benefits of bilingualism in the classroom that enable the teachers and students to create an effective teaching and learning environment, thereby challenging deficit theories that always viewed native language as a hindrance to process of learning and teaching. These new theories also began to link the language of the bilingual to cognition and, therefore, to academic achievement (Cummins, 1979). Cummins, in particular, criticized the notions that bilingualism produced negative intellectual or academic consequences and theorized further that bilingualism, when achieved at high levels of proficiency, may even enhance cognitive functioning (Cummins, 1986). The notion that bilingualism is a detriment to academic achievement is no longer supported by research (Sue & Padilla, 1986).

Policies and theories implemented in instructional practice generated the proliferation of "transitional bilingual education" for Chicanos/as. The goal of these approaches was to use Spanish as a means to learn English and to begin subject matter learning in areas such as literacy and mathematics (August & García, 1988). Teachers in bilingual programs began to teach reading to young children first in Spanish and to develop instruction in Spanish related to other subject matter learning goals. Even so, the explicit intent of such instruction was to move the students from bilingual programs into English-only instruction, making the transition in the early or late elementary grades without the specific goal of maintaining Spanish. Gone from accepted practice were the days when students were punished for speaking Spanish and Spanish-speaking parents were requested to speak and teach English to their children. The return of the child's and family's language into the curriculum had an important impact on the remainder of the curriculum. It became clear that equal access through opportunities to use the native language was not the only stimulus driving educational interests for culturally and linguistically diverse students.

MULTICULTURAL EDUCATION

Another important educational thrust of particular consequence to Chicano/a students came from the educational establishment and minority groups themselves. Aimed primarily at curriculum reform, multicultural education initiatives suggested that curriculum in this country should reflect the diverse character of the nation's cultural and linguistic groups. Educators recommended multicultural education for several reasons (Sue & Padilla, 1986). First and foremost, they argued, the curriculum should better represent the actual contributions by various cultural groups to this country's society. Curriculum in schools was criticized for its unbalanced emphasis of Western European values, history, literature, and general worldview (Banks, 1982). The United States was not a monolithic culture, and the curriculum should reflect its cultural diversity. Second, they suggested that a multicultural curriculum would inform majority children of minority group contributions and at the same time reaffirm minority group significance to society, thus helping minority students develop positive self-esteem. Third, as Grant and Sleeter (1987) suggest, multicultural education was perceived as a school reform movement aimed at changing the content and instructional processes within schools. Its goal was not only to provide equal educational opportunity, but also to enhance the schooling experience for all students.

Multicultural education as a concept took several distinct approaches to the instruction of students in general, and Chicano/a students in particular. However, the major impact of this reform movement has been in the area of curriculum—that is, the area of schooling that addresses the content of instruction. In essence, this major reform attempted to address what knowledge students should be gaining. Further, it made quite clear that we needed to know more about the United States' diverse cultural groups and that we needed to dispense this knowledge in our everyday schooling endeavors. While there was overall agreement about the importance of including curriculum that addressed racial/ethnic diversity, there was some disagreement regarding the goals of such activity. For Chicanos/as, issues regarding maintaining and developing Spanish-language skills, cultural nurturance, and overall educational equity came to the foreground.

Sleeter and Grant (1987) have provided an excellent review of these discrepant goals and the overall limited consequences of the multicultural education reform movement on American education, which is useful in understanding the role of such reform for Chicanos/as. Within a model described as "teaching the multiculturally different," the original goal was to teach educators to support culturally different students academically to facilitate their success in mainstream schooling. Although not directly implying the need to "change" or "assimilate" children of different backgrounds into the mainstream, this goal seemed to serve as a foundation for this form of multicultural education. This prescription was usually subtractive in nature. That is, children with different cultures and languages were asked to leave their cultural attributes behind through the use of bridge-like educational programs that promised access and success in academic and, later, societal domains. Within this view, multicultural education was seen as a temporary, highly directed educational endeavor that would lead to a melting pot filled with a successful and more homogeneous student population.

Early vestiges of Head Start reflect this multicultural approach. For preschool children ages three to four, Head Start and its extension for the early elementary student, Follow Through, were perceived as bridges to the mainstream academic environment. Other compensatory education programs such as Title I (which address underachievement directly) are in this same category of educational programs meant to bridge non-achieving students with those who are achieving academically. They are temporary in nature, with goals of transitioning unsuccessful students to success through a process likened to natural cultural assimilation. In this process, immigrants with very diverse cultures and languages come to embrace mainstream American values and acquire English as their main mode of communication. Schools were meant to serve as an organized vehicle to hasten this natural form of assimilation.

These multicultural educational efforts did consider important the cultural diversity of the students, families, and communities they served. In this way, they were distinct from earlier Americanization educational strategies. Some multicultural education efforts combined the bridging goal with another enhancing human relations (Colangelo, Foxley, & Dustin, 1982; Perry, 1975). In so doing, it was assumed that diverse populations would better understand each other, and this better understanding would enhance communication and social relations. In contrast to the assimilation and bridging goals and procedures, educational programs reflecting this approach to multicultural education asked students to add knowledge about other groups not like their own and use it in ways that would enhance social accommodation of diversity—"Let's learn to get along better." The most dramatic example of a large-scale program of this type is in the Canadian province of Quebec, where French-speaking populations (Francophones) were in constant social and economic dispute with English-speaking populations (Anglophones). The Canadian solution to this social relations problem was Bilingual-Bicultural Immersion Education (Lambert, 1969). Anglophone children were placed in French-only programs for the first three years of their educational experience. The goal of the program was for children over time to acquire knowledge of both the language and the culture of Francophones with the expected product of better human relations. Program evaluations indicate that these expectations were achieved without any academic achievement cost to children learning academic content in a language other than their own home language (Swain & Lapkin, 1991).

Another approach to multicultural education has been much more "activist" in nature. Its goals aim to promote respect for diversity. Beyond just acquiring and disseminating information regarding cultural diversity, this approach aims to develop intellectual and societal acceptance of cultural diversity as a goal in and of itself (Banks, 1981, 1984; Fishman, 1989; García, 1979; Gay, 1975; Gollnick & Chinn, 1986; Sleeter & Grant, 1987). This approach has been the most popular and most influential in the last decade, and has attempted to bring together issues of race, ethnicity, gender, and social class. The thrust of such initiatives has been to permeate the curriculum with issues of diversity in literature, social thought, scientific approaches, and historical construction while serving up criticism of standardized curricula, particularly those that reflect Western European contributions as the standard. A corollary of this approach is the overall multicultural and social reconstructionist perspective that researchers espoused (Appleton, 1983; Suzuki, 1984). In essence, students are asked by their instructors and related curriculum to become social critics, particularly in relation to issues of social injustice. For Chicanos/as, the development of Chicano Studies programs in institutions of higher education and the call for similar curricular offerings within the K-12 sector are examples of this educational movement.

It is important to keep in mind that the theoretical underpinnings for this type of multicultural activity for Chicanos/as rests in the importance of "ethnic identity" and "positive self-concept" for enhancing academic outcomes (García, 1994). Moreover, theory regarding cultural and social organization of minorities in the society began to receive attention. Ogbu and Matute-

Bianchi (1986), for example, in *Beyond Language: Social and Cultural Factors in Educating Language Minority Students,* called for bilingual educators to carefully consider cultural and language issues if they were to serve Chicano/a students effectively.

In practice, education of Chicanos/as became more than language and transitioning concerns. Embedded in teachers' repertoires is the importance of recognizing and nurturing cultural attributes of students and families. Curriculum that is more relevant to the "Chicano" experience is more likely to be produced and used in schools serving Chicano students. Proactive multicultural education has emerged from the bilingual education community in the United States. In the last five years, dual immersion programs have been introduced into large Latino school districts in California, New York, Texas, Illinois, and Florida. These programs aim to produce a student population that is bilingual and bicultural. For Anglo and English-speaking students, the goal is to acquire English and Spanish language and literacy. Dual Immersion programs generally begin at the kindergarten level. Anglo and English-speaking students are exposed to Spanish-language instruction in classrooms with Chicano/a Spanish-speaking students, in addition to a curriculum that presents and addresses bicultural concerns, for example, the case of codeswitching (moving between Spanish and English), an acknowledged form of communication among Chicanos/as. For Chicano/a students in these programs, the goals are the same. These goals are in concert with the notion of actively promoting cultural diversity, with a healthy academic respect for the linguistic and cultural attributes of the diverse students involved (García, 1994).

Similar programs in the San Francisco, San Diego, Detroit, New York, and Chicago public schools are housed in magnet schools. These schools strive to expose a culturally diverse set of students to a thematically designated multilingual and multicultural curriculum. These programs attempt to integrate African American, Latino, Asian, and other culturally diverse student populations into these schools by recognizing diversity as a potential contribution. Attention to equal educational opportunity and multicultural education agendas is important to these programs.

Attention to multicultural education in this country over the last two decades has produced a set of debates and substantive accomplishments. New curriculum efforts by publishing companies have been launched to address concerns of "bias" raised by proponents of multicultural education (Gollnick & Chinn, 1986). Several states require teacher-training programs to provide language and cultural training at the pre-service level. Magnet and dual immersion bilingual education programs can be linked to the values and goals of multicultural education. The above discussion has attempted to place multicultural education into three broad categories based on the goals of distinct but not necessarily exclusive goal agendas: bridging/assimilation for culturally diverse students; enhancing human relations; and actively promoting cultural diversity as a societal goal. These goals build upon previous historical and ongoing initiatives dealing with equal educational opportunity that maintains that no child should be denied the benefits of education. These two educational initiatives have individually and together changed the nature of educational response to the growing presence of cultural diversity in our schools.

BEYOND MULTICULTURAL EDUCATION

Since the time of Socrates, educators and philosophers have argued for teaching that does more than impart knowledge and skills. Knowledge and skills are important enough, the argument goes, but true education and real teaching involve far more. They involve helping students understand, appreciate, and grapple with important ideas while developing a depth of understanding for a wide range of issues.

Yet teaching aimed at these important goals is presently most notable for its absence from the majority of U.S. classrooms. Tharp and Gallimore (1988) and García (1994) have attempted to provide evidence of this continuing trend in U.S. classrooms. Goodlad (1984) articulates it best in his classic study of U.S. schools when he reports that

> a great deal of what goes on in the classroom is like painting-by-numbers— filling in the colors called for by numbers on the page. . . . [Teachers] ask for specific questions calling essentially for students to fill in the blanks: "What is the capital city of Canada?" "What are the principal exports of Japan?" Students rarely turn things around by asking questions. Nor do teachers often give students a chance to romp with an open-ended question such as "What are your views on the quality of television?" (p. 108)

If this portrait is a true depiction of mainstream American classrooms, it may be even more true in classrooms serving low-income, linguistically and culturally diverse children. The perception is that these students require drill, review, and redundancy in order to progress academically, so their learning opportunities are likely to be excessively weighted toward low-level skills and factually oriented instruction. While such academically related skills and knowledge are important, equally important are the opportunities for students to be exposed to more cognitively demanding learning situations that promote "enlarged understanding of ideas and values" (Adler, 1982, p. 23). To that end, in the following discussion I will attempt to consolidate the more theoretical issues addressed earlier in this chapter.

The legacy of an equal educational opportunity and multicultural education era has left us with some clearly identifiable results. First, educational endeavors related to culturally diverse students have been pragmatically oriented—that is, they have focused on discrimination, desegregation, underachievement, low self-esteem, and non-English proficiency, and have advanced programs to address these problems. In doing so, these efforts tend to lack any substantive integrated theoretical underpinnings. Instead, the proposed solutions are driven by the social values associated with educational equity and pluralism. Conversely, a more theoretical approach would still consider discrimination, underachievement, and desegregation, but would attempt to first understand why such problems exist and then address solutions from that set of understandings (García, 1997).

The extended case study approach to cultural diversity is another legacy of the last three decades of educational activities that center on culturally diverse populations through multicultural education endeavors. Through this approach, the educational community has produced an extensive literature on the characteristics of different racial, ethnic, and ethnolinguistic groups. This work aimed at documenting the cultural and linguistic attributes of different groups in this country so these attributes could be understood and used to better serve these populations. It was not uncommon to learn that American Indian children were non-verbal (Appleton, 1983), Asian American children were shy (Sue & Okazaki, 1990), Mexican American children were cooperative (García, 1983), African American children were aggressive (Boykin, 1983), and Anglo children were competitive (Kagan, 1983). Although this case study work was meant to further advance our understanding of culturally diverse students, it often had the effect instead of promoting stereotypes. Moreover, it did not recognize the broader, well-understood axiom of social scientists who study culture: there is as much heterogeneity within any cultural group as there is between cultural groups. Unfortunately, descriptively useful indicators took on explanatory values: if that student is Chicano/a, she must be cooperative and speak Spanish. Educational programs that were developed to address these cultural attributes soon discovered that many Chicano/a children were not cooperative and did not speak Spanish. If all Chicanos/as are not alike, if all African Americans are not alike, if all American Indians are not alike, then what set of knowledge about those groups is important educationally? What overarching conceptualizations of language, culture, and schooling are useful in understanding the educational framework of linguistic and culturally diverse Chicano/a students?

NEW THEORETICAL PERSPECTIVES

Mehan (1987) distinguishes between ethnic studies (the study of ethnic groups) on the one hand, and the sociocultural approach to language, culture, and education on the other. This distinction does not diminish the significance of ethnic studies. From the point of view of schooling, approaching the subject of social and cultural contexts of learning for culturally diverse youth with a focus on ethnic studies poses difficulties and can even be dangerous. Because an educator cannot possibly acquire a sufficient ethnological knowledge base of the groups he or she will encounter, the knowledge they do acquire tends to be stereotypic. These stereotypic notions often lead to a cultural deprivation view; that is, because a culture is characterized as different, it is characterized as deficient. With that in mind, the focus of educators should be on understanding the intersection of the school with the family, home, and community, rather than only on understanding the ethnic cultures of our diverse student bodies.

Schools, and certainly the classroom arrangements within them, can be seen as roughly analogous to a culture. The classroom has many, if not all, of the characteristics that anthropologists and sociologists tell us belong to culture, including tacit rules, patterns, formal structures of organization, and an ecological component. Most important are the tacit dimensions, the hidden dimensions that Philips (1984) and others (García, 1994; Tharp & Gallimore, 1988; Trueba, 1988) have described. We tend to think that school is about learning academic skills, but teachers, parents, and children often recognize that there are also numerous cultural demands of the school.

Some classic work has been done in this area by Labov (1972), who looked at the same children across different social domains of the school culture. Specifically, he observed educational testing encounters arranged in a number of ways. The theme of school culture is clear in his work: depending upon the context in which one observes a child, one gets a different view of that child. Much like Philips (1983), who found communicative differences between Warm Springs Native students and school, Labov found significant communicative differences between the domains of the school. In short, if you look at a child in only one situation, you get only one kind of picture.

Moll and Díaz (1986) contributed to this understanding of context specificity. They observed children, not at home and at school, but under different constraints of instruction. The children were enrolled in a bilingual program, the goal of which was to allow Spanish-speaking children to acquire English as quickly as possible. At this school, the children had two teachers, and were taught by one in English and by the other in Spanish. Moll and Díaz videotaped lessons in both settings and asked each teacher to watch the videotapes of the other. The Spanish-speaking teacher was appalled when she saw the children in the English-speaking teacher's classroom: they were not reading. They were engaged in drill and practice activities with very little cognitive activity taking place. In the Spanish-speaking classroom, where the children were given comprehension activities, they were reading in Spanish. Moll and Díaz discussed this situation with the Spanish-speaking teacher and hypothesized that reading is specific to the domain of language. So they performed some experiments. They had the children use the reading comprehension skills they had acquired in Spanish in reading English. In doing this, they violated one of the basic tenets of bilingual education—that the two languages be kept separate. When they let the children call upon all resources they had available, their progress was remarkable. They began comprehending written English very well, even though they did not have complete mastery of the language. A bridge between the two cultures was developed to the school's goals.

Gallimore, Boggs, and Jordan's (1974) study of the Kamehameha Early Education Program (KEEP) is another example of how cultural bridge-building can be accomplished. Inherent in this approach is the idea that one does not ask children to leave their cultures at the classroom door. One recommendation is to allow cultural elements that are relevant to the children to enter the classroom. Through this approach, known as "scaffolding," the school constructs a set of supports for children that enables them to move through relevant experiences from the home towards the demands of the school, as representative of the society. It is not a subtraction of culture, and is not an attempt to reproduce home environments in the context of the school. The idea is to allow the child to respect the demands of the classroom while preserving the integrity of the home. For Chicanos/as, it means adopting educational respect for the social and cognitive roots of human development that are present in the home and family (García, 1997; Valdez, 1996).

At this time it seems conceptually appropriate to frame this discussion in a broad, educationally relevant theoretical continuum. At one end of this continuum, it can be argued that addressing culturally diverse populations calls for a deeper understanding of the interaction of a student's culture and the prevailing school culture (Tharp, 1989). This cultural significance position is supported by a rich contribution of research that suggests that the educational failure of "diverse" student populations is related to this culture clash between home and school (Boykin, 1986; García, 1988; Heath, 1983; Rodríguez, 1989; Vogt, Jordan, & Tharp, 1987; Wiesner, Gallimore, & Jordan, 1988). In essence, researchers have suggested that, without attending to the distinctiveness of the contribution of culture, educational endeavors for these culturally distinct students are likely to fail. Theoretically, students do not succeed because the difference between school culture and home culture leads to an educationally harmful dissonance—that is, to a home-to-school "mismatch." Directly enunciating this position, Sue and Padilla (1986) argue, "The challenge for educators is to identify critical differences between and within ethnic minority groups and to incorporate this information into classroom practice" (p. 62).

At the other extreme of this theoretical continuum lies the position that instructional programs must insure the implementation of appropriate general principles of teaching and learning. The academic failure of any student rests on the failure of instructional personnel to implement what we know "works." Using the now common educational analytical tool known as meta-analysis, Walberg (1986) suggests that educational research synthesis has identified robust indicators of instructional conditions that have academically significant effects across various conditions and student groups. Other reviews (Baden & Maehr, 1986; Bloom, 1984; Slavin, 1989) have articulated this same position. In this vein, a number of specific instructional strategies, including direct instruction (Rosenshine, 1986), tutoring (Bloom, 1984), frequent evaluation of academic progress (Slavin, Karweit, & Madden, 1989), and cooperative learning (Slavin, 1989), have been particular candidates for the "what works with everyone" category. Expectations play an important role in other formulations of this underachievement dilemma. Levin (1989) and Snow (1990) have suggested that students, teachers, and school professionals in general have low academic expectations of culturally and linguistically diverse students. The popular dramatization of high school math instructor Jaime Escalante in the film *Stand and Deliver* exemplifies this position. Raising student motivation in conjunction with enhancing academic expectations through challenging curriculum is a prescribed solution. Implied in this "general principle" position is that the educational failure of diverse populations can be eradicated by the systemic and effective implementation of these general principles of instruction understood to work with "all" students.

Interspersed along this continuum are other significant conceptual contributions that attempt to explain the academic underachievement of culturally and linguistically diverse students. Freire (1970) has argued that educational initiatives cannot expect academic or intellectual success under oppressive social circumstances. He and others (Cummins, 1986; Pearl, 1991) suggest that such oppression taints any curriculum or pedagogy, and only a pedagogy of empowerment can fulfill the lofty goals of educational equity and achievement. Similarly, Bernstein (1971), Laosa (1982), and Wilson (1987) point to socioeconomic factors that influence the organization of schools and instruction. Over generations, extensive exposure to poverty and related disparaging socioeconomic conditions significantly influence the teaching/learning process in the home, the community, and schools. The result is disastrous, long-term, educational failure and social disruption of family and community. Ogbu and Matute-Bianchi (1986) offer an alternative, macrosociological perspective with regard to the academic failure of culturally and linguistically diverse students. Their conceptualization interprets this country's present social approach to several immigrant and minority populations as "caste-like." In this theoretical attempt to explain underachievement, they argue that these populations form a layer of our society that is not expected to excel academically or economically and is therefore treated as a "caste-like population." These expectations are transformed into parallel self-perceptions by these populations, with academic underachievement and social withdrawal as the result.

Clearly, the above conceptualizations are not presented here in any comprehensive manner. Moreover, the "cultural match/mismatch" to a "general principles" continuum need not be interpreted as a set of incompatible approaches in the attempt to understand the educational circumstances of culturally diverse students. These conceptual contributions have not espoused multicultural education principles or educational equity policies. Instead, they have attempted to address the educational issues of educating a culturally diverse population by searching for explanations for educational underachievement. For Chicanos/as, this means directly understanding and educationally acting upon the linguistic and cultural characteristics that are unique to them as an ethnic group and as individual students.

These contributions take into consideration the work of Freire (1970), Bernstein (1971), Cummins (1979, 1986), Heath (1986), Ogbu (1986), Trueba (1987), Levin (1988), and Tharp and Gallimore (1988), who have suggested that the schooling vulnerability of culturally diverse students must be understood within the broader contexts of society's circumstances for students in and out of schools. That is, no quick fix is likely under social and schooling conditions that mark students for special treatment of their cultural differences without consideration of the psychological and social circumstances in which each student resides. This approach warns us against the isolation of any single attribute—whether it be poverty, language difference, or learning potential—as the only variable of importance. This more comprehensive view of the schooling process includes an understanding of the relationship between home and school, the psycho-sociocultural incongruities between the two, and the resulting effects on learning and achievement (Tharp & Gallimore, 1988).

A NEW PEDAGOGY

Since the end of the nineteenth century, "act psychology" has generated a set of understandings that focuses on the assertion that perceiving, remembering, and organizing—ultimately, knowing—are all acts of construction. These assertions take into consideration that our knowing is related to the circumstances we come to know. This "constructionist" perspective is rooted in the notion that knowing is a result of continued constructions—the give and take between old information, its organization or structures, and new information, processes of organizing that information, and the specific circumstances in which all occurs. Embedded in a "constructionist" perspective for Chicano/a students is the understanding that language, culture, and their accompanying values are constructed in home and community environments (Cummins, 1986; Goldman & Trueba, 1987; Heath, 1981); that children come to school with some constructed knowledge about many things (Goodman, 1980; Hall, 1987); and that children's development and learning is best understood as the interaction of previous and present linguistic, sociocultural, and cognitive constructions (Trueba, 1988). A more appropriate perspective of learning, then, is one that recognizes that learning is enhanced when it occurs in contexts that are socioculturally, linguistically, and cognitively meaningful for the learner. In other words, they bridge previous "constructions" with present "constructions" (Díaz, Moll, & Mehan, 1986; Heath, 1986; Scribner & Cole, 1981; Wertsch, 1985).

Such meaningful events, however, are not generally accessible to culturally diverse children. Those schooling practices that contribute to the academic vulnerability of this student population and tend to dramatize the lack of fit between the student and the school experience are reflected in the monolithic culture transmitted by the schools in the forms of pedagogy, curricula, instruction, classroom configuration, and language (Walker, 1987). These practices include the systematic exclusion of the students' histories, language, experience, and values from classroom curricula and activities (Giroux & McLaren, 1986; Ogbu, 1982); "tracking," which limits access to academic courses and learning environments that foster academic development and socialization (Durán, 1986; Eder, 1982; Oakes, 1990) or a percep-

CHART 1 *Conceptual Dimensions of a Responsive Pedagogy: Addressing Cultural and Linguistic Diversity in High-Performance Learning Communities*

Schoolwide Practices

- A vision defined by the acceptance and valuing of diversity—Americanization is NOT the goal
- Treatment of classroom practitioners as professionals, as colleagues in school development decisions
- Characterized by collaboration, flexibility, enhanced professional development
- Elimination (gradual or immediate) of policies that seek to categorize diverse students, thereby rendering their educational experiences inferior or limiting for further academic learning
- Reflection of and connection to the surrounding community—particularly with the families of the students attending the school

Teacher Practices

- Bilingual/bicultural skills and awareness
- High expectations of diverse students
- Treatment of diversity as an asset to the classroom
- Ongoing professional development on issues of cultural and linguistic diversity and practices that are most effective
- Basis of curriculum development to address cultural and linguistic diversity:
  1. Attention to and integration of home culture/practices
  2. Focus on maximizing student interactions across categories of Spanish and English proficiency and academic performance
  3. Focus on language development through meaningful interactions and communications

---

tion of self as a competent learner and language user; and limited opportunities to engage in developmentally and culturally appropriate learning that are not limited to teacher-led instruction (García, 1988).

The implication of this rethinking has a profound impact on the teaching/learning enterprise related to culturally diverse students (García, 1991). This new pedagogy redefines the classroom as a community of learners in which speakers, readers, and writers come together to define and redefine the meaning of the academic experience. It might be described by some as a pedagogy of empowerment (Cummins, 1986), by others as cultural learning (Heath, 1986; Trueba, 1987), and by others as a cultural view of providing instructional assistance/guidance (Tharp & Gallimore, 1988). In any case, it argues for the respect and integration of the students' values, beliefs, histories, and experiences, and recognizes the active role that students must play in the learning process. This responsive pedagogy expands students' knowledge beyond their own immediate experiences while using those experiences as a sound foundation for appropriating new knowledge. For many minority students, this includes the use of the native language and/or bilingual abilities that are a substantive part of a well-functioning social network in which knowledge is embedded.

A responsive pedagogy for academic learning requires redefinition of the instructor's role. Instructors of Chicano/a students must become familiar with the cognitive, social, and cultural dimensions of their students' learning. They also need to recognize the ways in which diversity of instruction, assessment, and evaluation affect learning. They should become more aware of the classroom curriculum, its purpose, and its implementation, and should recognize that the configuration of the classroom environment and the nature of interaction of students with the teacher and with other students is significant. Further, instructors must also recognize that the acquisition of academic content requires helping students display their knowledge in ways that suggest they are competent as learners and language users. Analysis of these dimensions will underscore the potential for equipping the classroom for the particularly sensitive task of insuring academic success with Chicano/a students.

Finally, teachers must destroy preconceived myths about learning processes and the potentially underprepared student, and, in particular, about those who come from lower socioeconomic households and/or homes in which English is not the primary language. For educators embracing this new concept of responsive pedagogy, new educational horizons for themselves and their students are not only possible but inevitable. Chart 1 summarizes these important dimensions of a responsive pedagogy within a high-performance learning community. This theoretical recasting of education for Chicanos/as is based on a distinct and important shift in understanding the future of education for this population of students, viewing their language and cultural differences as assets to be considered seriously in their education, as opposed to problems to be overcome.

NEW NATIONAL EDUCATIONAL POLICY IN 1994

From this theoretical context, specific changes in policy and practice with regard to Spanish-speaking Chicano/a students developed in the reauthorization of the Elementary and Secondary Education Act (ESEA) in 1994. This reauthorization influences the way the federal government articulates its role regarding the support of U.S. education and how it disperses federal resources in support of that articulated role. Typical rationales for changes in national educational policy are often related to crisis intervention: there is a problem and it must be addressed quickly, usually with more political and philosophical rhetoric than action. In the past, national policy for serving linguistically and culturally diverse students and their families was driven to a large extent by this "crisis" rationale. Accordingly, crises policies in this arena have been shortsighted, inflexible, and only minimally cohesive or integrated; they are not always informed by a strong conceptual, empirical, or practical knowledge base. Past articulations of Title I and Title VII of ESEA—both prime examples of the crisis intervention approach related to providing services to Chicano/a language-minority students—have suffered from these disadvantages.

New policies that emerged under the 1994 reauthorization of ESEA recognized the acute need to serve this student population, but they also recognized the need for the following in developing new policy:

- a new conceptual and empirical knowledge base;
- consultation within the field to capitalize on the wisdom of current policy, administration, curriculum, and instructional practice;
- cohesive policies and programs that integrate services and reflect the partnership between national, state, and local educational systems; and
- recognition of current demographic and budgetary realities that will be operative throughout this decade.

New policy directions, primarily those related to Title I and Title VII, will be implemented in line with the presuppositions mentioned above (see *Teachers College Record*, 1995, for a comprehensive description of the policy foundations for this reauthorization).

Knowledge Base The theoretical and empirical foundation established by recent findings has documented effective educational practices related to linguistically and culturally diverse students in selected sites throughout the United States (García, 1994). These descriptive studies identified specific academically successful schools and classrooms that served language-minority students. The case study approach adopted by these studies included examinations of preschool, elementary, and high school classrooms. Researchers interviewed teachers, principals, parents, and students, and conducted specific classroom observations to assess the "dynamics" of the instructional process.

These studies provide important insights with regard to practice: general instructional organization, literacy development, academic achievement in content areas like math and science, and the views of the students, teachers, administrators, and parents. In summary, studying these effective curricula, instructional strategies, and teaching staffs suggests that academic learning has its roots in sharing expertise and experiences through multiple avenues of communication. Effective curricula provide abundant and diverse opportunities for speaking, listening, reading, and writing, along with scaffolding, in order to help guide students through the learning process. Further, effective instruction encourages students to take risks, construct meaning, and seek reinterpretation of knowledge within compatible social contexts. Under this knowledge-driven curriculum, skills are tools for acquiring knowledge, not ends in themselves. The curriculum recognizes that any attempt to address the needs of these students in a deficit or "subtractive" mode is counterproductive. Instead, this knowledge base recognizes that educators must be "additive" in their approach to these students, adding to the rich intellectual, linguistic, academic, and cultural attributes and skills they bring to the classroom. Moreover, programs for these students are integrated and comprehensive and consider mastery of English and academic content equally important. Educational goals are the same as for all students. In short, linguistic and cultural diversity are treated as assets, not as problems.

Wisdom of Practice Too often, in the heat of legislation and the political process, policy development is highly centralized in the domains of various interest groups and professional policymakers. Therefore, the reauthorization initiative was crafted in consultation with diverse constituencies. In linguistically and culturally diverse communities, the federal government consulted the usual players, in particular educational groups, such as the National Association for Bilingual Education, and the Mexican American Legal Defense Fund.

This new ESEA legislation also organized broader efforts of school reform. Of particular significance was the Carnegie Foundation for the Advancement of Teaching's 1995 report, "The Basic School: A Community for Learning," which acknowledged the key components of an effective school that need to be brought together in an integrated and cohesive manner. It recognized that a good teacher alone, even in a good classroom guaranteeing effective teaching/learning, is not enough. Good schools are effective teaching/ learning communities that underline the significance of the early schooling years and place a high priority on the development of language and knowledge. "The Basic School" is based on the idea of best practice, a comprehensive plan for educational renewal. The work of the Stanford Working Group was of particular significance. This group, funded by the Carnegie Corporation of New York, consulted many individuals who represented a broad spectrum of theoretical, practical, and policy expertise. In published reports and various forums, they analyzed and articulated precise recommendations for policy and legislation related to linguistically and culturally diverse populations. Thus, new policy proposals were shaped with the consultation of others and incorporated shared wisdom from various established perspectives. Any proposed changes, if they are to be effective, must be embraced by those individuals and organizations presently in the field.

Cohesiveness The proposed policies have also attempted to view the provision of services to students in an integrated manner. Through new legislation in Goals 2000, the U.S. Department of Education has set the stage for the state-by-state development of standards. The passage of the Improving America's Schools Act (IASA), the specific 1994 title for the reauthorization of the ESEA, achieved an alignment of specific goals and standard initiatives with specific resource allocation policies. This alignment also recognizes the need for integration of federal, state, and local government efforts to enhance effectiveness and efficiency. Moreover, the federal role must allow flexibility at the state and local levels while requiring that all children achieve at the highest levels.

Title VII reauthorization—which addresses services to limited-English-proficient (LEP) students as a component of the IASA—is also highly congruent with the alignment principle. It is a key component of the integrated effort to address the educational needs of students effectively. Specifically, it will continue to provide for leadership and national, state, and local capacity-building with regards to educational services, professional development, and research related to linguistic and culturally diverse populations. Other programs, particularly Title I, are also important and will more directly increase the services needed by all students living in poverty, including those with limited English proficiency.

Demographics and Budget Realities The number of LEP students in our schools has increased over the last six years by nearly 70 percent, or approximately one million students. It is important to recognize that the national presence and diversity of this population is substantial, and that this trend will probably not subside. In the last decade, the number of states having LEP students as more than 2 percent of their student populations has increased by ten. Today, twenty states can be counted in such a column, and half of these have LEP student populations that vary between 5 percent and 25 percent. Presently, over 180 language groups are represented in programs funded under Title VII. The growth is highest in the five southwestern states (California, Arizona, Texas, New Mexico, and Colorado) that have the largest concentrations of Chicanos/as.

Unfortunately, the fiscal resources available to meet the growing and diverse demands of this population are not likely to increase significantly. National, state, and local funding for these populations has not grown in proportion to their increase. Critics of bilingual education such as Linda Chávez and Congressman Bill Light of New York have indicated that bilingual education costs taxpayers anywhere from $5.5 to $15 billion dollars yearly. How they arrive at those figures is a mystery, since federal funding for bilingual education programs in the last decade has ranged between $125 and $200 million annually. The Clinton administration requested a 4 percent increase in these federal funds in 1996, but no major increases in this program area will likely be requested in the near future because of the politically volatile budgetary processes and the political debate regarding bilingual education (García, 1994). Although new legislation in the IASA regarding the dispersal of Title I funds to high-poverty areas should bring more resources to Chicano/a language-minority students, such funding will still be limited. This means that present resources must be used more efficiently.

RETURN TO "AMERICANIZATION"

English Only At this writing, the U.S. House of Representatives has passed H.R. 123, the English Language Empowerment Act of 1996, by a 259 to 169 vote; the Senate has not yet acted on similar legislation. This legislation would permit states to craft "English only" laws that could restrict the use of languages other than English in any form of governmental services, including education. It would also prohibit production of election materials in languages other than English. Such a national legislative provision would affect the use of Spanish in bilingual education programs that serve Chicano/a students.

Future federal legislation seems related to a recent U.S. Supreme Court decision regarding a case in Arizona. In March 1997, the Supreme Court declined to rule on the constitutionality of Arizona's English Only amendment. Article 28 of Arizona's constitution, also known as Proposition 106, was adopted by voters in 1988 and required all levels of state and local government to "act in English and no other language." Two lower federal courts overruled the measure as a violation of the First Amendment right to freedom of speech for state employees and elected officials. The Supreme Court threw out those decisions on procedural grounds—in effect dismissing the case after eight years of litigation without ruling on its merits.

For now, the practical impact will be negligible. A 1989 opinion by Arizona's attorney general minimized the restrictive impact of Article 28, arguing that it would not prohibit employees from using languages other than English "to facilitate the delivery of government services." A separate challenge to this article is under consideration by the Arizona Supreme Court, and the measure has already been ruled unconstitutional by a lower state judge. Until that case is resolved, the English Only amendment will not be enforced. Any decision by the Arizona Supreme Court will, of course, be appealed to the U.S. Supreme Court—further delaying a final disposition of the case.

"English Only" State Initiative   A new California state initiative is the most recent effort to restrict the use of a language other than English in the delivery of educational services to non-English-speaking children. The new ballot measure, identified as "English for All Children," passed by 61 percent of the vote in June 1998. It proposes to:

1. require that all children be placed in English-language classrooms, and that English-language learners be educated through a prescribed methodology identified as "Structured English Immersion";
2. prescribe methodology that would be provided over a temporary transition period, not normally to exceed one year;
3. allow instruction in the child's native language only in situations in which a waiver is granted, done so in writing, done so yearly by parents, and also requiring a school visit by a parent; and
4. allow native-language instruction only if the student already had mastered English, was over ten years of age, and such instruction was approved by the principal and the teacher.

The English Only initiative would additionally allow native-language instruction only through an exclusionary and complicated process: twenty or more parents at each grade level at each school would have to request waivers for native-language instruction; then each year they would have to request such instruction again and personally come to the school to negotiate written consent to continue native-language instruction. Moreover, teachers, administrators, and school board members would be held personally liable for fees and damages by the child's parents and guardians for not implementing any or all provisions of Proposition 227. These provisions, taken together, are the most restrictive measures yet proposed for serving language-minority students either nationally or within any state, via legislation or the courts. The initiative is presently being adjudicated in both state and federal court venues. These court rulings will have a substantive impact on the future of bilingual education policy and its practice within and outside the state of California. This articulation of policy and practice returns the education of many non-English-speaking Chicanos/as to the earlier days of Americanization policy, practice, and theory. Paradoxically, such policy and practice is completely at odds with recent federal policy, effective classroom practices, and new theoretical formulations for these same students.

CONCLUSION

In summary, the education of bilingual Chicano/a students remains a tapestry of theory, policy, and practice that historically and presently ranges from Americanization, equal educational opportunity, multicultural education, and the more encompassing approach I have identified as a "responsive pedagogy." This continuum of education addresses these students in very different ways and relies on distinct theories of linguistic, cognitive, and social development, teaching/learning, and the role of schooling. At one end of this theory/policy/practice continuum is the acceptance of linguistic and cultural diversity as a resource in schooling, while at the other end lies the notion that diversity is a problem in achieving the goals of an educated society. With regard to the education of Chicanos/as, this continuum poses an ongoing tension and debate that is likely to remain unresolved in the near future.

Therefore, for those of us dedicated to continuing this debate in a way that can inform better educational outcomes for Chicano/a students, I outline a research agenda designed to pursue the challenge of addressing cultural and linguistic diversity that focuses on improved teaching and learning for Chicanos/as. Certain elements of schoolwide and individual teaching practices increase the likelihood that culturally and linguistically diverse students can be academically successful. The literature reviewed in this chapter also provides considerable guidance in the particular research questions that can serve as a starting point for developing useful strategies for schools.

Beginning with the core issue of student engagement in the classroom, we know from the literature on language acquisition and effective instruction for language minority students that these students are much more likely to be engaged learners in environments in which the curriculum and teaching approaches build on the diversity of the students and teachers (Pease-Alvarez, Espinosa, & García, 1991; Wong-Fillmore, 1991). This also means that most teachers must have a familiarity with or close connection to the home communities that the students represent in the schools if they are to develop practices that reflect experiences that will allow students to build an understanding of complex ideas and new concepts (Pease-Alvarez et al., 1991). In addition, as discussed previously, engaged learning for culturally and linguistically diverse students necessitates considerable time devoted to interactions with each other and with the adults in the school community to develop improved social and communication skills, as well as to create a "safe" learning environment. Finally, assessments of student progress in learning various subjects, developing conceptual understandings of subjects, and acquiring particular skills need to be aligned with curricular and instructional goals; assessments also have to involve all students as a means of truly gauging the quality of the learning environment. In other words, if linguistically and/or culturally diverse students are systematically left out of regular schoolwide or classroom assessments, the results of such efforts cannot begin to address all of the learning that goes on in a school—or, more importantly, the areas in which further attention should be devoted.

With these elements in mind, a set of critical questions helps guide a systematic assessment of responsive learning communities at the school-site level:

- How are language, culture, and student diversity addressed in the instruction, curriculum, and assessment practices? What are the effects of these practices?
- What are the resources, experiences, and structures that contribute to the professional development of the school community? How are these related to student achievement?
- What is the school vision and mission(s)? How are issues of language, culture, and diversity addressed in these? How are these articulated for/to teachers, students, district and school administrators and policy bodies, and parents?
- How do power relationships in society and the educational and local community get embedded in the school?
- What are the prevailing norms and underlying theories that shape the roles, expectations, and standards? How do these change as schools create and implement new policies and practices aimed at developing responsive performance learning communities?

This agenda is not all-inclusive, but it should guide us in the new generation of research, theory, policy, and practice, and could make a difference in the future education of Chicanos/as.

REFERENCES

Adler, M. (1982). *The Paideia proposal: An educational manifesto.* New York: Macmillan.

Appleton, C. (1983). *Cultural pluralism in education: Theoretical foundations.* New York: Longman.

August, D., & García, E. (1988). *Language minority education in the United States: Research, policy and practice.* Chicago: Charles C. Thomas.

Baden, B., & Maehr, M. (1986). Conforming culture with culture: A perspective for designing schools for children of diverse sociocultural backgrounds. In R. Feldman (Ed.), *The social psychology of education* (pp. 289–309). Cambridge, MA : Harvard University Press.

Banks, J. (1981). *Multiethnic education: Theory and practice.* Boston: Allyn & Bacon.

Banks, J. (1982). Educating minority youths: An inventory of current theory. *Education and Urban Society, 15*(1), 88–103.

Banks, J. (1984). *Teaching strategies for ethnic studies.* Boston: Allyn & Bacon.

Bernstein, B. (1971). A sociolinguistic approach to socialization with some reference to educability. In B. Bernstein (Ed.), *Class, codes and control: Theoretical studies towards a sociology of language* (pp. 146–171). London: Routledge & Kegan Paul.

Bloom, B. (1984). The search for methods of group instruction as effective as one-to-one tutoring. *Educational Leadership, 41*(8), 4–17.

Boyer, E. L. (1995). *The basic school: A community for learning.* Princeton, NJ: Carnegie Foundation for the Advancement of Teaching.

Boykin, A. W. (1983). The academic performance of Afro-Americans. In J. T. Spence (Ed.), *Achievement and achievement motives: Psychological and sociological approaches* (pp. 143–164). San Francisco: W. H. Freeman.

Boykin, A. W. (1986). The triple quandary and the schooling of Afro-American children. In U. Neisser (Ed.), *The school achievement of minority children* (pp. 57–92). New York: New Perspectives.

Brown v. Board of Education, 347 U.S. 483 (1954): 686.

Civil Rights Act of 1964, 88-352 (1964).

Castañeda v. Pickard, 648F. 2nd 989 (1981), (1007 5th Cir 1981); 1035. ct. 3321.

Colangelo, N., Foxley, C. H., & Dustin, D. (Eds.). (1982). *The human relations experience.* Monterey, CA: Brooks/Cole.

Cummins, J. (1979). Linguistic interdependence and the educational development of bilingual children. *Review of Educational Research, 19,* 222–251.

Cummins, J. (1986). Empowering minority students: A framework for intervention. *Harvard Educational Review, 56,* 18–36.

Dewey, J. (1921). *Reconstruction and philosophy.* London: University of London Press.

Díaz, S., Moll, L. C., & Mehan, H. (1986). Sociocultural resources in instruction: A context-specific approach. In Bilingual Education Office (Ed.), *Beyond language: Social and cultural factors in schooling language minority students* (pp. 197–230). Los Angeles: California State University, Evaluation, Dissemination, and Assessment Center.

Durán, R. (1986). *Improving Hispanics' educational outcomes: Learning and instruction.* Unpublished manuscript.

Eder, D. (1982). Difference in communication styles across ability groups. In L. C. Wilkinson (Ed.), *Communicating in the classroom* (pp. 245–263). New York: Academic Press.

Elam, S. (1972). Acculturation and learning problems of Puerto Rican children. In F. Corradasco & E. Bucchini (Eds.), *The Puerto Rican community and its children on the mainland* (pp. 83–99). Metuchen, NJ: Scarecrow Press.

Elementary and Secondary Education Act of 1965, Title II, Pub. L. 89-10, Stat. 27(1965).

Equal Educational Opportunities and Transportation Act of 1974, Pub. L. 93-830, Stat. 514(1974).

Fishman, J. (1989). Bias and anti-intellectualism: The frenzied fiction of "English only." In J. A. Fishman (Ed.), *Language and ethnicity in minority sociolinguistic perspective* (pp. 146–169). London: Multilingual Matters.

Freire, P. (1970). *Pedagogy of the oppressed.* New York: Seabury Press.

Gallimore, R., Boggs, J. W., & Jordan, C. (1974) *Culture, behavior and education: A study of Hawaiian-Americans.* Beverly Hills, CA: Sage.

García, E. (1983). *The Mexican-American child: Language, cognition, and socialization.* Tempe: Arizona State University, Center for Bilingual Education.

García, E. (1988). Effective schooling for language minority students. In National Clearinghouse for Bilingual Education (Ed.), *New focus* (Monograph). Arlington, VA: Author.

García, E. (1991). *The education of linguistically and culturally diverse students: Effective instructional practices.* Santa Cruz, CA: National Center for Research on Cultural Diversity and Second Language Learning.

García, E. (1994). Addressing the challenges of diversity. In S. L. Kagan & B. Weissbourd (Eds.), *Putting families first* (pp. 243–275). San Francisco: Jossey-Bass.

García, E. (1997). The education of Hispanics in early childhood: Of roots and wings. *Young Children, 52*(3), 5–14.

García, R. (1979). *Teaching in a pluralistic society.* New York: Harper & Row.

Gay, G. (1975). Organizing and designing culturally pluralistic curriculum. *Educational Leadership, 33,* 176–183.

Giroux, H. A., & McLaren, P. (1986). Teacher education and the politics of engagement: The case for democratic schooling. *Harvard Educational Review, 56,* 213–238.

Goldman, S., & Trueba, H. (Eds.). (1987). *Becoming literate in English as a second language: Advances in research and theory.* Norwood, NJ: Ablex.

Gollnick, D. M., & Chinn, P. C. (1986). *Multicultural education in a pluralistic society.* New York: Maxwell Macmillan International Press.

González, G. (1990). *Chicano education in the segregation era: 1915–1945.* Philadelphia: Balch Institute.

Goodlad, J. (1984). *A place called school.* New York: McGraw-Hill.

Goodman, Y. (1980). The roots of literacy. In M. P. Douglass (Ed.), *Reading: A humanizing experience* (pp. 286–301). Claremont, CA: Claremont Graduate School.

Grant, C. A., & Sleeter, C. (1987). An analysis of multicultural education in the United States. *Harvard Educational Review, 57,* 421–444.

Hall, N. (1987). *The emergence of literacy.* Portsmouth, NH: Heinemann.

Heath, S. B. (1981). Towards an ethnohistory of writing in American education. In M. Farr-Whitman (Ed.), *Variation in writing: Functional and linguistic cultural differences* (vol. 1, pp. 225–246). Hillsdale, NJ: Lawrence Erlbaum.

Heath, S. B. (1983). *Ways with words: Language, life, and work in communities and classrooms.* Cambridge, Eng.: Cambridge University Press.

Heath, S. B. (1986). Sociocultural contexts of language development. In California Department of Education (Ed.), *Beyond language: Social and cultural factors in schooling language minority students* (pp. 143–186). Los Angeles: California State University, Evaluation, Dissemination, and Assessment Center.

Kagan, S. (1983). Interpreting Chicano cooperativeness: Methodological and theoretical considerations. In J. L. Martínez & R. H. Mendoza (Eds.), *Chicano psychology* (2nd ed., pp. 289–333). Orlando, FL: Academic Press.

Labov, W. (1972). *Sociolinguistic patterns.* Philadelphia: University of Pennsylvania Press.

Lambert, W. E. (1969). Psychological studies of the interdependencies of the bilingual's two languages. In J. Puhvel (Ed.), *Substance and structure of language* (pp. 163–181). Berkeley: University of California Press.

Laosa, L. M. (1982). School, occupation, culture and family: The impact of parental schooling on the parent-child relationship. *Journal of Educational Psychology, 74,* 791–827.

Lau v. Nichols. (1974). United States Supreme Court, 414 US 563.

Levin, H. M. (1989). Financing the education of at-risk students. *Educational Evaluation and Policy Analysis, 11*(1), 47–60.

Levin, I. (1988). *Accelerated schools for at-risk students* (CPRE Research Report Series RR-010). New Brunswick, NJ: Rutgers University Center for Policy Research in Education.

Mead, M. (1939). *Culture of the islander.* New York: Academic Press.

Mehan, H. (1987). Language and schooling. In G. Spindler & D. Spindler (Eds.), *Interpretive ethnography of education at home an abroad* (pp. 109–136). Hillsdale, NJ: Erlbaum Associates.

Moll, L., & Díaz, S. (1986). Bilingual communication and reading. *Elementary School Journal, 6,* 146–171.

Nieto, S. (1992). *Affirming diversity: The sociopolitical context of multicultural education.* New York: Longman.

Oakes, J. (1990). *Multiplying inequalities: The effects of race, social class, and tracking on opportunities to learn mathematics and science.* Santa Monica, CA: Rand.

Ogbu, J. (1982). Cultural discontinuities and schooling. *Anthropology and Education Quarterly, 13,* 168–190.

Ogbu, J. (1986). The consequences of the American caste system. In U. Neisser (Ed.), *The school achievement of minority children: New perspectives* (pp. 118–141). Hillsdale, NJ: Erlbaum Associates.

Ogbu, J. (1987). Variability in minority school performance: A problem in search of an explanation. *Anthropology and Education Quarterly, 18,* 312–334.

Ogbu, J., & Matute-Bianchi, M. E. (1986). Understanding sociocultural factors: Knowledge, identity and school adjustment. In Bilingual Education Office (Ed.), *Beyond language: Social and cultural factors in schooling language minority students* (pp. 73–142). Los Angeles: California State University, Evaluation, Dissemination, and Assessment Center.

Pearl, A. (1991). Democratic education: Myth or reality. In R. Valencia (Ed.), *Chicano school failure and success* (pp. 101–118). New York: Falmer Press.

Pease-Alvarez, L., Espinoza, P., & García, E. (1991). Effective instruction for language minority students: An early childhood case study. *Early Childhood Research Quarterly, 6,* 347–363.

Perry, J. (1975). Notes toward a multicultural curriculum. *English Journal, 64,* 12–18.

Philips, S. U. (1983). *The invisible culture: Communication in classroom and community on the Warm Springs Indian reservation.* New York: Longman.

Philips, S. U. (1984). *The invisible culture.* New York: Longman.

Rodríguez, C. E. (1989). *Puerto Ricans born in the U.S.A.* Winchester, MA: Unwin Hyman.

Rosenshine, B. (1986). Synthesis of research on explicit teaching. *Educational Leadership, 43*(3), 60–69.

Scribner, S., & Cole, M. (1981). *The psychology of literacy.* Cambridge, MA: Harvard University Press.

Skinner, B. F. (1957). *Verbal behavior.* Englewood Cliffs, NJ: Prentice-Hall.

Slavin, R. E. (1989). The pit and the pendulum: Fadism in education and how to stop it. *Phi Delta Kappan, 70,* 19–23.

Slavin, R., Karweit, N., & Madden, N. (1989). *Effective programs for students at risk.* Needham Heights, MA: Allyn & Bacon.

Sleeter, C. E., & Grant, C. A. (1987). An analysis on multicultural education in the U.S. *Harvard Educational Review, 57,* 421–443.

Snow, C. E. (1990). The development of definitional skill. *Journal of Child Language, 17,* 697–710.

Spener, D. (1988). Transitional bilingual education and the socialization of immigrants. *Harvard Educational Review, 58,* 133–153.

Sue, S., & Okazaki, S. (1990). Asian-American educational achievements: A phenomenon in search of an explanation. *American Psychologist, 45,* 913–920.

Sue, S., & Padilla, A. (1986). Ethnic minority issues in the United States: Challenges for the educational system. In California Bilingual Education (Ed.), *Beyond language: Social and cultural factors in schooling language minority students* (pp. 35–72). Los Angeles: California State University, Evaluation, Dissemination, and Assessment Center.

Suzuki, B. H. (1984). Curriculum transformation for multicultural education. *Education and Urban Society, 16,* 294–322.

Swain, M., & Lapkin, R. (1991). The influence of bilingualism on cognitive functioning. *Canadian Modern Language Review, 47,* 635–641.

Tharp, R. G. (1989). Psychocultural variables and k constants: Effects on teaching and learning in schools. *American Psychologist, 44*, 349–359.

Tharp, R., & Gallimore, R. (1988). *Rousing minds to life: Teaching, learning, and schooling in social.* New York : Cambridge University Press.

Thomas, S. V., & Park, B. (1921). *Culture and personality* (2nd ed.). New York: Random House.

Trueba, H. T. (1987). *Success or failure? Learning and the language minority student.* Scranton, PA: Harper & Row.

Trueba, H. T. (1988). Peer socialization among minority students: A high school dropout prevention program. In H. Trueba & C. Delgado-Gaitan (Eds.), *Schools and society: Learning content through culture* (pp. 54–71). New York: Praeger.

U.S. Department of Health, Education and Welfare. (1970, May 25). Memorandum regarding 1964 Civil Rights Act. Washington, DC: Author.

Valdez, G. (1996). *Con respeto.* New York: Teachers College Press.

Vogt, L., Jordan, C., & Tharp, R. (1987). Explaining school failure, producing school success: Two cases. *Anthropology and Education Quarterly, 18*, 276–286.

Walberg, H. (1986). Synthesis of research on teaching. In M. Wittrock (Ed.), *Handbook of research on teaching* (3rd ed., pp. 15–32). New York: Macmillan.

Walker, C. L. (1987). Hispanic achievements: Old views and new perspectives. In H. Trueba (Ed.), *Success or failure? Learning and the language minority student* (pp. 15–32). Cambridge, MA: Newbury House.

Weis, L. (1988). *Class, race and gender in American education.* Albany: State University of New York Press.

Wertsch, J. V. (1985). *Vygotsky and the social formation of the mind.* Cambridge, MA: Harvard University Press.

Wiesner, T. S., Gallimore, R., & Jordan, C. (1988). Unpackaging cultural effects on classroom learning. Native Hawaiian peer assistance and child-generated activity. *Anthropology and Education Quarterly, 19*, 327–353.

Wilson, W. J. (1987). *The truly disadvantaged: The inner city, the underclass, and public policy.* Chicago: University of Chicago Press.

Wong-Fillmore, L. (1991). When learning a second language means losing a first. *Early Childhood Research Quarterly, 6*, 323–347.

Staying in the Race:
The Challenge for Chicanos/as
in Higher Education

Patricia Gándara

The problem of underachievement among Chicanos and Chicanas and their noticeable absence from the rolls of college graduates is often referred to as a "pipeline problem," and the loss of Chicano/a students from the educational system throughout primary, secondary, and post-secondary schooling is characterized as "leakage" in the pipeline. The metaphor conjures images of a benign system in which some weakness or defect in the pipe simply allows these students to slip out. If there is any blame to be assigned, then it is toward a failure in the system to identify and "fix" the leakage points. The evidence, however, does not support this metaphor of a benign system. Rather, a review of the research on Chicano/a school failure points to a far more intentional system of obstacles placed in the path of students who enter the race full of optimism, but more often than not fail to navigate the hurdles and thus fall by the wayside. A more apt metaphor is that of a footrace with hurdles placed on the track. Hobbled at the outset by a history of poverty and disadvantage, most Chicanos/as fall victim to the hurdles and, calculating the odds against winning, take themselves out of the race. Hence, the challenge for Chicano/a students is not simply to avoid the breaks in the pipeline, but to actively surmount the obstacles placed before them and to stay in the race. The challenge for the system is to acknowledge the obstacles that have been placed in these students' paths and to remove them. More recently, however, the public has been reluctant to acknowledge that all students do not play on a level field, or run on the same smooth track. Actions have been taken by the electorate and the courts in California and Texas that have discounted the unequal circumstances faced by some minorities, and by Chicanos/as in particular, and compelled them to compete in a race with the odds stacked against them.

Chicanos/as are at the highest risk for school failure of all ethnic groups, in spite of the fact that their school performance is *not* the lowest among all groups. The reason for this is that Chicanos/as leave school without a diploma at significantly higher rates than any other group (De La Rosa & Maw, 1990). In 1995, Hispanics[1] trailed both White and African American students by 30 percentage points (57% versus 87%) with respect to high school completion, and only 8.9 percent of Hispanics in the 25- to 29-year-old age category had completed four or more years of college, while the figure for African Americans and Whites was 15.3 percent and 26 percent, respectively (Carter & Wilson, 1997).

After slow but relatively steady progress in college attendance and degree completion over the last several decades, Chicanos/as are now faced with the prospect of a rapid erosion of those gains. In 1980, a year in which Latinos (about two-thirds of whom are of Mexican origin nationwide) were about 6.5 percent of the U.S. population, they accounted for only 2.3 percent of all bachelor's degrees conferred. By 1994, with a population share in excess of 10 percent, Latinos garnered only 4.3 percent of all bachelor's degrees, a substantial improvement, but still far below population parity. Moreover, in 1993, the Latino Eligibility Task Force, a working group of faculty researchers mandated by the University of California Regents to review the problems of eligibility for the state's Chicano/Latino population, found that at the current rate of advancement, it would take forty-three years for Chicanos/as to reach population parity in the UC system (Latino Eligibility Study, 1993).

In July 1996, however, the Regents of the University of California passed SP-1, a resolution prohibiting the use of race/ethnicity and/or gender among the criteria that could be used for university admission. Only one year later, this action was followed in California by Proposition 209, which barred the use of race/ethnicity and/or gender as criteria for hiring or contracting with state entities and for admissions decisions to state colleges and universities. Many predicted that these actions would decimate the numbers of Chicanos/Latinos and other minorities admitted to the University of California. If anything, the early predictions fell short of the mark. The University of California reports that in the year before Proposition 209 and SP-1 took effect, 53 percent fewer Chicanos/Latinos were admitted to the entering freshman class for 1998 at UC Berkeley, and 33 percent fewer were admitted to UCLA. For the two flagship campuses of the UC system, this translates into a freshman class comprised of 8.6 percent Chicanos/Latinos.

Some supporters of the ban on affirmative action were quick to note that the decline in percentages of underrepresented minorities at the flagship campuses had translated into higher percentages of Chicano/a and other students of color attending the other UC campuses.[2] However, it is important to note that UCLA and Berkeley traditionally enrolled many more Chicano/a students than any of the other campuses, with the exception of the small Riverside campus; hence, while most of the other UC campuses did indeed gain Chicano/a students as a result of this "domino effect," the net effect was still a 1998 freshman class with only 8.7 percent Chicanos/as across *all campuses* in a state in which 40 percent of the public school population is Chicano/Latino (California State Department of Education, 1997). Prior to the ban on affirmative action, Chicanos/as had comprised 9.6 percent of the 1997 freshman class (University of California, Office of the President, 1998).

Patricia Gándara

In 1997, the 5th Circuit Court of Appeals ruled in favor of Cheryl Hopwood, who contended that she was unfairly discriminated against because minority applicants who were "less qualified" than she had been admitted to the University of Texas School of Law while she was denied admission. The court's decision was interpreted by Texas Attorney General Dan Morales as outlawing the use of race or ethnicity as a factor in admissions, financial aid, and retention and recruitment programs in all institutions of higher education within Texas. Early returns on effects of the Hopwood case for Chicano/Latino admissions in Texas have been similarly distressing. The fall 1997 entering freshman class at the University of Texas included 12 percent fewer African Americans and 10 percent fewer Chicanos/Latinos than the prior year. The law school, however, saw a much more drastic effect, with only 52 percent of the previous year's proportion of Chicanos/Latinos and 19 percent of African Americans being admitted (Chapa, 1997).

While the theme of this volume is the legacy of the Treaty of Guadalupe Hidalgo and its consequences for the education of Chicano/a students throughout the Southwest, the discussion in this chapter is focused on Texas and California, the two states where contemporary higher education policy is causing reverberations throughout the Southwest and the nation. Because upwards of 85 percent of the region's Mexican-origin Latinos/as are concentrated in these two states (del Pinal & Singer, 1997), Chicanos/as have been hit especially hard by these decisions. Most Chicanos/as who aspire to higher education, especially those from lower-income families, cannot afford to leave the state, and so tend to apply to nearby colleges in their own state (Rendon & Hope, 1996). Unfortunately, if grades and test scores are the primary criteria for admission to the university, relatively few Chicanos/as will be admitted.

In the most recent round of admissions at the University of California at Berkeley, eight hundred underrepresented minority students with 4.0 GPAs and a mean SAT score of 1170 (the largest portion of whom, 616, or 77%, were Chicanos/Latinos) were turned away because their *relative* ranking, combining GPA and SAT scores, was lower than that of other students (Lee, 1998).[3] If Chicano/a students with such stellar academic records are deemed noncompetitive in this post–affirmative action era when compared to Asian American and White students, this bodes ill for future access to higher education for Chicanos/as and other underrepresented minorities. Table 1 below displays recent GPA data for Chicanos/Latinos and other ethnic groups.

TABLE 1   *Grade Point Averages by Ethnic Group: College-Bound Students in Three States, 1997, and All Students in California, 1990*

	CA, TX, NY *SAT Takers, 1997*	CA *All Graduates, 1990*
White	3.32	2.74
Asian American	3.37	3.11
Chicano/Latino	3.18	2.44
African American	2.88	2.33
Puerto Rican	2.84	—

Source: The College Board, 1997 SAT examinations, and Ludwig and Kowarsky (1994).

TABLE 2   *SAT Scores for Six Ethnic Groups: California, Texas, and New York, 1997*

	Verbal: *All Students*	Math: *All Students*	Verbal: *Top 10%*	Math: *Top 10%*	*% Scoring* *500+ Verbal*	*% Scoring* *500+ Math*
African-Am (31,068)	432	423	498	498	26	21
Mexican-Am (33,288)	444	453	510	534	29	32
Native-Am (3,366)	479	484	549	566	44	44
Asian-Am (41,389)	488	554	571	640	48	68
White (177,015)	523	529	599	612	61	62

Source: The College Board, unpublished data from 1997 SAT administration.

Among students intending to enroll in four-year colleges (SAT takers), as well as all high school students in California, Chicano/Latino GPAs are substantially below those of both Whites and Asian Americans, placing the Chicano/Latino students at a serious disadvantage when students are strictly ranked for college admissions. Unfortunately, adding SAT scores to the formula does not help. Table 2 shows average SAT scores for all test-takers, average SAT scores for students who scored in the top 10 percent of all test-takers, and the percentage of students who scored 500 or above on the SAT in 1997 for all major ethnic groups in the three most racially/ethnically diverse states—California, Texas, and New York. Disparities are great between Chicanos/as and African Americans and all other groups, but the disparities are especially wide in the upper ranges of the test—that is, among the students who compete for admission to selective four-year colleges and universities.

When SAT data for California are analyzed by income level, average scores for the highest income Chicanos/Latinos are only five points above those for the lowest income Whites (University of California Outreach Task Force, 1997). This suggests that similarities in class characteristics between Chicanos/Latinos and Whites or Asian Americans may be more apparent than real. Hence, in the absence of fundamental changes in class-based experiences, significant increases in test scores for Chicano/a students may be difficult to achieve in the short term.

Clearly, in order for Chicanos/as to increase their presence in higher education nationwide, and most particularly in California and Texas, either admissions criteria must be changed, or factors that depress GPA and SAT scores must be addressed in some significant and systematic way and with great urgency.

THE IMPORTANCE OF GREATER ACCESS TO HIGHER EDUCATION FOR CHICANOS/AS

A review of more than three hundred published statements made by college presidents during 1997, in the immediate aftermath of Proposition 209 and the *Hopwood* decision, revealed a surprisingly strong consensus in favor of affirmative action. Leaders of both public and private institutions of higher education were virtually unanimous in their support of it as a tool for achieving some measure of diversity in the nation's universities and colleges (Gándara, 1998a). Moreover, the chancellors of all nine University of California campuses, who were compelled to abandon affirmative action as a result of SP-1 and the passage of Proposition 209, openly disagreed with the decision to eliminate it, as did the president of the University of Texas when faced with the *Hopwood* decision.

The university presidents' positions were based on two explicit principles, and one less openly articulated concern: that diversity is intellectually healthy because it brings students and faculty into contact with a broad mix of perspectives; and that colleges and universities that more accurately reflect the composition of the population they serve are more just institutions, and that this kind of representation is not likely to be achieved without some kind of affirmative action. Most of the rhetoric in the press considers the first principle, the intellectual benefits of diversity, perhaps because this track is viewed as the least politically charged and the most defensible on purely academic grounds. Moreover, the beneficiaries of this position would appear to be the majority population, whose intellectual perspectives are presumably enhanced by faculty and student racial/ethnic diversity. One of the best examples of this perspective was articulated by Neil Rudenstine, president of Harvard University. President Rudenstine asserted that students are challenged by a diverse educational environment . . . to see issues from various sides to rethink their own premises, to achieve the kind of understanding that comes only from testing their own hypotheses against those of people with other views. Such an environment also creates opportunities for people from different backgrounds, with different life experiences, to come to know one another as more than passing acquaintances, and to develop forms of tolerance and mutual respect on which the health of our civic life depends. (*San Francisco Chronicle,* 1996, p. A21)

The second principle, that of social justice, was candidly described by the departing chancellor of UCLA, Charles Young, who was not shy in disagreeing with his regents' decision to abandon affirmative action in the university:

> What we're really trying to do is provide an opportunity for groups that have not been able to participate equitably in our society to make the kind of contribution they should, to reap the benefits they should, and to receive the education which will enable them to do so. We are trying to make enrollment in the university look more like the breakdowns in the population—not because that in itself is some ideal, but because those great disparities indicate serious problems. (Gable, 1995, p. 29)

More subtly coded in both President Rudenstine's and Chancellor Young's comments is another issue. Rudenstine refers to "the health of our civic life" and Young alludes to "serious problems." These are, no doubt, concerns of many university CEOs, for a nation that supports the disenfranchisement of large portions of its population, whether by restricting the vote, denying equal opportunity in the job market, or limiting equal access to education, has set in motion policies that undermine the social contract upon which a democratic nation must be based. How does a nation, or a state, reconcile the enormous disparities in education and opportunity that result from university admissions criteria that effectively, and systematically, shut out large <M%-1>sectors of the population? What are the consequences for race relations when those who are denied opportunity are overwhelmingly people of color? As Chicanos/as become a larger proportion of the school population—50 percent of the school-age population in California by 2005 (del Pinal & Singer, 1997)—such exclusion from the primary means of social mobility has important consequences, not only for the social fabric, but also for the economy.

A recent RAND study (Sorensen, Brewer, & Brighton, 1995) points out both the advantages of educating Latino students at a level equal to that of White students and the disadvantages of an inequitable education. Sorensen et al. conclude that:

> Hispanics with a bachelor's degree will pay more than twice as much in taxes as those with only a high school diploma, and Hispanics with a professional degree will pay an estimated three times as much as those with a bachelor's degree, [thus failing to increase the educational attainment of Hispanics] will exact a high economic toll for individuals and for society. Given the ex-

perience of other undereducated groups, there are certainly concomitant human, social and political costs. (pp. 2–3)

Inasmuch as Chicanos/as form the overwhelming majority of Latinos in the Southwest and their poverty rates are second only to Puerto Ricans among all Latino groups (del Pinal & Singer, 1997), the potential economic impact of increased education for Chicano/a students could have far-reaching effects on the economic health of the region.

LATINO FACULTY AND THE DIVERSIFICATION OF THE ACADEMY

Minority faculty may be more likely to take a personal interest in minority students (Martínez, dissertation in progress; McBay, 1986), they help to create a climate that is more inviting for students of color (Hurtado, 1990; McBay, 1986), and they provide important role models (Pascarella & Terinzini, 1991). Hence, some people believe that one important strategy for increasing Latino and other minority student presence on college campuses is strengthening the corps of faculty of color (Latino Eligibility Study, 1993). However, there are relatively few professors of color in the nation's historically White colleges and universities, due in part to the historically small pool of minority Ph.D.s. Table 3 shows the severe underrepresentation of minority faculty nationwide. Data from a new study (Moreno & Yun, in press) show that the representation of Latino faculty in Research I universities in the Southwest is higher than for any other region (although lower than for the University of California), registering 3.7 percent, which compares to a low of 1.1 percent in the Northwest and 1.6 percent in the Northeast in 1993–1994. Nonetheless, for a region in which nearly one-fourth of the residents are Latino (del Pinal & Singer, 1997), this is still an extraordinary under-representation.

Table 4 shows the growth in representation of minority faculty between 1985 and 1995 at the University of California, the premiere public institution of higher education in the nation's most populous and ethnically diverse state. Perhaps the most notable aspect of these data is the very minimal increase in Latino and other minority faculty during a period of active affirmative action, and in spite of a rapidly increasing Latino population and a larger pool of Ph.D.s (del Pinal & Singer, 1997; Carter & Wilson, 1997).

A recent study for the Association of American Colleges and Universities (Smith, 1996) calls into question the extent to which the low rates of hiring of minority faculty are, in fact, due primarily to the small pool of applicants. In this study of 298 Ford, Mellon, and Spencer fellowship recipients, 93 percent of whom received their Ph.D.s from elite Research I universities, Smith found that, although they were perceived to be "sought after," the great majority of these individuals (89%) in fact had few if any offers for tenure-track appointments—54 percent of the science Ph.D.s took post-doctoral positions

TABLE 3 *Full-Time Faculty in Higher Education, All Ranks, by Gender and Ethnicity, 1993*

	Percent of Population	Percent of All Faculty	Percent Male	Percent Female
African American	12%	4.8%	52%	48%
Latino	10%	2.3%	62%	38%
Native American	.9%	.4%	62%	38%
Asian American	3%	4.7%	75%	25%
White	74%	87.8%	67%	33%

Source: Carter and Wilson (1997).

TABLE 4 *University of California, Full-Time Ladder Faculty by Ethnicity, 1985 and 1995*

	Percent CA Pop. 1985	Percent All Faculty 1985	Percent CA Pop. 1995	Percent All Faculty 1995
African American	8%	1.8%	7%	2.5%
Latino	21%	2.9%	28%	4.5%
Asian American	8%	6.0%	11%	10.1%
White	63%	89.2%	53%	83.0%

Source: University of California, Office of the President (1997).

or sought positions outside of academe because no tenure-track offers were forthcoming. In her summary statements, Smith quotes one Chicana with a Ph.D. in American History as representative of the comments heard from many:

> I would say that I find it a little surprising that I do not regularly get phone calls with regards to recruitment. We are so few, it's amazing that most universities will say, "We can't find anybody," yet persons like myself are not recruited. I think I should be getting phone calls, and I don't get phone calls. (Smith, 1996, p. 134)

Of all of the reasons given for diversifying the academy at the faculty level, one that is not often articulated is the need for a voice for underrepresented minorities. Without faculty in the institution who represent or reflect the experiences of Chicano/Latino communities, how shall their concerns be voiced? Too often, the issues that most affect Chicano/Latino communities are articulated by individuals with no first-hand knowledge of those issues, and the message is thus filtered through the experience of others. The few faculty of color are often overburdened with requests to serve on various committees and to be the expert on every issue dealing with their racial/ethnic group, to the point that their research and teaching suffer (Torres-Guzmán, 1995), and still there are not enough faculty of color to form the critical mass necessary to have an audible voice in the academy.

While Latino faculty are almost certainly important in helping to create a more hospitable campus climate for Latino students, university administrators often hold more power in decisionmaking and have access to budgets that allow them to have a direct impact on minority student recruitment, retention, and well-being. Like the faculty, however, Latino administrators are in short supply in higher education, and particularly in Research I institutions where the need to improve the climate for students of color may be the greatest (see Table 5). Hence, the hiring of high-level Latino administrators must be viewed as an important priority in raising the profile of Latino issues within academe. A recent study by Haro (1995) of university CEO hiring practices, however, found that, while the popular perception was that Latino candidates were highly sought after, in fact they fared more poorly in the hiring process than both White males and females. The reason most often given for not making offers to highly qualified Latino applicants was a difference in "style" that did not fit with the expectations of the recruitment committee. Among the components of style that were especially significant to respondents in this study were appearance and access to important networks, two attributes that were almost certainly affected by the candidates' ethnicity. Other research has pointed to discrimination against Chicanos/as based on color and indigenous features (Telles & Murguía, 1990), demonstrating that opportunities in the labor market are indeed affected by ethnic appearance. Moreover, social networks have been shown to reflect class structure and to be differentially related to access to opportunity for working-class and middle-class individuals (DeGraf & Flap, 1988). The Haro study suggests that these findings are no less true for Chicanos/as in the academic labor market.

TABLE 5 *Administrators in Research I Universities by Race/Ethnicity: Twenty-Three Institutions in the U.S. Southwest, 1993–1994*

Racial/Ethnic Group	Percent of Total
White	85.3%
African American	4.0
Asian/Pacific Islander	3.1
Latino	6.1
American Indian	.9

Source: Moreno and Yun (in press).

THE SOURCE OF CHICANO/A UNDERACHIEVEMENT

Answers to why Chicano/a students fare so poorly in school exist on two levels. First there are the reasons associated with social-structural variables: poverty, mobility, low educational level of parents, inadequate schools, language differences, testing and sorting policies, and discrimination. At the second level are explanatory theories or frameworks that attempt to make sense of why poverty, cultural differences, and social disadvantage have the devastating effects that they do on most Chicanos/as, as well as why some Chicanos/as are able to overcome these impediments to social mobility. Chicano/a students are at risk educationally not just because of individual characteristics such as early school performance, but because of characteristics of their families, schools, and communities. It is now widely acknowledged that the various contexts in which children live shape their behavior and influence their academic success (Jessor, 1993). A report by the National Academy of Sciences on the problems faced by adolescents points out that it is important to focus on the high-risk settings in which many low-income adolescents live and go to school (National Research Council, Panel on High Risk Youth, 1993). For example, recent research has pointed to the powerful effects of community on academic outcomes for ethnic minority youth (Mayer & Jencks, 1989; Yancey & Saporito, 1997). Portes and Zhou (1993) have argued, however, that raising children within a strong ethnic cultural community can be an important protective factor for low-income immigrant students. In fact, they argue, it is the absence of this protective cultural milieu that undermines the successful adaptation of Latino students who grow up in communities populated by second- and third-generation families who have lost their ties to their native culture and language and for whom the immigrant dream of opportunity has died.

In 1995, 28 percent of all Mexican American families fell below the poverty line, while only 6 percent of White families were found in this category (del Pinal & Singer, 1997). Young Latino children three to five years of age were seven times more likely (27% versus 4%) than White children to have parents who had not completed high school (National Center for Education Statistics [NCES], 1997). Research has shown that both socioeconomic level and parents' high school completion have a strong influence on educational achievement. Preschool education, a factor that can help ameliorate the effects of poverty, was afforded to only 17 percent of Latino children in 1993, while 38 percent of White children attended preschools (Karoly et al., 1998). Moreover, while preschool attendance has been increasing steadily for White children, the percentage of Latino children attending preschool has been essentially the same for twenty years (NCES, 1995).

Latino children are also twice as likely as White children to attend schools in which a high percentage of the students live in poverty. Research has shown that both learning environments and resources differ markedly between such schools and those with low poverty rates (NCES, 1997). For example, teachers in schools with high poverty rates are more likely to report problems of student misbehavior, absenteeism, and lack of parental involvement than teachers in schools with low poverty rates. The standards and quality of instruction have been shown to be substantially lower in the former (Office of Educational Research and Improvement, 1994), and teacher salaries and advanced training are also lower in high-poverty than in low-poverty schools (NCES, 1997).

Mobility also has a powerful and negative effect on the academic fortunes of children, and many Latino children are especially prone to high mobility (Government Accounting Office, 1995; Rumberger & Larson, 1996) because their parents often lack stable employment. Of course, employment status is closely tied to educational level, and Mexican American parents have the lowest educational levels of all ethnic groups (Chapa, 1991). Table 6 shows the percentage of parents of students who took the SAT examination in 1997 who had less than a high school diploma and those with some college education for the major U.S. ethnic groups in California, Texas, and New York. Parents with some college tended to be the most affluent and well-educated of each ethnic group. Parents of Mexican American students were more than twice as likely as any other group to lack a high school diploma, and were also the least likely of all groups to have any college education.

Language difference is also an important factor in the academic success of Chicano/a students. While there is no inherent reason why language difference *should* result in lower academic achievement for Chicano/a students, in fact it is an important predictor of school failure (Steinberg, 1984). This is almost certainly related to the uneven quality of programs provided for language-minority students across the country, and especially in California, where the largest number of Spanish-speakers reside. Decades of political battles over the efficacy and legitimacy of bilingual education as a strategy for educating limited-English-proficient Chicano/a students has resulted in fluctuating public support and financing for these programs. As a consequence, only a minority of students who could benefit from bilingual programs are actually served by them, and many Chicano/a students are pro-

TABLE 6   *Parent Education by Ethnicity for College-Bound Students, California, Texas, and New York, 1997*

	Percent of Parents with Less than H.S. Diploma	Percent of Parents with At Least Some College
African American (31,068)	6%	46%
Mexican American (33,288)	31%	29%
Puerto Rican (3,907)	15%	34%
Native American (3,366)	4%	54%
Asian American (41,389)	14%	59%
White (177,015)	2%	68%

Source: The College Board, unpublished data for 1997 SAT administration.

vided no support at all to help them make the transition into an all-English curriculum (Council of Chief State School Officers, 1990).

Testing has proved to be a particularly troublesome area for Chicano/a students. Standardized tests have been used historically to misplace Chicano/a students into classes for the mentally retarded and as an effective filter to prevent them from gaining access to upper track curricula and programs for the gifted and talented (Valdes & Figueroa, 1994). Such tests have also been used to track large numbers of Chicano/a students into dead-end curriculum tracks that preclude entry into higher education (Oakes, 1986).

Finally, racism cannot be discounted as a factor in the underachievement of Chicano/a youth. The educational history of Chicanos/as in Texas is rife with examples of segregation, exclusion, and unequal funding of schools serving Chicano communities (Chapa & Lázaro, 1997). Although the tone and context have differed in California, as well as in the Southwest in general, the inequities have been no less real (Donato, 1997).

Unfortunately, the attitudes that drive unequal educational policies have not abated. In a 1990 national opinion poll of White attitudes toward African Americans and Latinos conducted at the University of Chicago, researchers found that 53 percent of White respondents thought Latinos were less intelligent than Whites, 54 percent felt that Latinos were lazier than Whites, and 72 percent said they thought that Latinos were more likely to prefer living on welfare than Whites. Such attitudes were also found to be correlated with a lack of support for affirmative action policies (Smith, 1990).

Given the numerous social-structural factors operating against the academic achievement of Chicano/a students, it is hardly a wonder that so many have difficulties in school and fail to surmount the hurdles to higher education. Yet some low-income and working-class Chicano/a students do find a way to navigate the hurdles on the racetrack, while at the same time, many Chicanos/as who appear to enjoy the advantages of the middle class do not finish the race. An explanatory theory is required to make sense of these seemingly contradictory outcomes. I offer two possible theories and a partial explanation based on existing data on Chicanos/Latinos and their presence in the labor force.

THEORIES OF CHICANO/A UNDERACHIEVEMENT

Numerous theories have been advanced to explain the pervasive underachievement of Latino students. Among these are social and cultural deprivation (Hess & Shipman, 1965; Valentine, 1968), cultural difference or discontinuities between home and school cultures (Carter & Segura, 1979; Buenning & Tollefson, 1987), the social construction of disadvantage in involuntary minorities (Matute-Bianchi, 1986; Ogbu, 1987),[4] bureaucratic rule-making (Mehan, 1992), social agency expressed as resistance to mainstream norms (Giroux, 1983; MacLeod, 1995; Willis, 1977), differences in social and cultural capital (Coleman, 1987; Lareau, 1987; Stanton-Salazar, 1997), and segmented assimilation that gives advantages to the children of immigrants who maintain close ties to parental culture, and disadvantages those who do not (Portes & Zhou, 1993).[5] No doubt, many or all of these theories explain some portion of the variance in Chicano/a achievement, yet none adequately addresses the propensity for Chicanos/as to take themselves out of the academic race, or the conundrum of *middle-class* Chicano/a underachievement.

Referring back to data from Table 1, the average GPA for African American students intending to go to four-year colleges in 1997 was 2.88, while that of the Chicano/a students with similar intentions was 3.18. Assuming that the standard deviations of the two means are similar, lower performing Chicanos/as are disproportionately absent from the college-going pool. This suggests that Chicano/a students with lower grades, grades more like those of the African American students, had already taken themselves out of the race and decided not to apply to a four-year college. Thus, Chicano/a students with lower grades and test scores, more like those of the African American students, were not applying to four-year colleges or making the necessary preparations to do so. We found similar data that tends to confirm this tendency for Chicanos/as to take themselves out of the race in an ongoing study of the development of aspirations among four major ethnic groups in the class of 2001 in two high schools (one urban, one rural) in California (Gándara, 1998b). Although Chicano/Latino students had somewhat higher GPAs than African American students at the beginning of ninth grade, substantially more African American students (56%, n=70) than Chicanos/Latinos (38%, n=112) stated that their intention was to attend a four-year college after high school graduation. (For White students, 48% intended to go to a four-year college [n=207], as did 50% of Asian Americans [n=84].) This may, in part, be attributable to the fact that Chicanos/as tend to have much less exposure to parents who have gone to college and therefore may not discuss the topic at home, although it does not explain the very large discrepancy between African American and Chicano/a aspirations.

Steele (1997) has proposed a theory he refers to as "stereotype vulnerability" that speaks directly to the issue of academic aspirations. He argues that because some ethnic minorities, notably African Americans and Chicanos/Latinos, are often stereotyped as intellectually inferior, academic situations in which they must perform competitively may be threatening. This produces performance anxiety in these students, which may significantly depress their test scores and other ability measures. Hence, devaluing academic prowess and "disidentifying" with the activity (academic endeavor) that may result in damage to self-esteem is seen as an adaptive response to a threatening situation. Steele contends that many minority students thus remove themselves from academically competitive situations as an effective means of protecting their self-image. As such, the observation of the resistance theorists (e.g., Fordham & Ogbu, 1986; Giroux, 1983; Matute-Bianchi, 1986; Willis, 1977) that many students of color resist trying to do well in school for fear of "acting White" is revealed as a strategy to save face and deny others the opportunity of confirming their stereotypes about ethnic intellectual inferiority.

While Steele developed his theory primarily as a way of explaining the underachievement of African Americans and their resistance to schooling, the data suggest that this theory may actually be most explanatory for Chicanos/as. One can speculate that Chicano/a students with lower GPAs simply do not feel that they can qualify for entrance into a four-year college, do not see themselves as "college material," and seek to protect their self-image by not engaging in activities (e.g., taking college entrance exams) that, in their minds, may lead to a loss of self-esteem. On the other hand, African American youth, having experienced consistent and overt discrimination in schooling, may have developed better coping strategies than have Chicanos/as, who are often the targets of more covert discrimination. While many African Americans may opt out of the race, as do Chicanos/as, the evidence suggests that more African American students are willing to confront the power structure and insist that they be given a chance to compete—a strategy that is less common among Chicano/a students.

The problem of middle-class underachievement for Chicanos/as has been addressed by Miller (1995), who suggests that many generations of under-education among Mexican-origin youth have created an illusory Chicano middle class. That is, because "middle class" is a designation generally based on income and education, many Chicanos/as may give the appearance of being middle class without actually having the social capital that middle-class status normally confers.

Hence, the likelihood is that Chicano parents who have newly entered the middle class were raised by parents with little education, went to inferior schools where standards may have been low, and have been taught by teachers ill prepared to meet their needs, and, if they went to college, attended community or less selective state colleges, a pattern quite different from that of most White and Asian students (Rendon & Hope, 1996). Moreover, because they form an uncapitalized class—individuals with few assets that can place them "one paycheck away from poverty"—many of these Chicanos/as may have only a tenuous grip on the middle class. They lack the traditions, the networks, the access to the power structure that characterize middle-class life in the United States, yet their children are considered to have entered the mainstream. Thus, argues Miller, many middle-class Chicano/a students perform on school measures very similarly to lower income minority students (see Figure 1) because their experience is more like that of a lower income individual than of a solid member of the middle class. Hence, to assume that the track has been cleared of obstacles by their parents' position in the middle class is to perpetuate a hoax on many Chicano/a students and leave them bewildered and self-doubting about their inability to compete in what appears to be, but is not, a race among equals.

In spite of all of the barriers to educational achievement, some Chicano/a students do excel in school and go on to the highest levels of education. What lessons can be learned from these students that might be applied to the situation we face at the end of the twentieth century?

FIGURE 1 *Average SAT Scores by Parental Income and Race/Ethnicity*

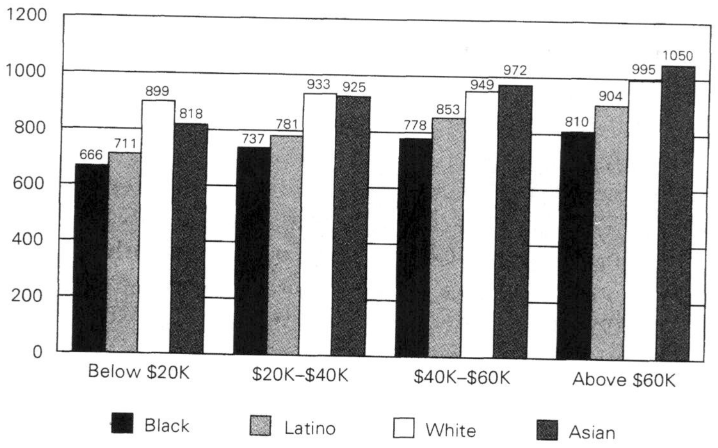

Source: University of California Outreach Task Force (1997).

SUCCESSFULLY NAVIGATING THE HURDLES TO HIGHER EDUCATION: VOICES OF EXPERIENCE

A 1995 study of fifty Chicanas and Chicanos from low-income backgrounds who had successfully leaped the hurdles of higher education and completed M.D., J.D., and Ph.D. degrees from Research I universities revealed a number of background characteristics that predisposed them to educational success (Gándara, 1995). Chief among these was a high value placed on, and exposure to, literacy, usually in Spanish, in the students' homes. While it seemed counterintuitive that students from homes characterized by low levels of parental education (between fourth and fifth grade on average) would be exposed to high levels of literacy, this indeed was the case for most of these individuals. Parents read to them in Spanish, from the Bible and sometimes from the classics. Parents themselves were consumers of print materials, avidly reading newspapers and paperbacks, and incredibly, in these low-income homes where the next meal was not always a certainty, 68 percent of families owned an encyclopedia, which was dedicated to aiding the children in their schoolwork. Virtually all of the women and most of the men in this study reported being avid readers themselves, usually modeling their interest after one or both of their parents or an older sibling. A Chicana whose father had dropped out of school before the sixth grade commented on the early literacy training she received from him:

> My father was an exceptional man. Education was very important to him. . . .
> When we started going to church, everything was in Spanish, and everybody

was supposed to read chapters and report. So I had a great deal of instruction in the Spanish language without knowing it. Also it sort of set the stage for literature. By the time I went into literature, that kind of stuff was not difficult at all. I would simply write in a biblical style. (Gándara, 1995, p. 43)

A second important commonality was the high incidence of attendance at desegregated schools, where the students were exposed to peers with much greater social capital than themselves. Two-thirds of the study subjects attended schools that were either mostly White or that were highly mixed racially/ethnically. This was especially unusual, since nearly 80 percent of these Chicanos/as lived in mostly Chicano/Latino neighborhoods and went to school at a time, and in places, where schooling was highly segregated. Parents, and sometimes the students themselves, frequently engineered ways out of the schools to which they had been assigned. As one subject noted, these schools were filled with kids "that were not going anywhere." Moreover, because most of these students who would eventually achieve at extraordinarily high levels already showed academic promise, they were usually tracked into college preparatory classes with other high-achieving White students, who formed an important network of peers with access to the social capital that these Chicano/a students lacked. It is important to recall, however, that these individuals were a tiny minority of all Chicano/a students in the school who had been "tapped" by their teachers, or who exhibited extraordinary persistence on their own part, to participate in the college preparatory track. Moreover, some subjects indicated that they believed they were selected for this special treatment because of a combination of good academic performance *and* the fact that they blended physically into the mainstream culture. The overwhelming majority of their Chicano/a peers were segregated into the lower tracked classes in their schools, a fact of which many of these individuals were acutely aware. Hence, White students were often the conveyers of information about opportunities that was never shared with the majority of Chicano/a students. These same White students were able to act as guides through the bureaucratic system of the school, which often operated to foreclose opportunities for Chicanos/as. One Chicana recounted the fateful day when she was introduced to the idea that her school had separate classes for students who planned to go to college, and that she, in fact, could aspire to such a future:

I had to go to school to register and there was this huge line and I was by myself. . . . The [White] girl in the other line was a girl I had gone to school with. . . . She said, "Don't get in that line, get in this line; this is for college prep." I told her that was not for me, and she said, "Yes, it is," and so I went with her because I didn't want to be alone. . . . When I got in the line, she talked me into it by saying, "Don't stand in that line because you will learn the same stuff you learned in seventh and eighth grade, just reviewing the same stuff." (Gándara, 1995, p. 74)

Additionally, the presence of White students in their classes allowed these Chicanos/as to form friendship groups at schools that facilitated a bicultural orientation—they were able to move easily in and out of different cultural milieu, which no doubt was a great asset as they moved into higher education, where success depended, to a large extent, on their ability to cross cultural borders (Phelan, Davidson, & Cao, 1991).

Third, the profound work ethic that characterized almost all of these households was channeled into dedication to studies and a strong belief that effort was more important than ability in achieving academic goals. Most of these individuals did not see themselves as the brightest student in their classes; they simply worked harder. As one respondent put it:

> I think that people admired the fact that I was an achiever when I really shouldn't have been. People would look at me and think to themselves, "There is no reason this guy should be as good as he is in everything." Academically, the counselors would look at me and say, "This guy has an IQ of 95; there is no reason he should be doing this well." And then I would work hard and I would get As and I would impress them. (Gándara, 1995, p. 83)

Parents modeled high standards in their own work, whether it was picking beans in the fields or cleaning offices on the night shift. Most of these Chicanos/as followed the model set by their parents and held themselves to equally high standards in school and an equally strong belief that effort could overcome others' assessment of their ability.

It is important to note, however, that not all of the respondents were equally dedicated to schooling, and there is an important lesson in this about trying to predict too early who will be academically successful. Twenty percent of the males in this study (n=30) who went on to become successful professors, physicians, and lawyers did not appear to be headed toward higher education as late as high school. This was a decision that was made late in their schooling careers, usually because someone saw potential in them and encouraged them. Had these individuals not been given the chance to redeem themselves, this would have resulted in a significant loss to the Chicano community, and to society in general. Given an extraordinarily competitive environment that turns Chicano/a students with 4.0 GPAs away from the university, we have reason to worry that a great deal of potential may be squandered because of adherence to a point system that gives no value to diversity and fails to acknowledge significant differences in opportunities to learn.

Finally, perhaps the most important contribution that the parents of these high-achieving students made to their children's futures was to tell family stories, legends, and perhaps myths, filled with hope. Most of these individuals could readily recount at least one family story or legend that was told often to explain the family's current circumstances and to create a sense of hopefulness in the children about the future. Most of the stories had to do with family exploits, esteemed and heroic relatives. All told tales of a family that was well regarded, wealthy, or powerful at one time, back in the "old country." The message seemed to be that although current circumstances were difficult, this represented an aberration of sorts in an otherwise illustrious history, and that certainly the family would someday be restored to its former prominence. The unstated message was that it was in the hands of these individuals to make this happen.

TRANSLATING THE LESSONS OF HIGH ACHIEVERS INTO STRATEGIES THAT WORK FOR CHICANO/A STUDENTS

The High School Puente (Bridge) program is an intervention modeled after a highly successful community college program that operates in about thirty community colleges in California. High School Puente has been introduced in eighteen high schools in the state and currently serves about 1,700 Chicano/a students. Its aim is to provide students with the skills, knowledge, and dispositions to pursue higher education at a four-year college or university. Students are invited to participate in Puente based on teachers' and counselors' recommendations. The program has few academic criteria other than good attendance and a reading level within two to three years of grade level.[6] The program has three major components: an intensive, enriched ninth- and tenth-grade English class that focuses on extensive writing instruction and exposure to Mexican American literature in the context of the regular freshman and sophomore curriculum; a counselor who ensures that students are registered in college preparatory classes and that they receive all of the information necessary to make successful applications to college; and a mentor, either an older peer or an adult who provides guidance, advice, and encouragement to keep them "on track" academically. The dynamics of the program, however, mirror in many ways the lessons learned from the cited study of academically successful Chicanos/as (Gándara, 1995).

The central focus of the program on literacy and on Mexican American literature aims to make the students avid readers and writers. Usually for the first time in their lives, these Chicano/a students are introduced to people from their own communities who are exciting, engaging, and well-known writers. In a sense, the students are reading the family stories of their culture, written by people who come from *their* family. Hopefulness is engendered in the students as they identify with the writers and begin to see themselves in the role of writer and storyteller. These classes are filled with students who cannot wait to tell their own stories and who write with a purpose. In a survey that asked ninth-graders what they enjoyed most about the program, the overwhelming first choice was Latino literature.

The job of the Puente counselor, first and foremost, is to provide the instrumental knowledge or social capital that is taken for granted in more advantaged communities. Most of the schools in which Puente operates do not have large numbers of upper-income students in college preparatory courses who can share their knowledge of the system with their peers; some Puente programs exist in communities that are almost entirely Mexican American. Moreover, the mere presence of upper-income students does not ensure that many Chicanos/as would profit from these encounters. In real life, these encounters are chancy at best; however, the counselor, who in most cases is also Chicano/a, does ensure that students and parents know how to navigate the system and are provided with the instrumental knowledge to allow these students to take full advantage of the opportunities that the schools can offer. When Puente students were surveyed about what they perceived to be the most important thing the program did to ensure their going to college, they indicated that it was the knowledge they got about what they needed to do to become eligible for admission to four-year colleges and universities. The Latino Eligibility Study (1994) confirms that lack of knowledge about how to become eligible was the greatest impediment to going to college for the Chicano/a students surveyed.

Because Puente does not select only the students who show the greatest potential for academic success, classes are heterogeneous. Outstanding performing students sit next to average performing students, and over the two years that they are in class together, many form strong friendships. This creates a learning community in which students often form study groups and help each other outside of class. It surrounds them with students of different academic backgrounds who share a common goal of doing well in school and going on to college. The tracking of students into college preparatory classes alongside other students with similar goals serves much (although not all) of the same purpose that the desegregated schools with high-achieving White students provided for the successful Chicanos/as studied.

The Puente mentor is either an older and academically successful student or a successful adult from the community who provides much of the social capital that Chicano/a students typically lack. In the early years of high school, an older student can show the younger student the ropes, and introduce him or her to supportive peers and activities that will enhance the high school experience and keep the student engaged in school. In the later years, the adult mentor provides knowledge of the traditions, the networks, and the access to the power structure that the students' own parents may not be able to provide in guiding the student towards higher education.

We have studied the Puente program for a four-year period and have found that there are four significant outcomes, in addition to improved academic preparation, that Puente can provide for Chicano/a students: 1) high aspirations; 2) positive attitudes toward schooling; 3) instrumental knowledge; and 4) a strong academic identity. We surveyed 970 students: 480 Puente students, 245 non-Puente Chicano/a students, and 245 non-Puente "other" students (about equally divided among Whites and Asians, plus thirty African Americans). Surveys were anonymous; therefore we were unable to verify GPA data for all students in order to establish equivalence of samples. However, we believe that the Puente and non-Puente students represented reasonably equivalent samples for the following reasons: Surveys were administered to both Puente and non-Puente comparison students in the *same* non-honors and non-remedial history classes across the state of California in which they were both enrolled. GPA data gathered from a sample of seventy-five Puente respondents from three schools yielded a mean GPA of 2.5, and data cited in Table 1 suggest that the non-Chicano/a comparison students (mostly Asian Americans and Whites) probably have a mean GPA somewhat higher than this, while the Chicano/a comparison students probably have a mean GPA slightly lower than 2.5.[7]

ASPIRATIONS

Table 7 displays the percentages of students across all grades who responded that they intended to go to a four-year college when asked about their post–high school plans. Aspirations to attend a four-year college were substantially higher for Puente students than for other Chicano/a students, and all others.

Although both Puente and non-Puente students in the ninth grade have high aspirations to go to four-year colleges (74% for Puente students versus 41% for all non-Puente), this changes over time, with a much steeper decline for non-Puente students (from 41% to 25%) than for the Puente students (from 74% to 53%). We believe that the exceptionally high aspirations of the Puente ninth-graders is the result of being in a program for nearly one year (they were surveyed in May) in which they are constantly told that they are being prepared for college. However, students adjust their aspirations over time to match the reality of their school performance and the expectations of those around them. Puente students maintain consistently higher aspirations across grades, and a much higher percentage of Puente students still intend to go to college even at the end of twelfth grade, when most students have made their decisions about their futures. It would appear that the consistent message that "you can do it" was having a significant impact on the Puente students' aspirations. Unlike the data presented earlier, most of these students appear to be staying in the race.

ATTITUDES TOWARD SCHOOLING

While it is easy to say "I want to go to college," an important test of this commitment is to ask what a student is willing to give up in order to do well in school and make the aspiration a reality. Hence, we posed four questions to students, asking them whether they'd be willing to sacrifice something to make their college aspirations a reality. We asked them: Would you be willing to give up 1) a friend who was holding you back; 2) a job; 3) hanging out with friends after school and on weekends; and 4) a sport or other activity that is important to you? Table 8 displays students' responses. It is typical of adolescents that loyalty to a friend is a strong value, and Puente students were only a little more likely than non-Puente students to be willing to give up a friend who they felt was holding them back. Although, when we analyzed this question by grade level, over time, Puente students became increasingly more likely to respond that they would give up a friend, while other students did not show the same progression in willingness to do so. This finding suggests that Puente students, while exhibiting a normal adolescent value of loyalty to friends, were developing over time a stronger value for achievement than the

TABLE 7 *Percent Students Intending to Go to Four-Year Colleges*

Category	N	Percent
Non-Puente Chicano	245	26.5%
Non-Puente "Other"	245	43.0%
Puente	480	67.0%

TABLE 8 *Percent Students Who Would Give Up (Grades 9–12 Combined)*

	N	Friend	Hanging Out	Job	Sport/Activity
Non-Puente Chicano	250	50%	64%	63%	43%
Non-Puente Other	245	53%	65%	65%	36%
Puente	500	57%	75%	82%	52%

$\chi^2 p < .05$

non-Puente students. On all other items, however, Puente students professed to be significantly more willing to make trade-offs in their life in order to achieve their academic goals.

INSTRUMENTAL KNOWLEDGE

In order to assess how much students knew about what was required to apply to college, we asked them to tell us if they knew "everything," "most of what they needed to know," "still had a lot of questions," "didn't know much," or "didn't know what was needed and didn't care." Table 9 displays the percentages of students, Puente and all non-Puente combined, by grade level, who responded that they either knew all or almost all of what they needed to know to go to college. By the spring of eleventh grade, the most critical point for students who are going on to college to be preparing to fill out applications, more than twice as many Puente students as non-Puente students stated that they knew all or almost all of what they needed to know to apply to college.

ACADEMIC IDENTITY

Perhaps the greatest challenge with minority students who have, in Steele's words, "disidentified" with schooling is to help them see the role of being a good student as a positive choice. This requires that students overcome fears

TABLE 9   *Percent Who Know All or Amost All Needed to Apply to College*

	9th Grade (n)	10th Grade (n)	11th Grade (n)	12th Grade (n)
Non-Puente	26% (171)	41% (141)	36% (113)	62% (93)
Puente	42% (182)	65% (198)	75% (110)	78% (58)

TABLE 10   *Value for Being a Good Student: Percent Choosing Each Response* *(Grades 9–12 Combined)*

	N	Good Student	Cool Student	Nice Person	Popular Student
Non-Puente Chicano	266	24%	36%	31%	9%
Non-Puente Other	262	26%	39%	25%	10%
Puente	549	35%	31%	31%	3%

χ^2 p < .001

of being rejected by some peers because of appearing to "act White" (Fordham & Ogbu, 1986). In order to protect students from this threat, it is important that they have friends who support the "good student" identity. Puente attempts to build cohorts of students who provide this kind of affirmation for each other. In order to assess whether Puente students would more readily identify with the role of "good student," we surveyed them to see which of the following four people they would most like to be: 1) a really cool student who is funny and fun to be around; 2) a really nice person who will always listen to your problems; 3) a really popular student who always gets invited to the best parties; or 4) a really good student who is always willing to help others with their homework. We tried to imbed the core student type into a phrase that would make each of the types appear attractive to adolescents. Table 10 displays the students' responses. The highest ranked response for Puente students was "good student," whereas this was only the second- or third-ranked response for non-Puente students. By a considerable margin, Puente students were more anxious to identify with the role of good student than were other students, suggesting that, at the least, a substantial portion of the Puente students were not disindentifying with doing well in school and in fact actively identified with this role. This finding is potentially very powerful, given that we know that peer norms among many low-income Chicano/a students often result in a reluctance to excel in school for fear of being singled out as "different" or "acting White."

The data suggest that Puente has an impact on shaping the aspirations, attitudes, and instrumental knowledge that will make it possible for these Chicano/a students to pursue higher education. We believe that this is because the program reflects our current knowledge base about the reasons why Chicano/a students do not go to college in large numbers, as well as capitalizing on the kinds of things that we know have worked for successful Chicano/a students in the past.

CONCLUSIONS:
"NO HAY MAL QUE POR BIEN NO VENGA"

After decades of relatively minuscule progress in providing equal opportunity for Chicanos/as in higher education, we are told by the courts and by the electorate that the track is now free from hurdles, that the race is the same for all groups, and that the clock has run out on affirmative action. Admission rates for Chicanos/as in Texas and California universities in the aftermath of Proposition 209, SP-1, and the *Hopwood* decision reveal the lie in this contention. The starting line has been set back and the whistle has been blown before Chicanos/as could even enter the race. Perhaps because of the perception that it is an unwinnable race, many Chicanos/as who are not forced out of the competition by other factors beyond their control, like poverty, inadequate schools, and risky communities, appear to be taking themselves out of the race. By the time other students are preparing for college, Chicanos/as are already in the work force. The situation could have continued in the same way it has over the last several decades for perhaps a couple of decades more before Chicanos/as became such a large portion of the population that their under-education became a serious economic threat to the states in which they reside, but recent events have changed that.

The devastating reversals in admissions eligibility for higher education have given rise to a new and more urgent conversation. Even the most conservative legislators know how to read the numbers and have begun to listen to the message that the nation's university presidents have been articulating en masse: no one will want to live in the society that results from the enormous disparities in opportunity that have been set in motion by historic and recent events. Although Texas has long taken a back seat to California with respect to state policies affecting Chicanos/as, ironically it is the Texas legislature that has been the first to respond to challenges posed by the demise of affirmative action in higher education.[8] House Bill 588, introduced by State Representative Irma Rangel and designed by a working group of university administrators, legal scholars, and minority legislators, was signed into law in May 1997. Known as the "Ten Percent Plan," HB 588 requires that the top 10 percent of graduating seniors from each school in Texas be granted admission to the University of Texas, regardless of their performance on standardized tests. Moreover, it sets out criteria by which students who have suffered "educational or economic disadvantage" may also be granted admission. Factors that may be considered in the admission of such students include attending a low-performing school and having bilingual proficiency. HB 588 sets out eighteen additional factors that can be included in admissions decisions. These criteria cover most of the demographic variables that divide low-income and disenfranchised communities from more affluent ones (Chapa, 1997). Unfortunately, because the 5th Circuit ruling also disallowed the awarding of financial aid using ethnicity as a factor, the fall 1998 University of Texas at Austin freshman class includes no more Chicano/a students than in the previous two years after the *Hopwood* decision. In fact, the campus has experienced a 12 percent decline in the number of Chicano/Latino students between 1996 and 1998 (Weiss, 1998). Hence, while more Chicano/Latino students may be admitted using the HB 588 plan, without the resources to attend the university, it does not appear that more can be expected to attend.

A similar proposal was made to the Regents of the University of California; however, this was a scaled-back version that would have admitted only the top 4 percent of students graduating from each high school in the state. This proposal was recently rejected by the Regents on the basis that it "would displace more qualified students from better schools—and also lower standards at the prestigious nine-campus university" (Weiss, 1998). The use of socioeconomic disadvantage as a factor in admission to the University of California has not had a significant effect on qualifying more underrepresented students. While all ethnic groups—including Whites—registered declines in proportions of students who intended to enroll in the university in fall 1998, the percentage of students who declined to state their ethnicity rose from 4.7 percent in 1997 to 14.1 percent in 1998 (University of California, Office of the President, 1998). Several studies conducted at the individual campuses confirmed that these were almost all White and Asian American students. Hence, any advantage accruing from the use of socioeconomic criteria as a factor in admissions would appear to have gone to either White or Asian American students or both.

Ironically, the Chicano/a students who may be the best equipped to succeed in a competitive university environment—those who have been raised in the middle class and exposed to mainstream culture, but whose grades and test scores have not yet reached a level of competitiveness due to residual educational disadvantage—are passed over when socioeconomic status is used as a factor in admissions decisions. This results in a kind of double jeopardy. The lowest income Chicano/a students, who might qualify on the basis of socioeconomic disadvantage, usually cannot qualify academically because pervasive educational and social disadvantage precludes them from receiving the kind of preparation and encouragement to consider college as an option. On the other hand, "middle-class" Chicanos/as, who may have a very tenuous hold on their middle-class status but who are at the threshold of eligibility, cannot be considered for admission because their alleged class membership excludes them from special consideration.

The political environments are clearly very different in Texas and California, as they also differ in other parts of the Southwest (e.g., New Mexico's treatment of its Latinos tends to be considerably more progressive than Arizona, and a new wave of conservatism in Colorado, exemplified in newly imposed restrictions on bilingual education, make it look more and more like California). The attention being paid to issues of equal access to higher education in Texas, however, will surely pose a challenge to the rest of the Southwest and to California in particular. We now have considerable evidence about what can work to keep more Chicano/a students in the race for higher education. Programs such as the Puente project have pointed the way. Greater attention and support for these strategies will almost certainly increase the numbers of Chicano/a students who will become eligible for college and who will stay the course. If we can combine this knowledge base with progressive legislative proposals such as those being experimented with in Texas, and if we can find ways to both fund low-income Chicanos/as who do gain eligibility and to include those Chicano/a students from the middle class who are insufficiently enabled by their alleged class membership, but also seriously disadvantaged by socioeconomic status criteria, the future will surely not look like the past. And, *no hay mal que por bien no venga* (there is no ill that does not also bring benefits).

REFERENCES

Buenning, M., & Tollefson, N. (1987). The cultural gap hypothesis as an explanation for the achievement patterns of Mexican American students. *Psychology in the Schools, 24,* 264–272.

California State Department of Education. (1997). *California basic educational data system.* Sacramento: Author.

Carter, D., & Wilson, R. (1997). *Minorities in higher education, 15th annual status report.* Washington, DC: American Council on Education.

Carter, T., & Segura, R. (1979). *Mexican Americans in school: A decade of change* (2nd ed.). New York: College Entrance Examination Board.

Chapa, J. (1991). Special focus: Hispanic demographic and educational trends. In D. Carter & R. Wilson (Eds.), *Minorities in higher education* (pp. 11–18). Washington, DC: American Council on Education.

Chapa, J. (1997, December). *The* Hopwood *decision in Texas as an attack on Latino access to selective higher education programs.* Paper presented at the Latino Civil Rights Crisis Conference sponsored by the Civil Rights Project, Harvard University, Washington, DC.

Chapa, J., & Lázaro, V. (1997). *Hopwood* in Texas: The untimely end of affirmative action. In G. Orfield & E. Miller (Eds.), *Chilling admissions: The affirmative action crisis and the search for alternatives* (pp. 51–70). Cambridge, MA: Harvard University, Civil Rights Project, and Harvard Education Publishing Group.

Coleman, J. (1987). Families and schools, *Educational Researcher, 16,* 32–38.

Council of Chief State School Officers. (1990). *School success for limited English proficient students: The challenge and state response.* Washington, DC: Author.

DeGraf, N., & Flap, H. S. (1988). "With a little help from my friends": Social resources as an explanation of occupational status and income in West Germany, the Netherlands, and the United States. *Social Forces, 67,* 453–472.

De La Rosa, D., & Maw, C. (1990). *Hispanic education: A statistical portrait.* Washington, DC: National Council of La Raza.

del Pinal, J., & Singer, A. (1997). *Generations of diversity: Latinos in the United States.* Washington, DC: Population Reference Bureau.

Donato, R. (1997). *The other struggle for equality: Mexican Americans during the civil rights era.* Albany: State University of New York Press.

Fordham, S., & Ogbu, J. (1986). Black students' school success: Coping with the burden of "acting White." *Urban Review, 18,* 176–206.

Gable, M. (1995). Not fair. *UCLA Magazine, 7,* 24–28.

Gándara, P. (1995). *Over the ivy walls: The educational mobility of low-income Chicanos.* Albany: State University of New York Press.

Gándara, P. (1997). *High School Puente evaluation report no. 3.* Davis: University of California.

Gándara, P. (1998a). *Priming the pump: A review of programs that aim to increase the achievement of underrepresented minority undergraduates* (Report to the Task Force on Minority High Achievement of the College Board). New York: College Board.

Gándara, P. (1998b). [Peer influences on academic aspirations of ethnically diverse high school students]. Unpublished raw data.

Giroux, H. (1983). *Theory and resistance: A pedagogy for the opposition.* South Hadley, MA: Bergin & Garvey.

Government Accounting Office. (1995). *Student mobility.* Washington, DC: Government Printing Office.

Haro, R. (1995). Held to a higher standard. Latino executive selection in higher education. In R. V. Padilla & R. Chávez Chávez (Eds.), *The leaning ivory tower* (pp. 53–66). Albany: State University of New York Press.

Hess, R., & Shipman, V. (1965). Early experience and the socialization of cognitive modes in children. *Child Development, 36,* 869–886.

Hurtado, S. (1990). *Campus racial climates and educational outcomes.* Doctoral dissertation, University of California, Los Angeles. (University Microfilms International No. 9111328)

Jessor, R. (1993). Successful adolescent development in high risk settings. *American Psychologist, 48,* 117–126.

Karoly, L., Greenwood, P., Everingham, S., Hoube, J., Kilburn, R., Rydell, C. P., Sanders, M., & Chiesa, J. (1998). *Investing in our children: What we know and don't know about the costs and benefits of early childhood interventions.* Santa Monica, CA: RAND.

Lareau, A. (1987). Social class differences in family-school relationships: The importance of cultural capital, *Sociology of Education, 60,* 73–85.

Latino Eligibility Study. (1993). *Report no. one.* Santa Cruz: Regents of the University of California.

Latino Eligibility Study. (1994). *The anchor study.* Santa Cruz: Regents of the University of California.

Lee, H. (1998, April 17). Oakland teachers decry UC rebuff of top students. *San Francisco Chronicle,* p. A21.

Ludwig, J., & Kowarsky, J. (1994). Eligibility of California's 1990 high school graduates for the state's public universities. In A. Hurtado & E. García (Eds.), *The educational achievement of Latinos: Barriers and successes* (pp. 259–297). Santa Cruz: Regents of the University of California.

Martínez, G. (in preparation). *The effects of an undergraduate mentoring project on the production of minority scholars.* Doctoral dissertation, University of California, Davis.

Matute-Bianchi, E. (1986). Ethnic identities and patterns of school success and failure among Mexican-descent and Japanese American students in a California high school. *American Journal of Education, 95,* 233–255.

Mayer, S. E., & Jencks, C. (1989). Growing up in poor neighborhoods: How much does it matter? *Science, 243,* 1441-1445.

McBay, S. (1986). *The racial climate on the MIT campus. A report of the Minority Student Issues Group.* Boston: MIT, Office of the Dean for Student Affairs.

MacLeod, J. (1995). *Ain't no making it: Aspirations and attainment in a low-income neighborhood.* Boulder, CO: Westview.

Mehan, H. (1992). Understanding inequality in schools: The contribution of interpretive studies. *Sociology of Education, 65,* 1–20.

Miller, L. S. (1995). *An American imperative. Accelerating minority educational advancement.* New Haven, CT: Yale University Press.

Moreno, J. F., & Yun, J. (in press). A demographic profile of the top U.S. research universities. In G. Orfield & E. Miller (Eds.), *Diversity challenged.* Cambridge, MA: Harvard University, Civil Rights Project, and Harvard Education Publishing Group.

National Center for Education Statistics (NCES). (1995). *The condition of education 1995.* Washington, DC: U.S. Dept of Education, Government Printing Office.

National Center for Education Statistics (NCES). (1997). *The condition of education 1997.* Washington, DC: U.S. Dept of Education, Government Printing Office.

National Research Council, Panel on High Risk Youth. (1993). *Losing generations: Adolescents in high risk settings.* Washington, DC: National Academy Press.

Oakes, J. (1986). *Keeping track. How schools structure inequality.* New Haven, CT: Yale University Press.

Office of Educational Research and Improvement. (1994). What do grades mean? Differences across schools. *Education Research Report.* Washington DC: U.S. Department of Education. (ERIC Document Reproduction Services No. ED 367 366)

Ogbu, J. (1987). Variability in minority school performance: A problem in search of an explanation. *Anthropology and Education Quarterly, 18,* 312–334.

Orfield, G. (1996). *Dismantling desegregation: The quiet reversal of Brown vs. the Board of Education.* New York: W. W. Norton.

Pascarella, E., & Terenzini, P. (1991). *How college affects students.* San Francisco: Jossey-Bass.

Phelan, P., Davidson, A., & Cao, H. (1991). Students' multiple worlds: Negotiating the boundaries of family, peer, and social cultures. *Anthropology and Education Quarterly, 22,* 224–250.

Portes, A., & Zhou, M. (1993). The second generation: Segmented assimilation and its variants. *Annals of the American Academy of Political and Social Science, 530,* 75–96.

Rendon, L., & Hope, R. (1996). *Educating a new majority: Transforming America's educational system for diversity.* San Francisco: Jossey-Bass.

Rumberger, R., & Larson, K. (1996, April). *The impact of student mobility on high school completion.* Paper presented at the American Educational Research Association, New York.

Serrano et al. v. Ivy Baker Priest, 2/87 P.2d 1241 (Cal. 1971).

Smith, D. (1996). *Achieving faculty diversity, debunking the myths.* Washington, DC: Association of American Colleges and Universities.

Smith, T. (1990). *GSS topical report no. 19.* Chicago: University of Chicago, National Opinion Research Center.

Sorensen, S., Brewer, C., & Brighton, E. (1995). *Increasing Hispanic participation in higher education: A desirable public investment.* Santa Monica, CA: RAND Corp., Institute on Education and Training

Stanton-Salazar, R. (1997). A social capital framework for understanding the socialization of racial minority children and youths. *Harvard Educational Review, 67,* 1–40.

Steele, C. (1997). A threat in the air: How stereotypes shape intellectual identity and performance. *American Psychologist, 52,* 613–629.

Steinberg, L. (1984). Dropping out among language minority youth. *Review of Educational Research, 54,* 113–132.

Telles, E., & Murguía, E. (1990). Phenotypic discrimination and income differences among Mexican Americans. *Social Science Quarterly, 71,* 682–696.

Torres-Guzmán, M. (1995). Surviving the journey. In R. V. Padilla & R. Chávez Chávez (Eds.), *The leaning ivory tower* (pp. 53–66). Albany: State University of New York Press.

University of California Outreach Task Force. (1997). *New directions for outreach.* Oakland: University of California, Office of the President.

Valdes, G., & Figueroa, R. (1994). *Bilingualism and testing: A special case of bias.* Norwood, NJ: Ablex Press.

Valentine, C. (1968). *Culture and poverty: Critique and counterproposals.* Chicago: University of Chicago Press.

Weiss, K. (1998, May 15). UC regents assail admissions plan. *Los Angeles Times,* p. A3.

Willis, P. (1977). *Learning to labor: How working class kids get working class jobs.* New York: Columbia University Press.

Yancey, W., & Saporito, S. (1997). Racial and economic segregation and educational outcomes: One tale—two cities. In R. Taylor & M. Wang (Eds.), *Social and emotional adjustment and family relations in ethnic minority families* (pp. 159–179). Mahway, NJ: Lawrence Erlbaum.

NOTES

1. Most federally collected data combine all Latino groups under the single rubric of "Hispanic." Therefore, in reference to federal data, the term Hispanic is used. The terms Hispanic and Latino are used interchangeably throughout this chapter to refer to data in which ethnic subgroups are not disaggregated. Where data are collected separately for ethnic subgroups, these groups are named separately. In California, approximately 80-85 percent of all Latinos/as are of Mexican origin (Latino Eligibility Study, 1993), or Chicano/a, as is the case in Texas, and thus these state data are described as referring to Chicanos/Latinos, or simply Chicanos/as.
2. "Underrepresented minorities" refers to African Americans, Latinos, and Native Americans.
3. The ethnic breakdown of the eight hundred underrepresented minority students with 4.0 GPAs was: 54 percent Chicano/a; 23 percent Latino; 17.6 percent African American; and 5 percent Native American.
4. Ogbu (1987) has coined the term "involuntary minorities" to describe groups who acquire minority status by virtue of political decisions that are out of their own hands, as opposed to groups who choose to immigrate. Such is the case of Chicanos/as, whose ancestors became minorities under the Treaty of Guadalupe Hidalgo when the U.S.–Mexico border was moved, creating a minority class out of individuals who were once a majority in the land. Similarly, African Americans are viewed as involuntary minorities in that they were brought to this country against their will.
5. Segmented assimilation is a concept described by Portes and Zhou (1993), wherein new immigrants are seen as assimilating into segmented sectors of the society—some into sectors that are "network rich" (such as Cubans and some Asian groups), and others into sectors that are "network poor" (such as Haitians and Chicanos/as). Network-rich sectors are able to provide social and economic support to transition newer immigrants from the group into American society. Network-poor sectors lack the social and financial resources to support this transition for their members, and these immigrant groups are especially vulnerable to downward assimilation and the development of oppositional stances to mainstream American society due to the isolation they experience in the society.
6. There is great variability in the selection criteria used from school to school. Students selected range in GPAs from 1.8 to 4.0, with a relatively even distribution along the continuum. Teachers and counselors generally refer students who they believe "can benefit" and show an interest in "doing well" or "doing better." Students are then selected by the Puente counselor on the basis of an individual or group interview. If they show up for the interview, with a parent, and express a desire to be in the program, they are usually accepted.
7. Data have been analyzed by gender and by grade in school as well. No significant gender differences were found; however, there are substantial differences by grade level, which are discussed elsewhere (Gándara, 1997).
8. For example, California has been perceived as being more progressive in desegregating schools for Chicanos/as, was ahead of Texas in providing bilingual education legislation, and led the nation in efforts to equalize school financing, notably brought forth by a Chicano family in *Serrano vs. Priest* (1971).

150 YEARS OF
CHICANO/CHICANA EDUCATION:
INTERGENERATIONAL PLÁTICA

As part of "150 Years of Chicano/Chicana Education: 1848–1998," a Forum cospon-sored by the Harvard Educational Review *and the University of California, Irvine, where the event was held in April 1998, six Chicanos and Chicanas graciously shared their own experiences and those of their families within the education system. We called this session the Intergenerational Plática, or dialogue, as we conceptualized the session as a conversation among Chicanos and Chicanas from different generations, in which they would share their schooling experiences with each other in much the same way many of us do at home with our parents, tíos y tías, abuelitos (aunts and uncles, grandparents), etc. The following is the edited transcript of that plática. Santana Ruiz, a UC Irvine and Harvard alumnus who served as the lead UC Irvine co-organizer and Master of Ceremonies for the Forum, introduced the participants. Facili-tating the plática was Antonia Darder, professor of education at California's Clare-mont Graduate University, who is a leading scholar and community activist for educa-tional equity and justice.*

SANTANA RUIZ: Our next segment is very special. In planning this Forum, besides having the research and the presentations and so forth, the commit-tee and the folks involved decided, "Let's have a regular old intergenera-tional plática like we have in our homes." We have Chicano students from dif-ferent eras in Chicano educational history, so the format's going to be a little bit different. We're going to be hearing them talk to each other. So allow me to introduce the participants.

We have Samuel ("Sammy") Ybarra, a descendent of the families involved in the *Alvarez vs. Lemon Grove District* case in 1931, which was a very important case in Chicano education history as it was the first successful challenge to segregation in the United States. Sammy's grandfather, Juan González, orga-nized the parents in Lemon Grove to start the process of ending segregation. Sammy is currently a field representative for U.S. Senator Barbara Boxer. We also have Sylvia Méndez, the daughter of Gonzalo and Felicitas Méndez of the *Méndez vs. Westminster School District* case. Sylvia was one of the students that went to the school and was not allowed to go in, *porque era Mexicana* (because she was Mexican). We have Maria E. García, a 1960's student activist from San Diego State University, currently principal at Audubon Elementary School in San Diego. We have Henry Gutiérrez, professor at San Jose State University in the social science department, and prominent in the 1960's East L.A. school walkouts. We have Enrique Sánchez, a high school student from Southwest High School in San Diego. Enrique will share his experiences as a current Chicano student in our educational system. And Beatríz Herrera, from Coachella Valley, California, currently a junior here at UC Irvine who is involved in MEChA.[1] She will share her experiences in Coachella and at UCI as a Chicana university student. Our moderator is Antonia Darder, an internationally recognized scholar and activist from Claremont Graduate University. Welcome!

ANTONIA DARDER: We are going to begin this discussion with Sylvia Méndez. Let's begin with some of the memories and impressions that you have of the events that were taking place in the Chicano community during the 1940s.

SYLVIA MÉNDEZ: During the 1940s there was a war going on. The Japanese [Americans] were interned in concentration camps at that time. My father always wanted to be a farmer, and he was able to lease a farm from an interned Japanese [American] farmer, so we moved to Westminster from Santa Ana, California. We used to take the money to the concentration camp to pay the lease—these camps were another injustice that went on then.

My dad was born in Chihuahua, Mexico, and raised in Westminster, California. He had gone to the all-White Westminster school because he was considered so intelligent that they moved him out of the Chicano school and placed him in the all-White school. And now that we lived in the district of the all-White school, my dad sent my Aunt Sally to the school to enroll us. When we arrived there, they told her, "Your children can stay in this school, but your brother's kids have to go to the other school." The reason for them not wanting us was because we were dark skinned, but my Aunt Sally's children were all light skinned and blonde. They said, "Your brother's kids have to go to the Hoover School." My Aunt Sally was acculturated, as she had lived here since she was a young girl, and she said—I can just envision her—"What do you mean my kids can stay here, and not my brother's?" So she said, "You will hear from us." She proceeded to go home and talk to my mother and father.

My father had become a naturalized citizen. He had studied the Constitution—the Constitution that tells you that we are all equal, that we all have the same opportunity in this country. My mother was Puerto Rican and she was also a citizen because Puerto Rico is a territory of the United States. She could not understand why they were doing this to her children. We had lived in a barrio in Santa Ana, where we had gone to an all-Mexican School. We were told we were going to the Mexican school because we lived in the barrio. But now we were in the Westminster district, an all-White district. There was no reason anymore why we couldn't go to that [White] school.

So my dad and mother proceeded to talk about it and said, "We are not going to stand for it." It was during the war, and my dad was making a thousand dollars a day. He had been exempted from the Army because we were growing tomatoes and asparagus for the armed services, so he had enough money. My mother took charge of the ranch for a whole year, while my dad dealt with the authorities. He believed in the system—he was not an activist—and he believed that you could do everything the right way. First, he talked to the school superintendent. Then he went to the school board. He tried to get the reason why we were not allowed to go to that school, but to no avail.

He approached an organization that's here today that would not help him at the time. They later joined in, but at the time nobody wanted to step in there and help him. So he formed an organization of his own in Westminster with all the *compadres* and *comadres*—all the friends and neighbors. We have some of the *ahijados* (godchildren) here today, whose parents were in that organization. They fought for that cause. It took my dad a whole year before they were able to go to court. He was trying to get all the people together; five people from the barrios went to court with him. My dad had enough money to hire a lawyer, and he heard about a lawyer who had been fighting discrimination in Los Angeles where the Mexicanos were not allowed to use the same swimming pool as Whites. They could only use it on Friday after all the Whites had used it, when it was dirty. That's when Mexicanos were able to go into it. The lawyer had fought that case and won.

My dad had heard from Henry Rivera, a family friend, that this was the lawyer to get and he got that lawyer. His name was David Marcus. Nobody helped him get that lawyer, but he hired him anyway, as he had the money. Then they went to court, and everybody else joined in. We are very grateful that they joined in, because after they won the case it was appealed by the school board. Thurgood Marshall of the NAACP wrote the brief for the appeal. I have a copy of it, if someone wants to see it. The NAACP, ACLU, the Japanese Americans, and the Lawyer's Guild all helped us in the 9th Circuit Court. They won the case at that time. [Applause].

ANTONIA DARDER: Of course, the case she's referring to is *Méndez vs. Westminster,* one of the most important desegregation cases in the history of the United States. Sylvia, in an earlier conversation you talked about your parents. You said that Gonzalo and Felicitas Méndez had incredible values that you kept. But what do you feel they wanted the Chicano community to remember about their struggle?

SYLVIA MÉNDEZ: My mother became very sad toward the end of her life because their struggle was rarely mentioned. So when the letter came from the *Harvard Educational Review* asking her to participate in this Forum, she was so excited. That was about two weeks before she died. She wanted everybody to know that we Mexican Americans are very assertive. We fight for our rights—like in the Lemon Grove case that was fought in 1930 and our case in 1940—and we'll continue to win. If we fight, we have to unite. We are not going to talk about each other. We are not going to pull one another down. We are going to go on continuing to fight and join each other, and we will become number one. [Applause]

ANTONIA DARDER: Thank you, Sylvia. I have to tell you, Sylvia, when I found out that Felicitas was Puerto Rican, that of course was very important to me, being Puerto Rican myself. Having grown up in the Chicano community since I was three years old, and having committed my life to the work within the Chicano community, it is important to understand that our work is really against human oppression, oppression of all kinds in every community. [Applause]

I want to turn to Henry and Maria, who were both very politically active during the 1960s. I want to ask you about your impressions of what was taking place in the Chicano community at that time. We'll start with Maria and then go to Henry.

MARIA E. GARCÍA: Well, I got to San Diego State in 1969. It was a wonderful year to get there because there were so many things going on. I was different in the sense that I'm fifth-generation, my dad's family were some of the original settlers of San Antonio, Texas. My mother was born in Yuma, Arizona, so I didn't have a lot of ties back to Mexico. But I had a real tie from my parents—*somos Mexicanos* (we are Mexican)—but we are part of this country. I have uncles who fought in World War II and came back with Purple Hearts. So there was never this, "You're not American." [We heard instead] "You are American. You have the same rights as everybody else." But then I went to school, and they let me know that that wasn't true!

We were a loving family—my parents and my aunts and uncles thought we were wonderful, and we grew up thinking we were so wonderful. You know, it was just a really nice thing: they loved us, we were cute, we were sweet, we were all these positives. And then we walked into a classroom and from being very positive we went to being very negative. And all of a sudden, my name was no longer Maria Elena, it was "Mary Helen." My mother was a high school graduate—she graduated in 1935 or 1936—and in those days, a high school graduate was a very well-educated person. She had taught me how to write cursive, and the first thing the teacher said was, "Where did you learn how to write like that? You have to learn how to print." I also took burritos for lunch, which made me different. So you know, it was constant. Everything I did was wrong. There was nothing I did that was right in school. I blamed it on the strictness of the nuns. I couldn't convince my parents that it was the most awful place that they had ever sent me to in my life. My dad had been a reluctant student, and he thought that I had inherited his reluctance. But it was really the way I was being treated. I can still remember [pauses for breath with tears in her eyes] eating burritos behind the ramps, so the nuns, not the kids, wouldn't make fun of my tortillas. Later on, in the sixties, we occupied a church camp. That was the best therapy I ever had, Okay!? [Applause]. Let me tell you about that.

At San Diego State in 1969 we didn't have "How to Picket 101," but we were always picketing. One of the first things that we occupied was this church camp. Some of the people who went to jail were friends of mine. We started picketing during the week: we would go to work in the morning, go to class, and then run out there, like twenty miles out of San Diego, so we could picket at this godforsaken camp.

Well, the people assumed we were not U.S. citizens, because they were used to seeing *braceros*² working out there. They just "knew" we weren't citizens, so they would bring the *migra* (INS agents), and here we were, all these college students who *were* citizens! They didn't really even want to serve us in the restaurants, because they were coming from the point of view of hate: "I'm here, and I belong here." It was very different for me to realize that they were looking at me funny as I walked into their cruddy little stores—you know, these little tiny towns where they have restaurants that are as big as this stage. So that was interesting.

Probably one of our blunders was when we were going to picket the Bishop's house in Mission Hills in San Diego. For those of you who are not familiar with San Diego, Mission Hills is a rather affluent area of the city. There were these two large mansions—that was the only way I could describe them to my young eyes. They were huge, you know, two stories, with a horseshoe shaped driveway. I was properly impressed. So we were out there, and in those days, you know, if you had had "How to Picket 101" you'd know you need a *guitarra*, the proper clothing, and because it was a church thing we also carried candles. At that time we also learned you do not carry a candle without putting it in something *porque te quemas las manos* (because you burn your hands). But you know, this all comes out of "Picketing 101."

So then we're picketing and the guitarras are going, and nobody's looking out the window. Now there's nothing worse than picketing a building and having no one pay attention to you. I mean, God, it's 6:00 p.m., it's 7:00 p.m., and they don't look out at us. We were really upset that we weren't really stepping on the Bishop's toes the way we had hoped to. Basically the issue was that the Catholic Church had not been responsible to the community the way it should be, and thus was part of the oppression in the community. So then, all of a sudden somebody drove up and said, "You guys have the wrong house! It's the house next door." [Laughter] If we had really paid attention, we would have noticed that there were swingsets in the backyard, and I'm assuming the Bishop did not need a swingset!

What came out of all our picketing, all that going back and forth, was the Father Hidalgo Center in San Diego. Now this did not happen overnight.

ANTONIA DARDER: Could I ask you a question, just as you're moving along, about these experiences? For you, in terms of your involvement as a young Chicana, what was the most important impact of the work you did?

MARIA E. GARCÍA: I think probably one of the most important is the friendships that formed—the unity that we formed together—although we always had to kind of shove the guys aside and say, "Hey, we have that ability too!" By the same token, there was a real respect built up with that group of people, both male and female. And I can't think of anybody that would call me that I wouldn't support in whatever endeavor they're in now. So we formed really strong bonds, really strong relationships that have lasted. We're not calling each other every day, but I do know that if they call me, or if I call them, we're there for each other. So I think that's one of the strongest things that came out of the Chicano Movement.

I also earned a reputation, and I think probably I'm still living with that reputation, because I have picketed the school district I work for. One of my favorite things to do when I get to a school as a new principal is to tell them I'm not "Hispanic," because I'm not "His- anything"—I'm Chicana! Okay!? [Applause] And I have to tell you that within two days the rumor gets back, "Well, I don't know what she is, but she's calling herself Chicana. She doesn't even call herself Mexican." But I am. You see, you earn your stripes and you use the title. So I'm Chicana! And the other thing I make sure they understand is that I fully support bilingual education. [Applause] Those are the two things that are not being changed in my mind. So other than that I'm open and flexible, but those are two of the things that I want people to know from the beginning—where I stand. Other issues don't matter.

We also learned a lot about the political system from that era. We would go to city council meetings with, you know, the plaques and the banners and the chants and the bad words and all of that kind of thing. Now we know how to pick up a phone and call a councilperson and say, "You know, this is not going to work!" But we have come to it as a process of growth.

ANTONIA DARDER: Maria, you mentioned in our earlier conversations that you were involved with the Chicano Federation.[3] Would you say a few words about the link between what was happening then in San Diego and what was happening in East L.A.?

MARIA E. GARCÍA: As a student I was on the Chicano Federation Board, the first elected board. There was an appointed board and then an elected board. When the moratorium[4] came up, the Federation sent up some two hundred people. That was the day when Ruben Salazar was shot.[5] The next day three of us from the Federation went to L.A. and spent the day writing writs, talking to people, going to the services, trying to find out what had happened. It was a real tie: I'd never felt so close to Latinos in Los Angeles as I did that day.

ANTONIA DARDER: Henry, since you were involved in the walkouts in East L.A., what are some of your impressions?[6] And could you talk a bit about your work now as a Chicano historian and educational historian?

HENRY GUTIÉRREZ: Thank you. In the spring of 1968, I was a second-year college student from East L.A. A lot of my friends were at school at Cal State L.A. and East L.A. College. I was hanging out with them and knew about what the high school students were planning. There was talk around the community that they were organizing, that they were formulating demands. They were going to do something. The issue for us as college students—and I recall meeting with my friends at East L.A. College—was were we going to support them? Were we going to be behind them? And thinking back on it now, I wonder what motivated me to get involved. What made me think that, "Yeah, the students were right," and "Yes, an action like a walk-out was the right thing to do"?

You know, I was a kid from East L.A. I went to Garfield High School, and by chance, really, ended up in college, because frankly our teachers didn't really care. I was also aware that Garfield High School had not adequately prepared me. I knew from my experiences of meeting other high school students from other parts of Los Angeles that Garfield High School was not giving me the kind of education that the same district was giving to other kids in other parts of the city. And, I already knew the disrespect that the administrators and some teachers at Garfield High School treated us with. I had felt that, I knew that first hand. But yet, what is it that pushes you over the line to say, "Yeah, I'm going to support students who are going to take to the street? I'm going to be there. I want to be there with them to be part of that protest." And I still have kind of a hard time answering why, other than having that gut feeling that I knew the students were right. And I knew we had to do something because this was 1968. The concept of Chicanismo was barely emerging as part of our consciousness. But I did see myself as part of the poor people of the United States. I did see myself as part of a class of people that were at the bottom of this country—and not by accident—and we had to do something about it. So that was the beginning that allowed me to relate to being Chicano—because I was poor and because poor people had to do something to change that situation. So that got me into supporting the students.

I was at Garfield when they walked out that day. I was at East L.A. College earlier that day, when we heard, "Hey, they're blowing out at Garfield!" Some of us were still asking ourselves, "Gee, well, should we? Should we not?" I took off and went to Garfield. After that I hooked up with the Educational Issues Coordinating Committee (EICC), and stayed with them from 1968 until the early 1970s.

The EICC was a community group that formed to support the students and their demands. We became kind of the conduit for all the energy and the mobilization for lots of other people like me, who all of a sudden decided, "Hey, I've got to go out and be part of this because we need to do something." We met every week on Tuesday evenings at a community center. People came with their grievances—we called them grievances. We formed grievance committees. We tried to get the L.A. school board to respond to their demands. We forced the school board to come to a meeting at Lincoln High School in

East L.A. It was the first time they'd ever come to acknowledge the Chicano community and meet with us in our community to hear our demands.

In the summer of 1968, they arrested *Los Trece* (The Thirteen) thirteen guys who were arrested for conspiring to disrupt the schools.[7] They were charged with felonies. This electrified all of us again. We picketed the police department—the L.A.P.D.—to support them, particularly Sal Castro.[8] I mean, the EICC really was behind Sal Castro. After he was released we had to fight to have him reinstated at Lincoln High School.

We sat in at the L.A. school board after picketing for ten or eleven days. I recall picketing day after day, marching around Lincoln High School with people. It was the biggest Chicano event I'd ever been to. That first day we picketed Lincoln High School and then we gathered at Lincoln Park, which is three or four blocks away from the high school. Then we marched up to the high school on North Broadway, and then up and down in front of that school. All kinds of people—students, college students, parents, professionals, and ministers—had been mobilized into that activity. We did that, as I said, day after day. We'd go back to the school board meetings twice a week and ask, "Okay, are you ready to take back Sal Castro?" They'd say, "No, get out of here." We'd go back to Lincoln High School and we'd picket some more. Then we'd go back to their next meeting and ask again, "Are you guys ready?"

Finally we decided, "Okay, we're going to stay here until you decide to take Sal Castro back at Lincoln High School." So we sat in at the school board for another ten or eleven days and camped out there. One thing that I always remember about that was the feeling of—and maybe it was similar to your experiences, Maria—this feeling of joy, of thrilling happiness, of taking some action to make a change. There was a sense of solidarity, the sense of possibility, that . . . I just cannot do justice to what that feeling is. I feel in a way that young people today miss something by not having had that kind of experience or not being able to see *la communidad en lucha* (the community in struggle). To see people who have been mobilized out of their run-of-the-mill activities to suddenly make history. I think that is just the most powerful thing that I can recall about that experience. [Applause]

What do I take away from that? I was just a young kid at the time. Like I said, it was my second year of college, and basically I was a kid from East L.A. who had never been anywhere. I was not fully appreciative at the time of how we were participating in a historic struggle that had been going on for decades. I didn't know about the Méndez case then. Now it's true that there were a number of people, Celia Rodríguez, for example, who were part of the EICC. So we had these older people, but again, I didn't appreciate their real historic role. I didn't know about the *Congreso*. I didn't know about the Méndez case. I didn't know about the struggles of the earlier generations. So that was one thing I was not fully appreciative of at the time that I can see now, that what we were doing was part of a very long struggle. Yet, we were being told that Chicanos just woke up yesterday and all of a sudden decided they valued education, or, like the teacher at Lincoln High School who was one of Sal's colleagues said, "Mexicans are Indians grubbing in the soil.

What's their culture? Their culture is *mañana*. Yeah, mañana for education." That's what he said.

So this was their attitude about us. They believed that we just showed up yesterday and decided, "Hey, we want to get an education." They wanted to say to us, "Hey, your culture is deficient" or "Your mental abilities are deficient." Back then I really wasn't fully aware that we were in this long historic struggle.

Maybe it's because I was a young kid, but how naive we were to think that if we changed the schools we were somehow going to get ourselves off the bottom of this society. Somehow we thought, "Well, gee, if we could get Chicano teachers, and if we get bilingual education, and if we get more Chicano administrators, then all of a sudden our kids are going to start making it. We're going to break out of the bottom of the society and work ourselves up into the middle or upper classes of society." Now I think, "No way!" The schools were doing, and are doing, exactly what the elite, the ruling class, wants them to do: to keep us down. To make us into the cheap, malleable labor that they need. So, in a way, we thought the schools were this nice institution that if we just fixed up a little bit, we'd do all right. We didn't realize it was really part of the oppressive mechanism that keeps us down. So now, as an older man, that is the other thing that I feel I take away from looking back on those experiences. [Applause]

ANTONIA DARDER: Moving to Sammy. Sammy, as a member of the family who filed the *Alvarez vs. Lemon Grove School District* desegregation case in 1930, what remains in your mind as the most important aspects of that community struggle?

SAMMY YBARRA: Let me first set the background. The Lemon Grove incident was named by Paul Espinosa, a producer out of San Diego State, who worked with the KPBS radio station. He did a documentary on the case, and called it "The Lemon Grove Incident." It was the first successful challenge to school segregation in the history of this country, preceding *Brown* by a couple of decades, but the school district didn't even appeal it. They know now that they probably could have won the appeal. But at the time they didn't appeal it, because it wasn't as dramatic, in the negative sense, as history seems to tell.

It was still a horrible situation in January 1930, when a few of my mom's ten brothers (she was about three years old at the time) went to school. The principal was standing in front of Lemon Grove Grammar School welcoming all the kids back from Christmas vacation. He was saying [pointing in two different directions], "You there. You there. You there. You there," pointing the White children into the school and the Mexican children to a barn—a barn! They were shocked. They were thinking, "Wait a minute!" They were used to this big beautiful school, where they had their books and their desks, and now they were going to this barn. The wood slats were separated by inches. It was horrible.

They all went home to Olive Street in Lemon Grove, which at the time formed a Mexican barrio, and said, "Hey, we can't go to the classroom!" Immediately their parents went to the school, and the school officials told them that their children were supposed to go to school in the barn. It all came out of that same rhetoric of Americanization that they talked about in this morning's panels—how the "Mexicans" were holding back the "English"—the "American" students, etc., etc., yet these children had all been born in Lemon Grove. So the Lemon Grove parents went and got a lawyer. My grandfather, Juan González, was instrumental in organizing the parents. They had their arguments. Some parents went away saying, "No, I'm going to go with whatever they say, because we can get in trouble. They'll throw us back [to Mexico]." That was a fear. But, thank goodness, we prevailed. They got the lawyer, and the lawyer went to court.

The fact remains, though, that this case was not as national as some of the other legal cases. My Uncle Jess says in "The Lemon Grove Incident" documentary, "Well, they picked Alvarez because he was the only one that had shoes on. Because the rest of them were barefooted. And he could speak English and Spanish." So they named the case after that student. The judge said, "You're crazy! They have to go to the same school. You can't do this." Thus, we won the Lemon Grove case, and it was fantastic. [Applause]

My parents were both born in San Diego and both attended San Diego High School. My father's high school years were cut short by World War II, when he, like many others, fought for our country. My mom was the only high school graduate in her family, which was very, very important and is still important to this day. Throughout my sixteen years as a printer, and over twenty-five years of singing and playing music throughout the States, including Mexico, through my work with the police department, and as a community representative now for the U.S. Senate, I am still a Chicano from Logan Heights. [Applause] I'll never profess to be anything other than a Chicano.

What the Lemon Grove incident created is something that you can still do today, in 1998, and it starts in the home. It has to start in the family. The families in Lemon Grove stood their ground for something that meant a lot to all of us. And I think that small significant thing carried over to our families, to my uncles, of which nine out of ten served in the military for the United States, five at one time in any given war.

Now there's racism of all kinds, whether it be Blacks or Asians, etc. But we have a strange one. During this morning's session, Dr. González referred to the theory that we have a defective brain, so why even waste their time. Well, that "defect" is so feared by that Europa, Manifest Destiny, Monroe Doctrine-oriented number 300 sunscreened flesh-colored crayon. [Laughter] I once had a crayon that said "flesh." It didn't look like any of us! [Laughter] Because we too are blond, blue-eyed, beautiful, brown skinned, six-feet, military, tax-paying, working, thinking, athletic, number 12 sunscreen, Mestizo, Latino, Hispanic, Chicano, Chicana, or whatever I call myself. And we do it all right here in our *tierra* (land) and we won't be denied! [Applause]

ANTONIA DARDER: Enrique and Beatríz, as you've been listening, the question comes up, "How aware were you about these different stories that you've just heard?" Were you aware of them, and if you were, where did you learn about them?

BEATRÍZ HERRERA: I have heard about every single event that we have been talking about. Unfortunately, I didn't learn about them until I got to UC Irvine. Before that, I had no idea what Chicanismo was. I had no idea about these very significant events in our Chicano history—and that is really sad. It really shows that we are, in fact, moving in a circular motion, as was mentioned earlier in the Forum. If we did at one point make some kind of advancement, we are right back where we started, in a way, because of Proposition 227,[9] and all the other propositions that attack us as Chicanos.

One thing that I did notice about everything that Sammy said was the concept of *familia,* and the close friendships that were formed—whether it was the actual familia to whom you are related, or your friends and your compadres, as in *Méndez vs. Westminster.* It makes me feel good in a way because being here at UCI, being a *Mechista* and seeing that same familia that I have come to be a part of through MEChA, makes me feel like we're getting somewhere. I mean, we have that strength. We trust each other, and it makes me feel that there is something positive that we are starting here at UCI. As we've heard about these successes, it just makes me feel like we're at the beginning of something that can happen once again. [Applause]

ENRIQUE SÁNCHEZ: Before today, I had never heard of any of these incidents. I barely learned about the Lemon Grove case when I heard Sammy and my dad talking at breakfast this morning. And the walk-outs and the Méndez trial—I had never heard of any of them. I wish that there were classes in my school so I could learn about this sort of thing, then I would have more to say right now. [Applause]

ANTONIA DARDER: To give you the opportunity, since they're right here—do you, Beatríz or Enrique, have any questions that you want to ask the other panelists?

BEATRÍZ HERRERA: I'd like to ask Maria, how or what experiences as a Chicana, and specifically what kind of gender issues, were present at that time, during the whole movement? For example, in the Chicano Federation Board, what was the working relationship you had with your fellow Chicanos?

MARIA E. GARCÍA: I love my fellow Chicanos, so let me start with that statement first, before I do a little bashing. I will be as kind as possible. They are the most stubborn group of men I've ever met! Right ladies? You know, they are a part of their environment. So, even though it's been hammered away and they may be saying the right things, I think that they fall back into it, without even knowing it at times. Sometimes I use humor. Sometimes it's a humor thing, you throw something out. Sometimes you just have to be angry. But yes, it's still there. And I don't know . . . I know for sure that in my lifetime we're not going to see it go away, but I hope that in your lifetime you do.

I think men always felt we were going to be the ones taking the notes. And, of course, if there was going to be a fundraiser, we were going to be the ones cooking the food. You know, the men would help carry it from the car, but the women were going to cook it. Although things have gotten better, I'm not sure if we've reached that point where it has actually gone away.

I think as Chicanas move up in positions, though, there is definitely a change, and a new respect. It's funny, something I do see in the school system though, when I'm talking to a parent—the mother, for example. She wants to move her child out of bilingual education or something, then after I explain to her why the child should stay in bilingual education, she nevertheless says, "Mi esposo quiere . . ." (My husband wants . . .). Does she think I'm going to be impressed with what her husband wants? So there's a lot of that still.

HENRY GUTIÉRREZ: I want to respond too, because I think we as Chicanos are not going to get past the gender issues, unless we start criticizing *la familia*. It is in la familia where the patriarchy is embedded. So, to the young people, I appreciate your desire to build community and solidarity, but I ask, what does familia mean? Does familia mean that we are reinforcing the patriarchy? I think that is what we need to be critical of. Unless we start moving beyond la familia, we are not going to get past these gender issues.

ANTONIA DARDER: Enrique, tell us a little bit about your own history as a student. You're in high school now: what has it been like for you? What has school been like?

ENRIQUE SÁNCHEZ: Well, I had an experience in elementary school when my parents went to enroll me. They were told that I would have to go to afternoon school. When my parents asked why, they said that it was because I did not speak English fluently. But that was a lie because I learned English before I learned Spanish. So, my parents had to fight them. They had to threaten them legally so they would put me in regular school. That was one experience.

ANTONIA DARDER: What is it like in your high school now?

ENRIQUE SÁNCHEZ: Well, I don't feel any discrimination there because there's all these teachers, they are White, but they do encourage everybody to go to college. They motivate us. But there are other schools in the same district that get more funding, I guess, and they've got better supplies and everything, like we should have. Our books are still in the Reagan years, 1985. They're still asking us what President Reagan should do.

And there is racism. In another incident where we went to a basketball game at another school, the majority of the people were White. During the game they threw tortillas onto the court. The teachers from that school did not say anything.

ANTONIA DARDER: Wow! Beatríz, what about your experience?

BEATRÍZ HERRERA: Like I said before, growing up in the Coachella Valley, there was never a doubt in my mind that I was going to college, and that was due to my mother pushing me. She did not go to college, and actually she didn't finish high school either. That's because they didn't let her. Going back to the family, la familia, that could be a negative thing. But I was always sure that I was going to college. I didn't know where or what college was exactly, but I knew I was going. I think that a lot of students with my background still go through the same thing. So getting here to UCI was obviously a culture shock because my community was predominately Mexicanos. Also, I did not expect the workload. I sincerely don't feel that I was prepared for college. But fortunately I'm doing fine, and still fighting to get my degree next year.

The one thing that I think gave meaning to that degree that I'm hoping to get next year is my involvement with my community. And I'm going to mention MEChA again, and I do that because it has become so important to me. It has given meaning to my degree because it makes sense to me now why I am going to get that degree. And that is to go back to my community so that what I went through won't repeat itself again. You know, we should not have students who don't know what college is! [Applause]

In response to your question, life at UCI is better because I have recognized the opportunities that I have to reach out to high school students, and I am taking advantage of them. So I feel good about being here at UCI and doing the things that I do.

ANTONIA DARDER: Enrique, what are your plans? Do you feel like you are going to go to college? Where are you now with that?

ENRIQUE SÁNCHEZ: I plan on going to community college and transferring and starting a career in the film industry.

ANTONIA DARDER: Are you concerned about having any problems?

ENRIQUE SÁNCHEZ: No, I think everything will be fair.

SAMMY YBARRA: What they both touched on is so important. If we could say we've accomplished anything from the Chicano days in the seventies, it's that we've got to go back to school. I became a history major in college, because they didn't teach me history in high school. The history they taught us had these big huge gaps, like somebody said earlier this morning, "Nothing happened in Texas at this time. Nothing happened in the Southwest." We all know that's baloney. There were human beings. A lot of things went on. So I had to go to college and learn history all over again. And then I said, "The heck with it! I'm going to centralize it and take Chicano Studies." And so we took Chicano Studies. My Chicano Studies professor was Gus Getner at Southwestern College in San Diego. Gus was German. He taught us Chicano Studies, which at that time was real important. He would say, "Your name is Enrique, not Henry. Juan, your name is not John, okay?" And then, as he was doing a roll call, he would state that there were two Ybarras in the class, and he would say, "Ybarra, Enrique; Ybarra, Samuel." That was his whole thing, not to do the typical thing, that is, to use the short name in English. That wasn't Chicano Studies; we were *creating* Chicano Studies.

And it's important that the students today don't have to start all over again. The game starts every day and you have to start from the beginning. If we can accomplish something here it's somehow to get [these issues discussed at the Forum] into the curriculum. If you are going to write the book, make it clear so these students can learn about themselves. Because you know, they [the dominant class] are hitting us from all sides. They are going to take and take and take. And we have to stop and say, "NO! You're not going to take anymore! Okay?!"

ANTONIA DARDER: I'd like to end with one last question for anyone who wants to answer. How do we as a community continue to move forward in terms of changes or improving our work, to better educational opportunities for Chicanos and Chicanas? What are some of the things that you feel we really have to do, and, given all the history and experiences we've discussed, where do we go from here?

HENRY GUTIÉRREZ: Well, I'm old so I can be cynical. But you know, I don't think we've come very far. Thirty years ago I was out in the streets protesting the poor quality of education that our young people got. From what I saw in today's presentations, we are as bad off, if not worse off, than we were then. [Applause] So the question for me is, do I think that for all the decades we've been at this, are we no better off now than we were thirty years ago? Or fifty years ago? Or seventy years ago? If that is so, then we need to do something more than what we have been doing up to now. As I suggested before, I think it is embedded in the nature of our society. We are embedded in a capitalist society that's based on inequality and exploitation, and unless that ends there cannot be educational equality.

SYLVIA MÉNDEZ: Well, I feel that the family is very important. The father and the mother must instill in their children that education will get them wherever they want, and that they have to study. Now with affirmative action gone we will have to work harder as Hispanics to try and get into the universities, into the Harvards. We have to instill in our children that they have to study hard, have perseverance and go for their goals. And they will be able to do it. We can do it. We can all do it. We just have to study. We have to help our children to make it, to get to those goals, to get to those schools. Sometimes, it is because they tell us that we don't have that 4.0 point grade average. Well, why don't we have them? The children have to study. Study and you will make it. Get that education. Have that goal. Go for whatever dream you have. Persevere and you will make it! This is a great nation and we have the opportunity. But if we go out there, we can do it. I know we can. Thank you.

MARIA E. GARCÍA: I think we need to emphasize the importance of college, and the doors that can be opened and the role models we have in our community. You know, I didn't go to college my first year after graduation because no one told me I could go. My mother told me she really felt bad because they couldn't afford it. But I didn't know there were grants and scholarships and all of that. My grade-point average certainly would have qualified me for it, but I didn't know what was available. And, in case we think we've made progress, I just last week sat on the HACER scholarship committee meeting for the McDonald's Latino scholarship fund. Normally we get 350 applications, but this year we received only 157. San Diego City Schools has the highest group of Latinos in San Diego County, and yet only five Latinos from that district applied for that $1,000 dollar scholarship. I am going to chair the scholarship committee next year. I will consider it my personal job to bug these counselors to death in order to get these kids to apply. [Applause]

I think we have to be aware that there are doors that can be opened. For anybody who "has made it"—and by the way, I don't consider myself to have made it—we need to open the door for someone else. Sometimes you may have to drag them through, or sometimes they will just walk on through. But we need to support each other. That's my biggest message.

SAMMY YBARRA: You know, Henry, I agree with what you said. It seems, at times, that thirty years have come and gone and we are still fighting for schools that are falling apart. But, there's a missing link. There is something missing. This morning they talked about heroes and said, "Well, it's what we've done as a people, etc." Well, let me tell you about some heroes: It's what we've all done as a people. We had more medal of honor winners in World War II than any other ethnic group. They all have names. Every one of them has a name. Cesar Chávez is another hero. He has a name. Okay!?

We can't just put it on the shelf. We have become complacent in our actions. In the sixties and seventies we had a fire. You know, we had *"¡Si Se Puede!"* (Yes, we can do it!) Since then we leveled off, but it's okay. We got some things done. And they [the dominant class] backed us up because they realized, "Oh man! Here they come. Those people. They're Mexicans and they're Anglos at the same time. We don't know what they are!"

Then you have legislation. We had smokescreens, and beware of those smokescreens. They think it's a march and a flag. And meanwhile legislation is going through and the votes are going through, and they're cutting all the visas and the immigrants. We made some ground but then we got complacent. Many people my age got the house in East Lake, and they got the house in Coronado, and they went off and the kids got bigger toys. That's where it went. The fire died.

People like Cesar gave their lives for the cause, and to show the injustices. And when we show up, people respond. But we've got to have that fire going. *¡Sí Se Puede y Que Viva Harvard Educational Review!*

BEATRÍZ HERRERA: We need to go back to our communities, because I think it's really important that as students we show up at the high schools that we went to and talk to the students that are there now, so that they can understand the importance of education. Today, I met the first principal of a school that isn't ashamed to call herself a Chicana, and I think that is what we need. We need more of that, so that we can start eliminating the self-hatred that a lot of our Chicanitos go through. You know, many are not proud of being Chicanos and I think that is something we really have to work at so that we can work together to meet our goals. [Applause]

ENRIQUE SÁNCHEZ: I think that family is important to better our opportunities. My parents, and my aunts and my uncles, they encourage me to do good in school. They are always asking me if I have finished my homework. We also need to take advantage of our school counselors. They are always encouraging me and because of that I have signed up for the SAT. And they have informed me about scholarships, too. We just need to take the help that they offer us. We need to listen to the people that want to help us. [Applause]

ANTONIA DARDER: It has been a tremendous honor for me to have had an opportunity to talk with you all. What is really clear for me is that the questions within the Chicano community illustrate that the Chicano community is a contested terrain. We have differences and there are issues. Listening to your stories we know there are different ways we look at what is going on. Part of our work ahead is to struggle with one another to figure out the direction our work should go.

These struggles within the Chicano community have a long history, 150 years of Chicano education and history. Some of you probably do know that it also happens to be 150 years since the Communist Manifesto. In saying that, I highlight the issue of class struggle. What does it mean to be poor in a society such as the United States? We must link our cultural struggles with class struggles. There are clearly issues that come up within our history that have to do with how Chicanos and Latinos in this country have been positioned, how we've been used as cheap labor. How that has affected our children and the kind of education we have received.

Many times we slip out and somehow evade this issue. I'm not sure of the reason, but it seems to be one of the most difficult issues for us to talk about.

We can certainly talk about the issue of language, which is more clear to us. And we can also address the issue of culture. But for some reason, at the point where we have to talk about money—the question of how capital shapes our lives, the way that we are positioned within the society, and the way that it takes away opportunities from our children and our communities—we often have a more difficult time. And yet the histories of Chicano and Chicana education and the Communist Manifesto are clearly linked to how we have been positioned within the context of capitalist America.

We also have to understand these educational problems and educational situations within the context of what is happening in the larger social reality. Everyone is talking about the globalization of the economy and the way money is moving all around the world. Yet the reality is that companies like Hasbro, a big toy company in Texas, closed down six months ago, and thousands of jobs were lost in an area that is predominantly Chicano. So the question becomes, where are those jobs going and how does the changing nature of work, the disappearance of jobs in particular areas, how do these things affect our community? How do they affect the educational programs that our children then find themselves in?

Lastly, the participation in social movements comes through clearly as we look at the history of participation in political movements, in political work. It is incredible how this work changes and politicizes the reality within our communities, and the realities within families. These movements have had a powerful impact on the social, cultural, and class formations of young Chicano and Chicana students throughout the last 150 years. More importantly, we have to link the struggles of Chicanos and Chicanas within schools and communities to the larger social issues so that we may seek to overcome the devastating impact of capitalism in the world today. We cannot see our conditions as isolated. We know, for example, that the language issues, the same bilingual issues that we are facing in this country, are similar to what the Basque are facing in Spain, the Quero are facing in Peru, and the Maori are facing in New Zealand. And that all of these issues, in one way or another, are truly connected to our struggle for social justice and economic democracy, not only in our communities, but in this country and in the world! Thank you. Thank you to all of you. [Applause]

NOTES

1. MEChA is a national student organization born out of the 1969 Santa Barbara Conference. At this conference, Chicano/a students, faculty, and community activists developed a master plan for higher education, including El Plan de Santa Bárbara, which called for the unification of Chicano student organizations into the Movimiento Estudiantil Chicano de Aztlán (MEChA). MEChA's goals are based on the ideals of the Chicano Movement, which include education as the foundation for achieving social, political, and economic justice for Chicano/a communities. A *Mechista* is a member of MEChA.
2. *Braceros* were Mexican laborers recruited/permitted to work in the United States under a Mexico–U.S. agreement during 1942–1949 and 1951–1964. It is estimated that several hundred thousand Mexican laborers participated in the Bracero Program.

3. The Chicano Federation is a nonprofit Chicano/Latino leadership development program in San Diego initiated by the Chicano Movement in San Diego in the late 1960s.
4. The Chicano Moratorium was a mass Chicano/a demonstration against the Vietnam War held in East Los Angeles on August 29, 1970, in part to protest the disproportionate draft and casualties of Chicanos.
5. Ruben Salazar was a vocal and active Chicano journalist for the *Los Angeles Times* killed by a tear gas projectile fired by Los Angeles Sheriff deputies into the Silver Dollar Bar in the aftermath of the Chicano Moratorium on August 29, 1970.
6. A protest in which some 10,000 Chicano/a high school students walked out of five East Los Angeles high schools (Belmont, Garfield, Lincoln, Roosevelt, and Wilson) during March 1968, in order to protest high dropout rates, lack of Chicano curriculum and faculty, and discrimination, among other issues.
7. *Los Trece* were Chicano activists who were arrested and charged with conspiring to disrupt the educational process of students through the East L.A. walkouts. All were subsequently found innocent.
8. Sal Castro was a social studies teacher at Lincoln High School who was one of *Los Trece*. He presently teaches at Hollywood High School in Los Angeles.
9. Proposition 227 was a California public referendum that sought to eliminate the use of bilingual education in the schools. The proposition passed by a vote of 61 percent "yes" to 39 percent "no" overall; among Latino voters, the results were 37 percent "yes" to 63 percent "no."

About the Authors

DOLORES DELGADO BERNAL is a President's Postdoctoral Fellow in the Chicana/o Studies Department of the University of California, Davis. Her research interests center around the politics of Chicana/o education, Chicana narratives and oral history methodology, and the socio-historical examination of Chicana cultural practices and identities. She is author of "Using a Chicana Feminist Epistemology in Educational Research" in *Harvard Educational Review* (1998), and "Grassroots Leadership Reconceptualized: Chicana Oral Histories and the 1968 East Los Angeles School Blowouts" in *Frontiers: A Journal of Women Studies* (in press).

ANTONIA DARDER is Associate Professor of Education and Cultural Studies and Director of the Institute for Bicultural Studies at Claremont Graduate University, Claremont, California. Her professional interests focus in particular on the impact of racism and economic inequality on the lives of Latinos in the United States. She is author of *Culture and Power in the Classroom: A Critical Foundation for Bicultural Education* (1991).

PATRICIA GÁNDARA is Associate Professor of Education at the University of California, Davis. Her research interests are education policy, educational evaluation, bilingual education, and minority student achievement. Her publications include "Choosing Higher Education: Educationally Ambitious Chicanos and the Path to Social Mobility" in *Education Policy Analysis Archives* (1994) and *Over the Ivy Walls: The Educational Mobility of Low-Income Chicanos* (1995).

EUGENE E. GARCÍA is Professor and Dean at the Graduate School of Education, University of California, Berkeley. He is interested in child development, language acquisition and bilingualism, and the education of non-English-speaking students. His publications include *Understanding and Meeting the Challenge of Student Diversity* (1994) and "Preparing Instructional Professionals for Linguistically and Culturally Diverse Students" in *Handbook on Research on Teacher Education* (edited by J. Sikula et al., in press).

MARIA E. GARCÍA is Principal of Audubon Elementary School in San Diego. She also serves on the board of Teatro Sin Fronteras for the Lycium Theater and on the Superintendent's Mexican American Advisory Committee. Her numerous awards include the Cesar Chávez Social Justice Award.

MANUEL N. GÓMEZ is Vice-Chancellor for Student Services at the University of California, Irvine. His previous professional efforts have included working with teachers and communities to improve educational opportunities and intercultural understanding. He is coauthor of *To Advance Learning: A Handbook on Developing K-12 Postsecondary Partnerships* (1990).

GILBERT G. GONZÁLEZ is a Professor in the School of Social Sciences and Chicano/Latino Studies, University of California, Irvine. His current research interests focus on the Mexican Diaspora and the rise of the U.S. empire. He is author of *Chicano Education in the Era of Segregation* (1990) and *Labor and Community: Mexican Citrus Worker Villages in a Southern California County, 1900–1950* (1994).

HENRY GUTIÉRREZ is Associate Professor in the Social Science Department at San Jose State University. His professional interests center around educational history and Chicano/a communities. He is coeditor of *Latinos and Education: A Critical Reader* (with A. Darder and R. D. Torres, 1996).

BEATRÍZ HERRERA is a senior at the University of California, Irvine, majoring in social sciences. A former Americorps volunteer, she is active in community citizenship drives and is a member of the Movimiento Estudiantil Chicano de Aztlán (MEChA).

MARTHA MENCHACA is Associate Professor in the Anthropology Department of the University of Texas at Austin. Her research interests are in the field of anthropology. She is author of *The Mexican Outsiders: A Community History of Marginalization and Discrimination in California* (1995) and "The Racial Implications of Another Broken Treaty" in *Reflexiones* (in press).

SILVIA MÉNDEZ is the daughter of Gonzalo and Felicitas Méndez, plaintiffs in the landmark case, *Méndez v. Westminster School District*. Now retired, she worked at the University of Southern California Medical Center for over thirty-three years as a registered nurse and Assistant Nursing Director of the Pediatric Pavilion. She continues to speak to high school students about the significance of the legal case in which she was involved.

GARY ORFIELD is Professor of Education and Social Policy at Harvard's Graduate School of Education and the John F. Kennedy School of Government. He is interested in the study of civil rights, urban policy, and minority opportunity. His publications include *Dismantling Desegregation* (with S. Eaton, 1996) and *Chilling Admissions: The Affirmative Action Crisis and the Search for Alternatives* (coedited with E. Miller, 1998).

ENRIQUE SÁNCHEZ is a senior at Southwest High School in San Diego. He is a participant in Access Via Individual Determination (AVID), as well as cross-country and track. He volunteers in community beautification projects and as an after-school tutor.

GUADALUPE SAN MIGUEL, JR., is an Associate Professor in the History Department of the University of Houston. His professional interests include the history of Mexican Americans, of American and minority education, and of Mexican Americans' struggles for educational equality. He is author of *"Let All of Them Take Heed": Mexican Americans and the Campaign for Educational Equality in Texas, 1910–1981* (1987) and coauthor of "From the Treaty of Guadalupe Hidalgo to *Hopwood:* The Educational Plight and Struggle of Mexican Americans in the Southwest" in *Harvard Educational Review* (with R. R. Valencia, 1998).

RICHARD R. VALENCIA is Associate Professor of Educational Psychology at the University of Texas at Austin. His research interests include the intellectual development and psychological foundations of minority children, and bias in testing. He is author of *The Evolution of Deficit Thinking: Educational Thought and Practice* (1997) and coauthor of "From the Treaty of Guadalupe Hidalgo to *Hopwood:* The Educational Plight and Struggle of Mexican Americans in the Southwest" in *Harvard Educational Review* (with G. San Miguel, 1998).

SAMUEL YBARRA is a San Diego field representative for U.S. Senator Barbara Boxer. He is also the grandson of the primary litigants in *Alvarez v. Lemon Grove School District,* the first legal challenge to school segregation in the United States. He has been involved in Chicano activism since the 1970s.

ABOUT THE EDITOR

JOSÉ F. MORENO is a doctoral candidate in Administration, Planning, and Social Policy at the Harvard Graduate School of Education, with a concentration in higher education. Born in Guasave, Sinaloa, Mexico, and raised in Oxnard, California, he earned a B.A. in social ecology from the University of California, Irvine, and a master's in education at Harvard. His primary research interests are educational history, and access, equity, and diversity in higher education. His dissertation research addresses whether university faculty believe that racial/ethnic diversity influences classroom dynamics, their pedagogy and curriculum, and aspects of their research. He is examining these beliefs within the context of legal and policy deliberations on the use of race-inclusive admissions policies.